TRUE LIFE IN GOD

VOLUME 1
1986-1987

Cover photo painted by Vassula Rydén ©

Nihil Obstat:
✠ Felix Toppo, S.J., D.D.
Bishop of Jamshedpur
Censor Librorum
Date: 28.11.05

Imprimatur:
✠ Ramon C. Arguelles, D.D., STL
Archbishop of Lipa
Date: 28.11.05

Volume 1 1986-1987

© Copyright Vassula Rydén

Published under license from
the Foundation for True Life in God Geneva, Switzerland

All rights reserved

Disclaimer: Vassula Rydén is not responsible for any errors in translation or variations in relation to the original English text that this publication may contain. With regard to quotes from the True Life in God Messages, please refer to the original handwritten publication for the day, month and year mentioned at the beginning of each messages for the original English text

ISBN: 978-1-63972-635-6

www.tlig.org

yet He is sending you into the world, to show the world the Heart of your God and that I Am who I Am, sent you, come now and rest in Me and allow Me to rest in you. ♥ ΙΧΘΥΣ ⳨

4. XII 90

Lord, You are All, and I am nothing. You are stupendously Great, so what are my praises for You the Holy of holies? No man can glorify You enough, yet my heart calls incessantly Your Name because You have set my heart on You.

your praises and your calls are not in vain; love Me and praise Me without cease, for as long as they come from your

Welcome

To the praise of Jesus and Mary

In reading the True Life in God Messages you hold in your hand, read them from the start, then follow the book in order so that you become immersed in God's Love for you. You will understand, while reading from the beginning that God is calling you to an intimate relationship with Him.

Jesus Christ asked me to tell you always to take my name, Vassula, out of the Messages and replace it with your name. You will hear Him then speaking to you, reanimating your soul to move, aspire, and breathe in His Glory. God will draw you very delicately into His Heart so that you no longer belong to yourself but to the One who moves you in union with Their Oneness (The Holy Trinity).

I want to thank everyone who supports and helps diffuse these Messages. Jesus said on several occasions: "My Message saves souls." Let everyone who is moved by the Holy Spirit become witnesses of God's infinite Love. May you, too, become a disciple of these End of Times.

Vassula Rydén

TRUE LIFE IN GOD: DIVINE DIALOGUE

I have read all the TRUE LIFE IN GOD books and meditated on their contents. I truly believe that the books contain the Divine Dialogue of the Holy Trinity, Our Lady and the Angels with humankind through Vassula Rydén. I have not found anything objectionable and anything contrary to the Church's authentic authority on faith and morals. Reading these books and meditating on the contents are spiritually beneficial to all. I recommend these books to every Christian.

Felix Toppo, S.J., DD
Roman Catholic Bishop of
Jamshedpur, India

Golmuri,
November 24, 2005

Editor's Note

The Holy Scriptures are quoted constantly in *True Life in God* yet, without acknowledgment. They are also perfectly flowing in syntax with the rest of the text. These two aspects give a living witness to the supernatural origin of what is said. No one can make a complaint that it is a private meditation because you can only meditate on what you know.

The vast quantity of Scripture quoted in sentences or phrases is beyond the mind of most people to memorize to such an extent as to quote unconsciously and constantly. These quotes are from all over the Scriptures and not simply from a few isolated Psalms or favourite Gospel passages. Moreover, many quotations and terms are essentially Hebrew and not translated accurately in some of our modern versions of the Bible. This is so especially where the texts, if they had been looked up, would have given non-Hebraic expressions. *True Life in God* uses the correct Hebraic expressions. We will consider some of these expressions alongside a little critique of the text where the Jewish/Hebrew dimension is affected.

There is very little grammar in Biblical Hebrew. It is rabbinical teaching that the absence of the grammar and the use of the "and" manifests that the work of God from the beginning of creation and all salvation history is one continuous unfolding act of God, and is therefore, expressed by one continuous sentence.

True Life in God has few full stops. The accurate reproduction of the text, therefore, is in itself a witness of divine authorship to Jews, scripture scholars and anyone who wishes to exercise discernment when reading *True Life in God*. A false prophet with no scriptural knowledge would, by writing naturally, include full stops.

The punctuation in this book follows the original handwritten Messages, where semicolons replace full stops and where sentences begin with lower case letters. Vassula says, 'I never understood why the text was punctuated in this manner until one day Sr. Anne Woods explained it in her book entitled Invitation to be One with Christ that the Old Testament in Hebrew was written in the same style.'

Throughout all Jewish Bibles and literature capital letters are used for pronouns when God is discussed. The Jewish reverence for the Name of God puts to shame a large number of Christians who have stopped showing this reverential exception in grammar. *True Life in God*, like Jewish literature, always gives the personal pronouns a capital letter when speaking of One of the divine Persons or to an Act of God when He intervenes.

At the back of this book, interested readers will find two appendices: the first contains a prayer of repentance and deliverance that our Lord wishes us to say; the second contains correspondence between Vassula and the Congregation of the Doctrine of Faith at the Vatican regarding the *True Life in God* Messages.

TABLE OF CONTENTS

1986 (Notebooks 1-6)...1
1987 (Notebooks 6-20)..11
Prayers..A-1
Vassula Rydén and the Congregation for the Doctrine of Faith................A-3

Vassula, have I not told you that we are united, we are one, beloved; call it: '<u>true life in God</u>'; live for me;
 here is what I want you to write;

June 10, 1987

1986

September 20, 1986[1]

Peace be with you;

Can I be with You?

yes, you are with Me; I am the Light;

Can I be near You?

you are near Me; you are in Me; I am the Light;

Can You shelter me?

you are sheltered by Me;

Can I lean on You?

you can lean on Me;

I need Your Strength to keep my Faith;

you are given Strength;

I need Your Love;

you are loved by Me;
I am the Light and I shine for everybody to see; have no fear, My Path is straight; My Path will lead you to Me; I will meet you and you will recognise Me, for I radiate Peace and Love;
come to Me; can you see Me? can you hear Me? do not be afraid; do not just stand there in the dark; see, your limbs are healed, you can walk again, see, your sight is back;[2] I healed you; I have healed your shame and your sins are washed away by Me; use your limbs to walk to

Me; your eyes to see Me, your faith to meet Me; I am your Redeemer; I am your Peace; I, Jesus, love all of you;

September 27, 1986

peace be with you; Vassula, come to Me, I am your Redeemer, your Peace; I lived on earth among you, in flesh; I am God's Begotten Son; come to Me and lean your head on Me; I am your Consoler; when you feel miserable remember, I am near you;
recite with Me this Prayer:

help me Father and lead me
to Your pastures of repose,
where everlasting pure water flows,
be my Light to show me the Way;
with You by your side will I walk;
with You illuminating me will I talk;
Father, Beloved, remain within me
to have Peace, to feel Your Love;
I will follow You in Your footsteps;
with You I will remain;
enlighten me, love me,
be with me here and forever after;
amen;

(Jesus had come to show me this prayer.)

September 28, 1986

(Today Jesus gave me a clear vision (intellectual vision) of myself in nowhere. My surrounding looked like I was in marshlands with no one around and my spirit seemed lost. Among the dry trees I saw Jesus looking for me.)

---

[1] This is written after the Purification.
[2] All of this is metaphoric.

I am here; it is I, Jesus; I have found you; come, let Me show you the way back; hear Me: I Jesus am the Way; every time you feel lost, call Me; I will come to you and I will show you the way; I am the Way;

September 30, 1986

peace be with you daughter;

Please, Jesus, give me light to be able to feel You and write.[1]

Vassula, lip-service means the call is meaningless;

(I realised my mistake. I asked Jesus this favour without love, without thinking, without really feeling it. I repeated it but really meaning every word and raising my soul to Him.)

deliver your call to Me, feeling Me[2] like this time; I, God, feel; I feel all; I must receive from your call, love from the depths of your soul, needing Me, loving Me, meaning every word you say; I, God, exist and I feel; any call which is lip-service might as well stay buried; lip-services are calls bellowing from graves; remember, I exist and feel; I wish that all My children work, giving Me joy;

October 5, 1986

(I'm reading a book in which many people reported "experiences with God", but almost all those people are told by 'experts' that they should forget what they experienced because it's not God; they tell them that only highly elevated souls experience these things from God and one has to be highly elevated too. As I know I'm none of this and far from good, I decided to stop these meetings by writing with God; I might as well 'pack-up' the whole thing.

They seemed to say that to reach God you have to be a saint and they made me believe God is so far. So I will drop the whole thing, leaving my hand to write for the last time what it wants, led by "the force" that has been writing all these months.)

Vassula! do not leave Me, beloved, be calling on Me and be learning from Me; remember, I am beside you all the time; I, God, am living in you; believe Me, I am the Almighty, the Eternal God;

No. It can't be. It can't be God. Those that know would prove to me that it is not God. Only highly pure souls who are worthy, God reaches giving such graces.

I am not beyond reach! Vassula, I do not refuse anybody; I blame all those who discourage My countenance to My children to come to Me; whoever teaches that to be able to be with Me or be accepted by Me should be pure or worthy are those who are damaging My Church; any man having found Me, but is discouraged by others, I, who am Infinite Strength, will support him, giving him My Strength; why, why do I have men who call themselves experts, judging whether I am or not, banning every possibility, leaving My children disconsolate and helpless and disillusioned, disregarding all My graces, pulling away My children from Me; why are all My given blessings rejected; blessings that I gave; I am Infinite Wealth;

daughter, when you had finally found Me, I was full of happiness; I was careful not to frighten you away; I was being gentle, treating you like a mother handling her infant; I made you approach Me; I was full of happiness calling you and meeting you, having you near Me, sharing everything I have, My beloved; and now, you come telling Me that you are thinking of leaving Me, because I, God, am impossible to reach and that you were given information that only worthy souls can reach Me and that you are

---

[1] I need to feel God's Presence.
[2] Being aware of God's Presence.

below the standard required! I never deny any soul; I offer My graces even to the most wretched;
 delight Me and meet Me in this way; I bless you, daughter; I am guiding you; you are eating from Me; Vassula, read today 1 Peter; read attentively, then I will relate it to you; read the first chapter; live with faith; Peter teaches you to have faith;

(Jesus made me understand many things with the word 'faith'; that one can make mountains move by faith. One has to believe blindly, if you wish.)

October 10, 1986

I am the Light; I, Jesus, want to warn you: never ever fall into traps set up by evil; never believe in any message which brings you unrest; do understand why evil is trying very hard to stop you; daughter, any message condemning My previous messages[1] is from evil; the devil is trying once again to stop you and discourage you; I, who am your Saviour, am confirming to you that all the messages bearing calls of love and peace, leading those that are lost to find their way back to Me, are all from the Father and Me; so do not get discouraged, have faith in Me; remember, do not believe in any message that will leave your heart worried; I am Peace and peaceful you should feel;

October 16, 1986

peace be with you; beloved, rest; do not burden yourself more; I can feel how you are straining;

I felt Your Presence! Were You emphasising Your Presence, Jesus?

I am, I emphasised My Presence so that you understand; Vassula, I am fully aware of your capacity;

(That day I was particularly tired but I could not stop reading and working. I felt Jesus' Presence everywhere. He was trying to tell me something.)

October 22, 1986

I, God, delight to have you near Me; I love you, daughter; have faith in Me; in less than two months you will be hearing Me distinctively,[2] I will give you the support you want; My aim is to guide you; you will progress enormously in less than two months, for this is My will; I am your Teacher; all My teachings will enlighten your soul; remain near Me; Vassula, every time you feel miserable come to Me and I will console you, for you are My beloved; I never want to see any of My children miserable; they should come to Me and I will console them;

October 23, 1986

Vassula, which house needs you more? I want you to choose;

Jesus, if You are asking me what is more important, Your House or mine, I would of course say "Your House"; and to choose, I choose Your House.

I bless you;

(Jesus seemed so pleased!)

I will guide you, little one;
 come, take with you My Cross and follow Me; remember, I will help you; you will be My disciple; I will help you to reveal Me; I am Holy, I am Holy, so be Holy, live Holy; I will give you My

---

[1] First editions before the approach of the Cross.

[2] Prediction which came true. After six weeks I could hear His voice clearer.

support; Vassula, are you willing to work for Me?

Name Yourself again.

Jesus Christ;

Yes, I will work for You.

I love you; call Me when you wish;

(I was agreeing without really realising what it means to work for God. Since I love God I wanted to please Him. I never realised my incapacity!)

hear Me, listen to My cries, listen to My cries, can you see My Cross? I am Jesus who brings forth this vision;[1] I call, I am suffering because I am counting you, My beloved, and I see you scattered and unaware of the dangers the devil has laid out for you; My Heart lacerates to see you so far away from Me!

(Jesus for a whole month was giving me images of His Cross. Wherever I turned my head and looked in any direction, a huge dark-brown cross was standing. If I lifted my eyes from my plate, while eating, this enormous Cross was there. If I looked from within my mosquito-net, the Cross again. If I walked out and went to another room, to sit, or whatever, the Cross followed and it was there. For a month; it was as though it was <u>haunting me</u>.
Then another thing started to haunt me. That all that's happening is perhaps not from God. But then, if it was from the devil, how dumb can he get? I started to fear what people would say of this, what will happen to me. I will be mocked!)

daughter, daughter, live in peace!

(I was suspicious.)

Who is it?

---

[1] I saw a huge dark Cross.

it is I, Jesus, remain near Me; I have been calling you for years; I wanted you to love Me, Vassula ...

Jesus, when was the first time You called me?

the time you were going to Lebanon; I called you in your sleep; you saw Me; remember how I pulled you towards Me, calling you?

Yes, I remember, I was very frightened. I was about 10. I was frightened by Your force that pulled me. It felt like a strong current, like a magnet pulling a small magnet. I tried to resist and pull away, but I couldn't until I found myself stuck on You, then I woke up.

(I found it strange that Jesus reminded me of this dream; and how I could remember it still.)

November 9, 1986

CRUCIFIXION

peace be with you; I am here, I am Jesus Christ; I am before you, I am your Teacher and I love you; evil was conquered by sacrificing Myself; sleep not because I am soon with you; I am the Revelations; I have tidings that will talk; talk to Me about My Crucifixion, Vassula;

What shall I say? Shall I think before or during?

before;

(Jesus gave me an image of the scourging.)

having scourged Me, they spat on Me and gave Me several hard blows on My head, leaving Me dizzy; they kicked Me in My stomach leaving Me breathless and falling to the ground; moaning with pain, they took sport in Me kicking Me by turn; I was unrecognizable; My body was broken and so was My heart; My flesh, which was ripped off, hung all over My body;

one of them picked Me up and dragged Me because My legs would not carry Me any longer; then they clothed Me with one of their robes; they hauled Me forward, repeating their blows, hitting Me across My face, breaking My nose, harassing Me; I listened to their insults; daughter, with such hatred and mockery their voices resounded, augmenting My cup; I listened to them saying, "where are your friends mustering while their king is with us, are all Jews as treacherous as these ones? behold their king!" and they crowned Me with a woven crown of thorns, daughter, "where are your Jews to hail you, You are king are you not? can you mimic one? laugh! do not cry, you are king are you not, behave like one then"; they tied up My feet with ropes and told Me to walk to where My cross was;

daughter, I could not go since they had My feet tied, so they hauled Me to the ground and dragged Me by My hair towards My cross; My pain was intolerable, parts of My flesh which hung from the scourging were ripped off;

they loosened the ropes off My feet and kicked Me to get up and lift My burden on my shoulders; I could not see where My cross was for My eyes were filled up with My blood which was streaking down My face from the thorns, which had penetrated My head; so they lifted My cross and laid it on My shoulders, pushing Me towards the gates; daughter, O how heavy My cross was which I had to bear! I felt My way to the gates, led by the scourge behind Me, I tried to see My way through My blood which burned My eyes;

I then felt someone wiping My face; women in agony came forth washing My swollen face, I heard them weeping and mourning, I felt them; "be blessed", I uttered, "My blood will wash away all sins of mankind; behold daughters, the time has come for your salvation";

I dragged Myself up; the crowds turned wild; I could see no friend around Me; no one was there to console Me; My agony seemed to grow and I fell on the ground; fearing that I would expire before the crucifixion, the soldiers ordered a man called Simon to bear My cross; daughter, it was not a gesture of kindness or of compassion; it was to save Me for the cross;

arriving on the Mount, they thrust Me on the ground, tearing off Me My clothes, leaving Me naked for every eye to see Me, My wounds opening again and My Blood flowing out on the earth; the soldiers offered Me wine mixed with gall; I refused it for deep inside Me I had already the bitterness given to Me by My foes; they quickly nailed My wrists first, and after allowing the nails to set in My cross, they stretched My broken body and with violence pierced My feet through; daughter, O daughter, what pain, what agony, what torment of My soul, forsaken by My beloved ones, denied by Peter upon whom I would found My Church, denied by the rest of My friends, left all alone, abandoned to My foes; I wept, for My soul was filled with sorrow;

the soldiers erected My cross, setting it in the furrow;

I gazed upon the crowds, from where I was hardly seeing; from My swollen eyes, I watched the world; I saw no friend among those who mocked Me; no one was there to console Me; "My God! My God! why have you forsaken Me?"; forsaken by all those who loved Me;

My gaze fell on My Mother; I looked upon Her and our hearts spoke, "I am giving you My beloved children to be your children too, You are to be their Mother";

all was ending, salvation was near; I saw the heavens open and every angel stood erect, all stood in silence, "My Father, into Your hands I commend My Spirit, I am with You now";

I, Jesus Christ, dictated you My agony;

bear[1] My Cross Vassula, bear it for Me, My cross cries out for Peace and Love; I will show you the Way for I love you daughter;

December 4, 1986

(Still I'm amazed and have enormous doubts of how this is happening. How could this happen? I mean how can I not control my writing hand. It's like I'm being used by another force. But I'm too realistic, that's why I doubt, and yet, it's happening, I'm confused ...)

I am here; it is I, Jesus; daughter, remember you are spirit and I am also Spirit[2] and Holy; I live in you and you in Me; remain in Me; I, Jesus, am with you always; understand this: be in My Light, for I am the Light and through Me you are receiving knowledge; you are progressing;

All right, You have convinced me that it is You. You have reached Your two goals: that I love You, was one, and that You are meeting me in this way is the other. You have seduced me. I know that I'm not more schizophrenic than the rest of the world, or psychotic than the psychiatrist himself. I know that it is not from the devils since I know how one feels when attacked by them, giving a disquieting feeling of torments.[3] I have not chosen to receive Your calls since I was totally aloof from You. You willed it My God. I do not regret, how could I, since I'm seduced now!

child, I elevated you to enable you to be with Me; I taught you to love Me; are you happy to be with Me in this way?

Oh yes!

I bless you from the core of My Heart;

December 8, 1986

Can I be in Your Light?

You are in My Light; I am Jesus, your Saviour; wearing My Cross[4] means bearing with you My sufferings, daughter;

December 10, 1986

daughter, will you follow Me? do not wander astray, lead a holy life;

Jesus, can't I be like I am?[5]

hear Me; list Me one person of holy creed who never chose the Church; list Me one person who was partial! ...

I can't think of any.

no, there were none;

(Jesus seemed to wait that I say something.)

You want me 'complete'?

yes, I do; fear not; what are you caring for, daughter?

(I must have sighed.)

What happens if I stay the same?

remain always the same and you will discover that I will not stop calling you to Me!

Can I ask you a question?

---

[1] First time Jesus talked about bearing His cross was on October 23, 1986.
[2] This does not deny His Glorious Body nor my flesh.
[3] That is when I was attacked before, so that I abandoned the writings.
[4] Jesus meant the cross one wears around the neck.
[5] Leading a jazzy life but also trying to be a disciple...

you may;

Do You really care if I change?

I do!

Is there a difference if I change, I mean to be holy like You say.

yes, there is a difference; turn to Me and remain with Me;

Can you see right now in the future?

I do, beloved;

Can I ask you a question?

you can;

Since you see in the future I would like to know something, if You don't want to answer me just draw me a heart – will I disappoint you in the end?

no, you will not disappoint Me;

(I was relieved ...)

How would you feel?

I, God, will feel glorified;

You would??

I would; do not fear, why are you fearing to be holy? remember, you are in the beginning of My call;

What does this really mean?

it means that you are still learning from Me; I will be teaching you and showing you My Works; I am only in the beginning of My call, you will discover later on how I work; I will call you later on at the appointed time to find Peace; are you fully aware of what Peace means?

I'm not really sure. Peace could mean death, could mean Church. I do not know quite...

I am Peace; I am here, near you; My right Hand holding your writing hand; My Left Hand on your left shoulder; I am present and you feel Me; I am your Teacher, daughter; walk with Me! work with Me for I have appointed you to be My bearer; do not let discouragement come from men; many of them do not understand, for darkness might have closed their heart, eradicating all understanding; have peace; I, God, love you to distraction; courage, daughter;

December 11, 1986

daughter, are you willing to be holy? do not fear;

(Jesus came back to the same subject of the previous message.)

What is it exactly to be holy?

to be holy is to be pure and completely devoted to Me; holy is to work with love for Me; holy is to love Me and stay near Me; holy is to obey the Law; holy is to be like I am;

Can one be holy in heart only?

yes!

Is the heart what counts more than the holy clothes?

yes, the heart is what is important; remain near Me, remain near Me;[1] you are not near Me like I wish! I feel you are evading Me;

(Jesus was not happy ...)

---

[1] 'Remain near Me' means that I was not concentrating on Him.

I am Holy, so I want you to be holy;

I really want to be nearer to You!

do you really mean it? are you really seeking Me?

Do not abandon me!

I will not!

Never?

never! daughter, do not fear; are you fearing that the habit[1] gives you sorrows? go on, say it!

(I took all my courage)

I really do not want to wear garments of nuns, I love You as I am also ...

you finally had the courage to say it, daughter! I am pleased with you for being truthful! I, God, love you; you realise you would have been lying in My Face if you would have said the opposite;

(I felt God so pleased but He might be sad for the result.)

I am not sad! listen to Me; I want you to be holy in heart, not in the habit;

What is partial? Wouldn't it be being partial not wearing the garments?

partial again teams up with the same meaning, one does not need holy garments to be holy; what worth are holy garments when the heart is unholy? it is like salt having lost its taste; I am going to you to be nearer to Me; I will bring you closer to Me; feel loved by Me, do not fear Me, I am Peace; I, Jesus, guide you, I lead you; pray more and work with Me in this way; augment your faith in Me; need Me; be watchful for the time is near;

---

[1] Nun's dress.

December 13, 1986

daughter, do you feel I have trapped you? I love you, beloved, do not fear Me; you seem to fear that I am trapping you!

(True, I mentioned to my friends this and used the word 'trap'.)

I know, I wished that you love Me;

Are You angry?

no, I am not;

Shall I be frank?

be;

You wanted me to love You?

I did;

You have reached Your goal?

I have;

You seduced me and I like it!

are you happy this way?

I am very! I wish I would be less blunt!

you are learning; eat from Me, be blessed;

Is it possible that I bless You too?

it is;

Then have my blessings, Jesus Christ!

I love you; I have brought you up to be My bearer; I wished that you love Me; since you are going to be My bearer, I wish you to be holy since I am Holy and you are willing to follow Me and work for Me, do not fear of being holy; why are you fearing it so much?

Are you angry?

no, I am not angry; holy is to be pure and to live in Me; holy is to follow Me, loving Me; holy is to be like I am; I will teach you to be holy if you are willing;

I'm willing to do as You wish, since I love You.

I will teach you then, daughter; remain near Me and you will learn; trust Me and have faith in Me; believe Me when I tell you that I am happy to have you near Me; you will learn, go in peace and remember, feel loved by Me;

December 14, 1986

I am your Consoler;

Tell me, Jesus, what good is this guidance and what for?

it will lead many to Me; it will revive My children to come back to Me, and read My Word;
 I am your Good Shepherd who calls you to Me; believe Me daughter, look at Me, look at Me; I have revealed My Face to you; do not feel uncertain, believe in Me; have you forgotten how I work, have you not heard of My Works, do not let your era destroy you; stay, daughter, as you are;[1] do not let them convince you now that you are awake and abiding in My Light; stay near Me;

Jesus, please will You stop them if they try to do this?

I will; I will not let anybody destroy you; hear, all those that have ears; be watchful for the time is near;

December 15, 1986

daughter, all Wisdom comes from Me, do you want Wisdom?

Yes, Lord!

I am going to give you Wisdom; hear Me, you will acquire Wisdom, I am the Lord Almighty and I will teach you; cling to Me and you will learn, have faith in Me;
 awake My children, daughter; live in Peace for every step you take, I, God, bless; full, you shall be many;[2] go in peace;

December 16, 1986

It took me a day to realise what You offered me! I was amazed with myself for just accepting without thinking what You were offering me! I want to thank You, Lord.

peace be with you; are you realising its importance?

Slowly, yes! But I'm not worthy for such a grace!

you will have to acquire Wisdom; do not get discouraged though; I will teach you to earn it; you are in My Light and being in My Light you will learn;
 listen to My Voice, try and recognise Me; I am Jesus Christ and I am your Teacher; I have taught you to work through the Holy Spirit; I have taught you to love Me; I have poured out My Works on you to enable you to understand Me; I am your Strength; you will be given Strength to surmount your oppressors who will be many My child;

(God seemed sad, and it scared me because God's Voice suddenly became grave and sad.)

---

[1] Easy to convince me to believe just about anything! These people are called naïve in our circles.

[2] This means that once filled with the Holy Spirit my witnessing will draw many to God, we shall multiply.

Why? Why?

why? because many do not believe that I work in this way too; some do not believe in Me at all; daughter, I have to warn you;[1] I am telling you this so that you are prepared and aware of these people, since they are deaf and blind and have closed their hearts; they will want to justify their cause; they will tell you that this is not Me, that all of this comes from your mind, they will feed you with venomous theories; they will find ways of showing you that you are wrong, they will let you read their theories[2] to prove to you that you are wrong; so I am warning you, daughter, do not let men discourage you; do not let your era destroy you;

Lord, what can I do? Unless You protect me with Your Hand!

I will be near you all the time; do not feel abandoned; I will teach you to be strong and you will overlook all your oppressors; I am preparing you; I will feed you to be full; have My Peace and abide in Me;

      ΙΧθΥΣ ⨉⟆[3] Jesus Christ

---

[1] God spoke very fatherly and intimately.
[2] Prediction that came true after a week or so.
[3] ΙΧθΥΣ - In Greek means *"Jesus Christ Son of God Savior"*

1987

January 8, 1987

peace be with you, Vassula; it is I, Jesus; Vassula, come to Me, come and live in the middle of My Heart;

Do you want me, Jesus?

O I do! I eagerly want you; I want to entice you!

But I'm not worth anything,

I love you as you are ... be My bride, Vassula;

How could I!

I love you;

I don't know how to be Your bride, Jesus.

I will teach you to be My bride, beloved;

Do I carry a symbol for this, Lord?

I will let you bear My Cross; My Cross cries out for Peace and Love;

I want to make you happy, Jesus.

give Me happiness by never leaving Me, give Me happiness by loving Me, give Me happiness by awakening My children;

I need Your strength for all this, especially the last one!

look at Me;

(I looked at Him; He was radiating strength, like an aura.)

I am Strength; I will help you, be blessed;

Are You happy with me? I never asked You before.

I am happy with you all the time I feel loved by you;

I wish I could see You materialise!

ask and it shall be given to you; augment your faith in Me;

(I decided to show the writings to a Catholic priest here. He condemned them saying it's the devil, and that I should stop. Jesus had asked him if he wanted to bear the Cross of Peace and Love with me. I told him that. He said it's evil. He gave me to read: St. Michael's prayer, and the Memorare of St. Bernard, and the Novena of confidence to the Sacred Heart; told Me to read these prayers for the following days then see what happens.[1] I did. I let my hand write and it came out: "I, Yahweh, am guiding you." Four days in a row.)

Lord Jesus I have done the priest's will, I stopped writing except letting these five words come out after praying. I stopped You from writing to obey the priest. I want to ask You Lord, why, why did You ask him, since you knew what will happen and what a lot of sufferings he would give me!

I am with you daughter, I asked him because I want him to learn, I want him to start to understand My Riches, I am Infinite Wealth!

---

[1] The priest had asked me to stop writing and so I obeyed him but when I took a pencil, God used my hand again.

"learn that I, Jesus Christ, am giving this guidance for My children; it is I, who am guiding Vassula; do not reject My given blessings; My messages cry out for Peace and Love; I want My children to fill up My sanctuaries; I want them to turn to Me, I want them to live holy; I come to shine on this dark world; I want to revive them and tell them that My Word is Alive! I want them to remember My Word which they put aside; I want to remind them how much I love them; I want to enkindle their hearts, I want to tell them to love each other as I love them; I love you, son, understand that by trying to stop Vassula you are unwillingly damaging My Church; I am the Lord Jesus Christ whom you love; I know you are doing this in good faith, but so was Saul before I came to tell him, that what he believed right, was wrong, and was persecuting Me; you believe that the charism I, Jesus, gave to My daughter is from evil; believe Me, son, do not feel frightened, for I am telling you again that it is My Will having Vassula learning from Me; she is flourishing now and later on her fruits will feed many lost souls; you will one day understand, son;[1] I, Jesus Christ, love you;"

(The priest, after having read this, blamed me, saying it's evil and divinations.)

I know; narrate Me by saying to him: "divinations are for fools, inspirations are for blessed children; divinations bear no fruits, inspirations bear good fruits feeding many;"

regain your courage, daughter, Wisdom awakes My children; I, God, love you;

January 21, 1987

(The priest gave me a lot of sufferings. Like God predicted to me on the 16th, he sent me pamphlets with all sorts of theories, to prove it's evil. He also sent me, as God predicted, a theory about subconscious mind, and occultism and satanism, plus a letter telling me to destroy the writings and warn people that this was all from the evil one, for my good and for the others. I told him that I obeyed his wish to pray those three prayers and that I did not write to see the result. But I do not think he believed me, because he went to tell the other priest (who believes the writings come from God and who supports me) that the writings are satanic, and that I am not even reading the three prayers he asked me to! He alarmed a lot of other priests, so the one who supports me asked me to leave him the latest two notebooks to read. The following day, having made up his own opinion, he told me to continue writing. Yet I know the one who believes it's evil, I know he does it because of the love of the Church, to protect the church; I only wish he would see clearer. He wants to save me too, because he believes it's evil. I hope one day he will understand. I pray to St. Mary. What am I doing wrong?)

O daughter how I pain for you;

Am I doing wrong if I desire the others to love God and show them this message?

no, you are doing nothing wrong; I am Mary, Mother of Sorrows; Vassula, I am near you, always; be with Us; come to Us for consolation; they do not understand Our Riches; they have closed their hearts forever, you are one of the many signs We have given them, but they do not seem to understand; God encouraged you to hear His call;

Vassula, every time you bring a soul near God, God is pleased with you; My Son Jesus and I are always beside you; be careful because evil is furious with you; evil is trying to discourage you, their way of fighting you is to add wrong words to mislead you; remember always this and never forget it; it is their weapon against you; I am near you protecting you;

---

[1] Prediction came true.

Would I be able to recognise the evil?

I will always tell you; trust Me; Jesus has trained you to recognise Him;

Why am I attacked?

I will explain this to you, My child; understand that you are being exposed in Hades,[1] beloved; your love to God is healing many strayed souls;[2] that is why you are attacked; I am near you protecting you; I have now told you this so that you may understand why you receive the wrong word; you are healing them with the love you have for Jesus and your Holy Father;

Am I working in this way too?

yes, you are healing them with your love; do not let men influence you to submit in their theories; every time you are told to stop writing, remember how you were unaware and living in darkness; many of our children do not recognise Our signs anymore; God has chosen you to be His bearer; please Him and hear Him;

Thank you, Holy Mary, may God bless you.

peace be with you;

Jesus?

I am; Vassula, I love you to a degree you are unable to grasp; Vassula, how I suffer to watch my children so arid; how can they forget the love I have for them? I laid out My Life for them; beloved, be near Me and feel Me; I will come to you in the appointed time to deliver you, but first you have a task to accomplish;
   I, God, have already revealed Wisdom to bless all mankind; O daughter, one day you will understand fully how I work; do not fear, for I, God, love you;

(Later:)

daughter, it is I, Jesus, I want you to read the three prayers every time before you write with Me because they keep away evil; believe Me, they are powerful prayers; do you still want to work for Me?

Jesus, if I say no, what will You do?

you are free to choose, do not fear, I will not take away the charism I gave you; I will always meet you to tell you how much I love you;

No, Jesus, I have already said that I'm willing to work for You; why should I change my word, You remember?

I am pleased with your answer, daughter; remain near Me and I will guide you;

Jesus, have I hurt You anytime?

yes, you have; I was hurt when you forgot how I came to save you from darkness; but I have forgiven you; I know how much you love Me; I am your Bridegroom; do not forget; do not forget either that by being My bride we share everything; Vassula, I am bearing My Cross of Peace and Love on My weary shoulders, take it, beloved, for a while; I will place it on your shoulders liberating Me from My burden; I want you near Me so that I am able to unload My Cross on you; I want you near Me because I know you understand how I suffer; when you will feel My Cross you will suffer too; I am your Bridegroom and I will share My sufferings too with you; I will feel rested whenever you liberate Me from My burden; before you accepted Me I was near you all the time watching every movement you made, beloved; I called you so many times, but you were unaware of My Presence; now, finally you heard

---

[1] Purgatory.
[2] Our prayers to God and our love for God is used as well by God to lift souls from purgatory. At the same time, our love to God makes Him give graces to strayed souls on earth to save them.

Me and came to Me, why then do you doubt?

(Doubts after my contact with the priest.)

every time you are weak, doubting, remember what I have just told you; bear My Cross of Peace and Love and do not leave Me; come and pray with Me;

(Jesus prayed with me. He was looking upwards while praying.)

Jesus, You know how much I love You. I will help You carry Your Cross and unburden You. We can share It.

daughter, how I always wanted to hear you tell Me this; come, beloved, let us continue our way;

(Jesus was so pleased. Happy.)

(Next day.)

(I heard my name. Jesus was calling me incessantly. I was painting. I threw the brushes in the air, got up, ran to the desk.)

Vassula, Vassula, Vassula; I, Jesus, called you; O Vassula how I love you; glorify Me; be with Me always; every time you love Me with such fervour I feel glorified; delight Me always, hearing Me like now; remember, I am with you soon; I am going to take you near Me soon, beloved, because I love you to a degree you can never imagine, but first you must deliver My Message to all nations as you are doing now, then I will soon fetch you; I will take you here where I am and will have you near Me forever; I, Jesus Christ, love you; I have given you this grace, Vassula, I have blessed you; I will never take away what I give;
– daughter, will you revive My Church?

Oh Jesus, You ask something I am unable to do for You!

trust Me!

I will cling on You, and depend on You entirely. You're my Teacher.

glorify Me, I will lead you;

January 23, 1987

O Vassula, how I love you, come to Me, I am your Eternal Father; feel My love I have for My children! I guided you to love Me; it is I who showed you the Way; I am a God of Love, I am a God of Peace, I am God of Mercy; I am Meek; I am the Good Shepherd; I am a Forgiving Father; how could I see you lost without Me coming to your rescue? I count each one of you; the Good Shepherd will lay down His life for His sheep; I am an abyss of Forgiveness; I will never abandon you;

January 23, 1987

If I stopped writing, Jesus, what happens?

Vassula, even if you stopped writing, I am always with you guiding you; I gave you this charism to meet Me in this way and teach you; I have asked you if you want to work for Me and your reply pleased Me; Vassula, I like it when you hesitate; you are beginning to learn to think before deciding;
I am your Teacher, accept My guidance; I am guiding you to stay aware of evil seeking the ruin of souls by feeding them his vanity; I am teaching you to understand how treacherous evil can be; I will teach you to accept; I will teach you to be humble, honest with yourself, faithful to Me; I will feed you with humility; I am reminding you that I am not favouring you from others; My guidance is to teach you to improve and purify your soul; do not think for one moment that I gave you this charism because I love you more than the rest of

My children; I gave you this grace to feed you and others who are in <u>desperate need</u>; I am the Lord Jesus Christ, the Good Shepherd who watches over His flock; I come to show you the way back; I come to shine on you and give you hope;

Vassula, it is true, I have assessed you before you were born; I have chosen you to be My bearer, revealing My Message to all mankind; are you hesitating because I asked you before to be My bride?

Yes, Lord ...

You have already accepted, remember?

I know, Jesus. But on second thoughts I can't, not that I don't want to, but I'm not worthy to be Your bride. How! How could I have accepted just like that without realising its value!

Vassula, I can teach you to become worthy of Me;

Even if I'm worthy, that's not enough.

why?

Because it's not just being worthy, there is more than that.

I know, to be worthy is not enough, but I will teach you to be worthy and holy; you will have to work and earn it; come, I will help you; you are going to remain My bride, a bride who needs forming; I have accepted you as you are because I love you, but you must let Me form you the way I want you to be; I will feed you to grow; I have revealed to you how evil works, delivering amounts of information; I want you to stay awake reading them carefully;
 learn to accept; every time I see you weak, bound to fall into traps, I will rush to your rescue, do not take My guidance as a treatment of penitence, I am guiding you so that you do not fall; I do not want to lose you; invoke Me in your prayers and pray more;

January 24, 1987

Vassula, Vassula, little one, beloved of My Sacred Heart, do not fear, I love you;
 daughter, were you able on your own to love Me?

No, Jesus.

you have learned to love Me because I approached you, enlightening you; I converted you by awakening you; Vassula, do you know why I love you?

No, I don't know, Jesus.

I will tell you then: I love you because you are helpless, wretched and guilty; children are My weakness; I love them because they let Me form them; Vassula, come and abide in My Sacred Heart where in its depths you will find Peace and will feel My ardent Love I have for all of you; you will be able to tell them of My Love I have for them; behold! every day that goes by, you come closer to Me!

January 30, 1987

peace be with you; every time you feel weak come to Me and I will give you strength;
 Vassula, do you know why I chose you?

No, I don't, Jesus.

I will tell you then; I chose you because you are helpless and by far the most wretched from any man I know of; wretchedness attracts Me because I can console you; you are helpless and insufficient, unable of mastering any language;

Lord, if I am that bad, why have you chosen me to take this guidance?

have I not told you before? children are My weakness, because they let Me form them, I have chosen you to manifest My love through you, a frail flower unable to grow on its own; a flower which I found in the middle of wilderness and which I took and transplanted in My garden of delights, letting it grow under My light; all I ask from you is love; love Me and be faithful to Me; I want fidelity from you; I want every drop of love you have in your heart to fill up My Heart; I thirst for love, for I am Master of Love; so all I ask from you is to love Me; when you love someone do you not burn with desire to be with Him every second of your life?

Yes, that's true.

so what more natural than giving yourself entirely to Me? come, come to Me, I am your Father;[1] I know you are helpless without Me, wretched when left by yourself, and weak on your own; let Me form you so that through you I may deliver My message; O daughter, how much you will have to learn ....

I know; I know I know nothing.

Vassula I love you, have no doubt; I will answer your question; I do not only choose those who are My brides[2] by choice, I also come and choose those who do not know Me; I come and knock on every door; I knock and wait hoping that I would be heard; Vassula, I long for every soul to receive Me and welcome Me; I love you all;

I thought you prefer to be among religious souls, who make You feel always happy.

Vassula, I love My religious souls and My priests and nuns as much as My other children; I love everyone including sinners and those who persecute Me; Vassula, I approach everyone irrespective to what they are and how much knowledge they have acquired in their life time; I can raise the dead with My power; I am giving you My strength to meet Me in this way; for I am Lord and the smaller you are, the easier I can handle; you know quite well that I suffice by Myself; your insufficiency will glory My suffice; your wretchedness is of little account in My eyes, leave yourself to Me and let My hands form you;

I have not chosen someone of authority for My Authority suffices in itself; My appeal for Peace and Love will come through you showing My Mercy to all mankind; I will manifest Myself through you; I ask nothing of My children that they have not already; if they have but faults and sins let them give them to Me and I will purify them, I will unburden them, I will forgive them, I will not blame them, I will only love them; I love all those who fall and come to Me asking for forgiveness, I love them still more; I will never reject them even if they fall millions of times; I will be there to forgive them and wash in My Blood their iniquities; never will I weary in pardoning them for I am a God of Love and Mercy, I am full of pity for the weak;

My Heart is Holy and an abyss of Forgiveness; do no more, daughter; I love you, trust Me Vassula and all I have to say <u>will</u> be written;

(Later on:)

do you know that I am happy to have you near Me? I, Jesus, love you from the depths of My Heart and because of this love I have for you, evil hates you; they will be setting traps for you, I will be near you to warn you;

I do not want to fall!

I will not see you fall; I will be near you to sustain your falls;

---

[1] Is. 9:5.
[2] Nuns.

I do not understand why the messages were given before my 'formation'.

Vassula, I, God, gave you My messages so that many would profit from them; if you only knew how valuable souls are to me;[1] I know what you have in mind, I will answer your question;

hear Me, I have come to you to give My message of Peace and Love, I have chosen a mere child, unfit for My task, helpless and small without prestige, <u>a nothing</u>, to manifest through you My passionate love and teach those that still do not understand the riches of My Heart;

I suffer to watch My teachers so withdrawn from what is heavenly and their indifference they give to My blessings; for charism is a blessing; how their hearts have become coarse, leading to spiritual deafness and aridity; once more I come appealing for Peace and Love, but how many more will reject Me? how many more of you will not respond? how many of you, especially My teachers, would turn away their eyes in the other direction looking for Me? O men of little faith how little do you know Me! have you forgotten that I am Infinite Wealth? why are you surprised at the kind of instruments I use? My power is great and limitless and I will let My words be known through wretched souls....

Vassula, many will ask Me for a sign, that this guidance comes from Me; but the sign that I will give is you; I have delivered you from evil awakening you; I raised you up and lifted you to My Heart, pouring on you many of My works; accept what I give you, for Wisdom is leading you;

Vassula, I love you; little one, you are Mine; daughter, give Me love and give Me rest; let Me rest in your heart; accept Me, Vassula, do not deny Me; Vassula do you know how many years I was waiting for you to accept Me? oh how alienated you were from My Heart, have I ever told you how I felt then?

I do not really remember, Jesus.

I will tell you; I have been fearing for you, you had drifted away from Me and My Heart was utterly torn with sorrow;

Vassula, how then could you resist My appeal, beloved? I have been waiting for <u>so</u> many years; Vassula, accept My love; My love heals you;

It's not that I refuse You, Jesus, it's just that I feel more comfortable to <u>give</u> and love rather than receive. I think You know me.

(I felt sad, because I hurt Jesus without willing. Jesus immediately felt this.)

come with Me, I have a secret I want to tell you; Vassula, do you know why I love you?

Yes, you told me already.

there is still one more reason; I love you because you love My children;

come now nearer to Me, will you let Me enter your heart?

Yes, do, Jesus.

how happy you made Me, for I know I can rest in you; do not deny Me again, for I but long to enter hearts;

You will probably find stains ....

all impurities I will find, I <u>will</u> wash away; beloved, My Blood will purify you;

February 1, 1987

Vassula, it is I, Jesus Christ; I love you;
any message bearing blames or harsh words, know that it is not coming from Me; I am love, love, love;

---

[1] It seemed like God did not want to spare a minute.

My heart is an abyss of love; the guidance I am giving you is adjusted for you; regard yourself as a toddler who has but started her first steps, no one expects a toddler to walk with confidence and self-assurance; My guidance is for a beginner, I teach you in gradual steps and every step you take with Me I bless; I am your Father,[1] helping you and teaching you My child to walk with Me;

here is My answer to your thought; I love you all in the same way;

You speak of specially chosen souls.

are you not a chosen one? I love you all;

daughter, I have longed to have you near Me; how I longed for you to love Me, how I long for the rest of My beloved children to love Me; I call them; I spend all day and night behind their doors, waiting, hoping for a response; I watch them incessantly, My eyes never leaving them; I watch them filled up with sorrow; if they only knew in what state of poverty their souls are, if they only knew how they are damaging and hurting their souls;

I am near you, I am calling you to come to Me; do not be afraid; I will not reproach you; I do not call you to reproach your sins; I call you to meet Me if it is but for just a few minutes; come to Me, you poor souls come and meet Me and get to know your loving Father;[2] He Himself will feed you with His own Body; He will slacken your thirst with His own Blood;[3] He will heal you if you are sick; He will comfort you if you are distressed; He will envelop you with His love and warm you if you feel cold; do not refuse Me; I am Love and I love you in spite of your wickedness; I say I love you even if you despise Me; I am a God full of pity, always ready to receive you and let you live in My Heart;

daughter, how I pain to watch them slumbering while they are slowly sinking deeper and deeper in vile depths of sin; if they could only know how their iniquities render their souls! I tell you that your life on earth is but a passing shadow, but your life in Heaven is for eternity there; there you will live eternally near your Creator in His glory, for let Me remind you that you are His own children;

Vassula, I will call all those who persecute Me and defile My Name in My following message;

Yes, Lord.

February 2, 1987

O daughter, all I ask from all of you is love; My Father created you because of love; He gave His only Son because of love; I suffered for you and died on the Cross for love; I saved you from dying because of love; so why, why do some of you hate Me and persecute Me? are you hating Me because of My given Laws; am I preventing you to live free and fall into rebellion? have you perhaps not heard of Me because no one was there to teach you? thus developing your own laws, languishing for earthly wealth and pleasures, following your own inclinations?

children, beloved ones, this is the beginning of your hatred for Me; it is because you do not know Me; come then and meet Me; I am Love, believe in Me; if you tell Me that you do not know Me, I tell you that I knew you before you were born and I have consecrated you; if you tell Me that you hate Me, I tell you I love you; if you have sinned, I have forgiven you; if you have profaned My name, I have shown My Mercy on you; if you have wounded Me, I still love you and offer you to share My Kingdom in Heaven; in spite of your iniquities I forgive you fully;

---
[1] Is. 9:5.
[2] Is. 9:5-6: 'For there is a child born for us (...) and this is the name they give him: Wonder-Counsellor, Mighty God, <u>Eternal Father</u>, Prince of Peace.'
[3] Look at Jn. 6:48-51.

Vassula, I love you, have rest, I will continue dictating to you later on;

(Later on:)

I am here, it is I, Jesus Christ; let Me dictate to you, daughter, My words; hear Me now and discern Me;
are you fearing Me, are you denying Me because My eyes see through you and can read all that your soul has done? do not fear Me, for I have already forgiven you; My Blood was shed for your salvation;
I was on earth in flesh; I lived among sinners, healing the sick and raising the dead; I have not forsaken you; for I am still among you, healing you; come to Me to be healed, I will raise your souls to Me; I will teach you to love Me and to love one another; if you are weak, My Strength will sustain you; if you are lost, I will be there and show you the Way; My Law is a <u>Law of Love</u>; follow it; by following it I will open your hearts to be able to receive Me;
I will inspire you, I will teach you how to love, how to forgive, how to be holy and live holy; come then, beloved ones, come and learn from Me; I am Love; I am Peace; I am Mercy; I am Meek and Humble; I am Forgiveness; I love you all;

February 3, 1987

Lord, I feel void, empty, not as usual. Cold as a stone!

Vassula, it is I who prunes your branches, giving strength to you; I am your Devout Keeper; by pruning you I strengthen you, so that your fruit may be plenty;

February 4, 1987

little one do you know why I love you? here is one more reason; because you are My flower, allowing Me to prune you; allowing Me to feed you and allowing My Light to shine on you;
I am helping you to grow to bear the fruits of Peace and Love;
I am your Lord and Master;

February 5, 1987

beloved, I am Yahweh and My ecclesiastical editions are from Me; I have fed you; I am forming you, daughter;
I am the Almighty; have no fear;
listen, daughter, fulfil My Word;
I came and delivered you from evil to be in My light for you are to be My bearer; I will give you strength, I am always beside you, never have any doubt;

My incapacity is GREAT and I am afraid of the circumstances.

you need not fear, for My power will envelop you, thus giving you My strength to tread on My foes;
be on your guard for many will try and discourage you saying that this guidance is not from Me; I know how little you are and helpless; so be near Me and let Wisdom lead you, all authority will come from Me;
understand that Wisdom comes from Me;
all those that have eyes, let them see; all those that have a heart, let them understand, that it is I, Yahweh Sabaoth, who speaks; I have never forsaken you; I am delivering Wisdom to re-establish My given Word; I come to remind you all of My love for you, blessing you all; I do not want to see you lost, woe to the unwise! purify yourselves for the time is near; listen to My words, for in doing what I ask you I will forgive you; I am guiding you to live in Peace and Love, for I am a God of Peace and Love;
live holy, pray for forgiveness and I will bless you;
you are all My children whom I have created with love;

come, bind My words in your hearts for it is I, Yahweh, who guides you;

Lord, I am helpless and do not know anything. I only see a big mountain in front of me!

fear not, Vassula, for you are not the first helpless messenger I raised giving My word; have faith in Me; trust Me and I am guiding you;

February 9, 1987

peace be with you; I love you child; I am Yahweh; I have chosen you mainly because I willed it but also because you are so helpless;

I love you, Father, very much.

I know and I love you too, daughter; hear Me, have you felt as happy as now, before you loved Me?

No, never!

love Me Vassula; it is I who taught you how to love Me; are you willing to progress?

Yes, Father, so that I am able to glorify you. I want to do all what you ask because I do want You glorified.

Vassula, I will progress you; I want to warn you of evils; they[1] hate you and are constantly setting traps for you; I am near you guarding you, so do not fear;
 Vassula, I love you and I love all My children, My love is like a consuming flame constantly ablaze; My love is a jealous love; I thirst for love; fear not, for it is Love I am talking about little one; I hold you and your littleness delights Me; little one, through your frailty I will manifest My appeal for Peace and Love; I will fill you with My words; I will breathe into you My revelations; little one cling to Me, trust Me and love Me with fervour;
 let them know, tell them of My love I have for them;

February 10, 1987

Vassula it is I, Jesus Christ; I am with you, beloved; do you know that I am guiding you through Hades?[2] have no fear, My light is on you, protecting you from evil; having you exposed in Hades many souls are healing;
 I have taught you to love Me; love Me, your love for Me is healing them;[3] I use your love as a remedy to cure them; heal them Vassula, heal them; you are bearing My Cross with Me, Vassula; these works are heavenly works that My Father is revealing to you, many heavenly works are still hidden and are but mysteries to you;

Many people will not accept this, Jesus. They will blame it on my fantasy.

Vassula, how many among them have understood fully My Father's works on earth?

Many Works are not understood and are still mysteries to us.

how then will they understand what is heavenly?
 Vassula, all Wisdom is given to mere children; My Father delights in children; be happy, daughter, and praise My Father for being good to you; daughter, be His bearer and glorify Him; do not worry, I am guiding you; work in this way; I am your Teacher;
 I will continue forming you, beloved; I am forming you as well as My other

---

[1] The demons.

[2] Purgatory. (My soul is 'exposed' in purgatory. By loving God, souls can be liberated from purgatory. Prayers liberate souls from purgatory too.)
[3] Extinguishing their fires.

children; go in peace and remember that you are guided by Me; hear Me, I love you and I want you to be with Me;
 Vassula, I am pleased that your faith has augmented; purify yourself by eating Me and drinking Me;

I will, Jesus. I will go to receive Holy Communion.

come to Me, all My love covers you; I love you child;

Jesus, I love You and I'll fight for You.

fight I do not want! for I am Peace and you will work with peace, for Peace;
 fill Me with joy remaining as close to Me as possible; will you kiss My feet?

(I took a picture of Jesus and kissed His Feet.)

I love you, go in peace;

February 11, 1987

Vassula, it is I, Jesus Christ; daughter your sufferings will be Mine and My sufferings will be yours; you will share all what I have, yes, even My sufferings; I will be near you, consoling you when you need Me, but I want to be consoled in return when I am suffering;

Jesus, You do not really <u>need</u> anybody, especially me!

no, I do not need anybody, I suffice by Myself; but do I not share everything I have with you? I am your Saviour, your Healer, your Father,[1] your Spouse; I am your God who will never ever abandon you;

(In the evening while in the hall downstairs and about to climb the stairs with my hands full of glasses I very clearly discerned a huge dark cross on the upper level of the staircase. Huge it was. Jesus hanged on it, moaning, with agony, covered in bruises and blood. I had to go by it. I didn't know what to do. While passing it I heard Jesus call saying: "oh help Me, Vassula, come near Me;" I ran quickly up, left those glasses on the table and ran and took my scrapbook and Jesus wrote: "My agony is great, My sufferings are many, will you not help Me, I who died for you? I am nailed on My Cross and I cannot come to you, so come, I want you nearer; Vassula, how I love you all, heal My children, call them, have them love Me; be blessed, be near Me, I love you". While He wrote this down He made me feel all alarmed and I had not realised that in a few seconds I was covered with sweat.)

Vassula, I, Jesus, suffer and you discerned fully My Cross and I on it;
 I want you to feel My agony, suffer with Me daughter; live in Me and I will let you feel My pierced Heart, wounded by the lance and wounded by so many beloved souls; I love you, would you deny Me? I who suffered and died for you, will your heart have the courage to resist Me? I have suffered for love; I have called you out of love; I blessed you; I fed you; so now since I chose you, I will expect you to console Me, to love Me ardently; I will expect you to respond to Me;
 Vassula, have no fear; abandon yourself fully to Me; yes, surrender completely, abandoning yourself entirely to Me and leave Me free to do with you whatsoever I want to;

I have already agreed to work for You, Lord. So now You can do what You please with me, Lord.

yes, surrender; I love you, it pleases Me to hear you surrendering; never ever refuse Me for My love for you is unlimited;
 I will continue My teachings in giving you a secret; Vassula take your scrap book; fear not for My teachings come from Wisdom, all mysteries have not yet

---

[1] Read Is. 9:5-6.

been revealed; all works are given to those who know how to love Me;

(*I will take my scrap-book now ... Jesus gave me the secret. Then He said: "I will reveal many more hidden works to you." That was the third secret.*)

every day that goes by, you come closer to Me;

what does this mean?

it means that I will soon be with you;

(*Death does not scare me at all!*)

February 12, 1987

God Almighty, I do not want to fall in vanity or self-interest, I ask you to help me! I want to remain a nothing. I want to remain plain and give <u>You</u> all Glory!

Vassula, I am Yahweh; I love you;
 all authority will come from Me, little one; I will always remind you of your littleness; I will let you understand how I work; find peace Vassula, I am soon with you;

(*I felt relieved knowing that God will always remind me of my nothingness! I had an awful day, only doubts, that this is quite impossible, and that the whole thing is untrue, I felt that what is happening is not happening, yet I heard God calling me, it is like its absolutely real and yet nothing real, I suddenly felt as really the most wretched among men. What <u>is</u> really happening?*)

Vassula, have you forgotten how you were a year ago; My beloved, let Me remind you; when I, Yahweh, was passing among the dead,[1] I saw you there among the wicked; they were holding you, tormenting you; I saw you lying there, struggling on your own, your soul close to death; I felt full of pity for you; you remembered My works of old times and you realised then that I could be your refuge and so I heard your plea from earth;
 daughter, I always loved you, but you had forgotten Me; I yearned to be loved by you, to hear you call Me Father; for how many years I have been outside your door waiting, waiting that one day you might hear Me ... I was at hand's reach; yes, I was so near you; then, My Heart could not resist your plea; I came <u>full of joy</u>; finally, you called Me; I lifted you to My breast, daughter, and I healed your wounds; I taught you how to love Me; I taught you how to receive Me by elevating you, and I let My Light shine upon you .. My flower, do not despair; I am teaching you step by step, <u>with the vocabulary that you understand</u>;[2]
 you are asking Me why has part of My guidance been written before your formation; I will answer your question after you reply to My question; do you know how valuable just one single soul is to Me?

I know it is valuable, but how much, that I do not know My God.

I will tell you then how valuable souls are to Me thus replying to your question; a soul for Me is as valuable as to have written part of My guidance just for that single soul who would have had no other opportunity before his departure; do you understand now?

Yes, I do, and I know whom You mean.

I love you daughter, have no doubt that this guidance is from Me; I will always remind you who awakened you from your slumber;
 I love you, be always sure of My love; work in peace and do not forget Me;

---

[1] The spiritual dead.

[2] God emphasised this.

February 13, 1987

peace be with you; I am here, it is I, Jesus, who guides you; have no fear; unite in Me, Vassula; all I want from you is love;

I am worrying about the messages, I feel responsible. I don't know how to work!

I am self-sufficient and I am able to help all My children without your help, but as a Spouse, I want to share everything; do not worry for I am Strength, beloved; lean on Me and let Me lead; remember that I it is who give you this force to meet Me; I ask from you to love Me faithfully; love Me fervently; comfort Me when I ask for comfort for there are many among you who wound Me; such a multitude of sins are committed daily, grieving My soul, embittering Me, filling up My chalice with sorrows; how have they forgotten Me? Vassula, when a Spouse feels grieved where would He turn to for consolation but to His bride who loves Him;

I will console you if I can, but what to do, I who am, I know unworthy, probably hurting you unwillingly, insufficient and embarrassed (timid) to talk to You, filled with indignity!

I know that all what you said is true, but have I not chosen you, knowing all your weaknesses? I love you, Vassula, and all I want from you is a response to My love;

I love you a lot. You are constantly in my mind. I live for You. I love You, I cannot measure how much but you can, I can only ask You to teach me to love You more so that it becomes immeasurable.

beloved, pose your head on Me and let Me anoint you with purity to become one of My saturated flowers having absorbed Me; come, I will feed you, from My hand you will eat;
I will teach you to love Me more;

February 14, 1987

(After reading The Memorare of Saint Bernard (a small prayer to St. Mary).)

all the guidance is from God;
Vassula, can you hear Me? listen again Vassula, it is I, St Mary, do not fear Me; Vassula, I know your difficulties to realise that all this is really happening, but I ask from you to trust God; augment your faith;
He is working in you child; do not restrain yourself from submission, abandon yourself in His hands and do what He asks from you; I am near you helping you; have peace for He is guiding you;
Vassula, Jesus is forming you to become strong to be able to resist temptation; He feeds you, giving you all that you are lacking;
remember, daughter, Wisdom has brought you up; do realise why;

It is not just for me? All this, it's meant for others, too?

yes, you are being formed to be God's bearer;

I do not know how to be God's bearer.

God has preached to you and has taught you to love Him; trust Him for His riches are innumerable and His Mercy unfathomable; He loves you with ineffable tenderness and watches over you with loving eyes; every heavenly word lives forever;

I have to learn to love You more.

I will teach you, have peace;

(Later on:)

Vassula, it I, Jesus; I am giving you strength to meet Me;
progress with Me for I will institute My given words so that many can read

them and profit from them; daughter, when My given guidance will be established, I shall prepare you to meet Me; I long to have you near Me;

Vassula, look at Me;[1] are you happy meeting Me in this way?

Yes, very, I don't deserve this charism at all.

accept it; <u>accept what I give, I give even to the most wretched souls</u>; Vassula, have you heard that I give wisdom to mere children and not to the learned and clever;

Yes, I have, why is this?

because children are My weakness, they let Me form them;

I chose unworthy souls to form, ones who know little or next to nothing; <u>I</u> will supply you, Vassula, for I am wealthy; with Me you will lack nothing;

I love you, do you realise how happy you make Me every time we meet? I feel happy having you finally near Me; would not a father rejoice having found his lost child? you were lost and My heart was utterly torn with sorrow; you had wandered away leaving Me in despair; I went to look for you and found you; how then would I not rejoice having you near Me? Vassula, near Me you will learn; I will teach you all virtues to enable you to glorify Me; My child, learn to absorb the dew of righteousness; learn to glorify Me; learn from Wisdom; I love you; leave now in peace and call Me when you wish; let us pray together,

(We prayed.)

be now My companion and keep Me in your heart;

February 15, 1987

I love you, but maybe I love you in the wrong way. What is right or wrong I don't know; I worship You.

Vassula, love is love; I want you to love Me without restraint; I am your Holy Father who loves you intimately; approach Me and love Me intimately; I want to be intimate with you;

do not fear, I want all your love; Vassula I want you today to repent;

Should I repent to You now?

yes, repent, I am listening;[2] yes, daughter, I forgive all your sins for they are many;

Vassula do you know that I am He who taught My teachers to repent? they are My instructions; I have given to My teachers the authority to have My children confess to them;

child, I wrote it;[3] Vassula, refuse Me nothing; I will demand from you many things; are you ready to follow your God and Saviour?

I will, as long as I <u>recognise</u> that it's coming from You. I will follow you because I love You.

Vassula, never fear Me, trust Me; I am preparing you to face bigger trials; are you ready to follow Me?

With Your help I will be.

have no fear for I am near you, supporting you;

daughter, leave yourself entirely in My hands; let Me use you beloved for healing souls; let Me bind you to Me with love's chains; let Me feel you are entirely Mine; let Me, who am your Creator, possess you;

---

[1] I looked in Jesus' face. He looked straight at me.

[2] I did.

[3] I tried to erase 'confess' but my hand was blocked by God. I am against the confessions.

I have longed for your love; let My love enkindle your heart now; be Mine entirely; I longed for you, I long for you; do you never long for Me, Vassula?

I do.

(Or do I think I do?)

Vassula, beloved, by giving yourself to Me will both glorify Me and purify you;
I now bind you to Me, I, God the Most High, will be with you till the end;
– I tell you truly, that I have chosen you knowing you are nothing, helpless, wretched and sinful, but in spite of all your faults I love you; yes, I love you all in spite of your iniquities;

Lord, did You bind me now?

yes I have; I love you; it is out of love, I want you always near Me; beloved, hear Me, My bonds are bonds of love, they are bonds of purity; I love you, let My children understand how much I can love them;
My clemency has no limits; My love is a consuming flame enkindling every heart which receives Me;
daughter, leave now and remember that I am leading you; remember who purified you,[1] have you forgotten? have I not anointed you Myself?

Yes, Lord, on the 13th.

Vassula, I have Myself given you My Bread and Wine; remember I chose the time for you to purify you child;[2]
love Me, let us work together;

(This reminded me of the first time I took Holy Communion in this Church. Again it was done in a mystical way. I was with Karl the priest, God had sent me to him to get Holy Communion. He was not sure whether he should give it or not because it was asked in this mystical way. Then Karl said that he will talk to God, pray, but not aloud so that I won't hear what he says and I should let my hand write, from God the answers. God wrote:

"I WILL"

I asked Karl what he had asked. He said he had asked whether he should make me give my confession to him. God answered that He will.[3] Karl without hesitation told me to simply come for Holy Communion in four days. In the meantime, God asked me to repent. I did not know how, so he explained to me what to say. I did it with Him. Then the next day I had Holy Communion.)

February 16, 1987

(I started to realise that really I can't live without God. I think He really attached me.)

I am Yahweh, child; it is I, turn to Me; I love you and because of this <u>great</u> love I have for you I hold you; do not fear, child; hear Me; because of My elate love I have for you, I bind you to Me; lean on Me, I want you to need Me Vassula;

Do you love us so much?

O daughter have you not felt My love?[4] My Love for you wants to consume you;
I feel glorified to feel how attached you are to Me; I for My part love you inexhaustibly and I will not part from you ever; but I have also made sure that neither will you; I made sure of our union; see? ... I delight to have prevailed;
I desired us to be united forever; you needing Me, loving Me and bound forever to Me and I bound to you; leaving Me free

---

[1] I couldn't understand so I hesitated.
[2] True for in Church I fully discerned Jesus at the Tabernacle chanting, with the others. He Himself gave Me Bread and Wine.
[3] Exceptionally this time.
[4] Yes, of course I have. It is unbelievable.

to love you without restraint and reign over you;

I who created you and I who nursed you, I who consecrated you and I who was first to lay eyes on you; I who filled you with My Spirit willed it; for I, Vassula, am your God, Yahweh, who brought you up;

I made sure that the bonds I have attached you to Me are for eternity; you will be unable to detach yourself from Me for I am the Most High;

It's frightening, even though I love you, Lord! Your Power and Wisdom are great!

Why Vassula, what have you to fear? Am I not Lord of Love?

I will care for you; I will soothe you if in pain; I will cover you with My blessings; I will provide what you lack; I am Infinite Wealth; you need not fear with Me, I am He who holds the earth's foundations; leave Me free to do with you whatsoever I want; I am so happy having you near Me, you so frail and weak, for I know that your heart will let Me do as I please with you; fear not, for I am your Heavenly Father, and I love you beyond any human understanding;

I am Yahweh and if you have not heard afore, I am telling you now, that I am known to be Faithful and My word stands secure;

child, I have revived you from death to let My Word be written, I have brought you up to be My bearer;

Since you are to be My bearer, you have to be formed; you must learn how I feel, how I work and how My love enkindles hearts; how else would you be able to tell My beloved children?

come; feel My presence the way I have taught you; I love you little one; discern Me; I want you to be intimate with Me;

Vassula, tomorrow I will dictate to you a message teaching My children how to be with Me; go now and fulfil your other duties; go in peace;

(Jesus came later on:)

Vassula write; you are now united with Me, you will work with Me, you will suffer with Me, you will help Me, yes, I will share everything I have with you and for your part you will do the same;

being united is being forever together; because My bonds are eternal bonds, My elate love binds you forever to Me; My love enkindles even the hearts out of stone and puts them ablaze consuming them;

daughter, I have prevailed; you need not fear, I have won your heart, beloved, and I made sure that you will forever be Mine; O Vassula how I longed to thrust you in the depths of My Heart and let all the flames of My love utterly consume you, leaving you in total rapture for Me, your God;

Do You love me as much as that? To have done this?

have I not laid out My life for you? I laid out My life out of love, I sacrificed Myself for your salvation, out of love; I shed My Blood for you, out of love;

now I made sure that you are bound to Me;

Why?

why, have you forgotten that I am All Faithful; having you bound to Me I will be sure that you too will remain faithful to Me;

now that we are united we will continue working together; I will use your love for Me to heal many souls who are bound to be engulfed in Satan's flames; you and I are going to help these souls; all you have to do is love Me fervently; there will be times where I will come to you entrusting you with My Cross;

But I am nothing!

Vassula, remain nothing and let Me be everything you lack; wherever I go you will follow; alone you will never ever be; you are now united to Me;[1] grow in spirit, Vassula; grow, for your task is to deliver all messages given by Me and My Father; Wisdom will instruct you;

Yes, Father.

how beautiful to hear you call Me Father! I longed to hear from your lips this word, Father;[2]

February 17, 1987

Vassula why, why were you avoiding calling Me Father? Vassula I love being called Father;[3] I am Father of all humanity;

I love you, Father.

I love you too;

February 18, 1987

peace be with you;
 Vassula you need not rush, learn that I work gently, keep close to Me; – remember we are in Hades;[4]

(Later on:)

My Light covers you; anyone [5] who approaches you cannot touch you or harm you; My Light is upon you as a Halo of All Redemption;
 your love for Me heals and saves many lost souls, on the way to perdition; Vassula, they[6] are like little children left on their own, not knowing which direction to take; they are lost; when I am with them, I feed them giving them love, some of them then follow Me, you are helping them to love Me and follow Me;[7] I am using you, Vassula, in this way;

Should I then be patient with them and pray daily?

yes, have patience with them for they are beloved to Me; heal them, love them, Vassula;
 I am teaching you Wisdom, Heavenly works are from Wisdom; understand when I am teaching you;
 come, lean on Me, do you wish to leave now?

No, Jesus, we go on.

O daughter, I love you beloved; work with Me and glorify Me; I love your littleness; you are My saturated flower having absorbed Me fully; child, need Me always for without Me you will perish; I will give you all that you lack till the end; let Me completely free with you for I know what your needs are;

(I felt as though I will be unable to take down God's guidance, for it is difficult as I have all the time interruptions and insults from evil. Sometimes I feel as though God abandoned me completely to be their sport. The more it advances the worse the insults, for a moment I thought God left me. The insults are the worst words one can tell!)

Vassula, will I ever abandon you? I am All Faithful, have you forgotten My words?

It's my fault. I'm weak!

---

[1] While writing, I was wondering why He says I should remain nothing now and before He said I must hurry and change, growing stronger etc. He must have read my thoughts because He answered immediately. Next sentence.
[2] I had made it a point while praying that night to avoid saying Father, but referred to Him instead as 'God', being careful to avoid the word 'Father'. I don't really know why, but maybe I thought I should put more formality in my prayers.
[3] Is. 9:5.
[4] Jesus again took me in spirit in Hades, to see the souls.
[5] Any persecutor.

[6] We are like lost sheep.
[7] With our love we can bring people back to Jesus.

give Me now your weakness and My Strength will dissolve it;
 come, I will sanctify you Myself, I have with you reached My heaven, for in you I find My rest; remember we are united and our bonds are bonds of peace and love; these cords which attach your wrists and feet to Mine are for eternity; for beloved you are Mine; I Myself have purified you uniting you to Me; I have triumphed over you;
 I wished that you love Me; have no fear for I am Jesus holding you; with Me you are to be and feel My Presence; all I ask from you is love; do you love Me?

You know I do, Jesus.

love Me without measure; look at Me, have My peace;
 is there something you want to tell Me?

Yes, Jesus.

(I felt guilty for having to say this to Him.)

Jesus, although I love taking down this guidance and being with you, I must do other things too!

Vassula, happy are those who withdraw from their occupations and follow Me; you are indeed devoting a lot of your time writing with Me, but let Me tell you something else too; I also love to see you work and accomplish minor duties, duties of small importance, so long as you do them with love; every little work you do, no matter how small and meaningless becomes great in My eyes and pleases Me, as long as these small acts are done with Love; be blessed;

(In the evening we had guests and I was counting plates, napkins etc. I thought I had everything on my tray. I hesitated, and asked, knowing Jesus was with me, "What do we need more?" He answered me without hesitation: "We need love, Vassula;")

February 19, 1987

Vassula, allow yourself to suffer; all My chosen souls suffered; by suffering your soul is purified like gold is purified in fire; so is the soul; your suffering is in your guidance;

How in my guidance, Jesus?

although I allow you to call Me any time in this way and thus be together, I also allow the gates of evil to be left open; your guidance will not be an easy task, for you will have evil fighting you by discouraging you, in giving you the wrong word;

But, Lord, Your guidance can mislead me!

no, it will never mislead you or anybody else; I have taught you to recognise Me, Vassula;
 I have chosen someone with an incapacity of mastering any language, one who will depend on My given words; I have taught you to hear Me, I am training your ear; come, be patient, learn to accept, learn from Me;

(I started to worry.)

Vassula, all <u>will</u> be perfect! Vassula edit;[1] it is I, Jesus;

(Doubts again!)

O come, I long to tell you something; My heaven is in you, because I feel glorified and rested;

Jesus, I love you. Yes a lot too, 24 hrs a day I do. Even when I wake up in the night, my first thought is You. I eat, it's You. I work at home, it's You. I drive it's You. I play tennis and You are in my mind and love is in my blood for You since my body aches from

---

[1] Jesus used the word I would have used and I realised how God adapts Himself to the soul's capacity.

love. But, I cannot accept that I can give You rest, or that You find heaven in me, for what am I? A speck of dust, impossible I am, and when You tell me this I feel even worse in Your presence and ashamed.

all that you said about yourself is true, but I love you and I do find rest in you; I have irrigated your heart with My Blood and placed it in Mine; I have purified it and given it My Peace and Love beloved; Vassula, I who came to you, always wanted your love; now I have prevailed, I delight in you; love Me without restraint making up for those who forget Me and are but multiplying My wounds; love Me, Vassula, healing My beloved souls; be My heaven;

(Later on:)

My God, I realise it is You, yet I do not think I fully realise!

Vassula, you will one day;

If I do, I think I will faint!

when My word will be established; Vassula, I have always been known to keep My word;
I, Yahweh,[1] come from above; Heaven is made by My grace; I will fulfil My word, trust Me Vassula; do not worry too much beloved; be near Me; feel Me; love Me and glorify Me; leave the rest to Me; live in peace;
I am forming you with Wisdom, have My grace; weary not in healing souls; are you happy being now united to Me?

Yes, Lord, I am very happy to feel I am united to You, although I could not dare think of it.

why, Vassula?

Why? because of my not being fit for You.

Vassula, I always longed to be united with you and be intimately close to you, nevertheless never forget that I am your God and Holy;
Vassula will you still work for Me?

I have given my consent already. I am willing to continue working for Yahweh.

I am Yahweh, be blessed;

(Later on:)

(I read the prayer to St. Mary: The Memorare of St. Bernard.)

daughter, it is Jesus who guides you, do not fear, Vassula My daughter; listen to Me, your Holy Mother, I am here, present, near you; I am helping you, I love you; I will help you understand the way Jesus works, do not worry;
Jesus has united you now to Him; rejoice, Vassula; you must believe Me when I tell you that your soul heals other souls in Hades;[2] Vassula, do as Jesus asks you; He knows your needs; all He wants from you is love; love Him without restraint, glorify Him, amend for those that embitter Him; call Him, always telling Him you love Him; forsake Him not; accomplish all your other duties too with love, for love, for acts of love are what counts most for Him, no matter how little and insignificant they appear to you, they are of great value in His eyes and thus become great; follow Him and amend for others who neglect Him;
daughter, by being now united to Him you will feel His Cross; you will feel His Heart; He will ask you to share His feelings; He will ask you to help Him; He will ask you for rest; He will ask you to share His Cross; suffer when He suffers, rejoice when He rejoices; your sufferings will be His; comply with His wishes for He is God; learn to recognise Him, remember all what He taught you, for He is a Loving God All Merciful; He loves you

---

[1] The Father was speaking now.

[2] Purgatory for me was known by the word Hades.

all with ineffable tenderness; He will never demand from you anything that would harm you; He is gentle and good; learn to recognise Him, Vassula;

He is a God full of Love, never harsh; He will watch over you protecting you from all evil; He will never abandon you;

Vassula, courage; daughter, call Me when you wish; I love you;

I love You too, Mother. Teach me to love You more!
Jesus, I love You.

I am here, beloved; it is I, Jesus;

(I surrender all over again.)

I love you; give Me your little heart in which I will sow the seeds of Peace and Love; I will form you like I desire you to be; nothing will go in vain; all will be for saving My children; do not fear, let Me lead you daughter;

(My love for Jesus was at its full this morning, also a fear that He'll abandon me, since I'm nothing, and a 'nothing' loving God is probably offending His Holy Name.)

O daughter, I love you; be with Me; I will never leave you, O My little one; few are those that glorify Me as you do;

Vassula, My Vassula, I care for you; when I have delivered My guidance I shall not wait further; My Heart longs for your little soul; O how I myself suffer to have you down on earth;[1] I shall take you back to Me, delivering you and rejoicing My Heart, for I burn with desire to have you again with Me; have My Peace, I am with you soon;

Vassula do you want to take in writing My next Message?

Yes, Lord.

are you ready?

(I had avoided this message for a few days but now I felt ready for it. Jesus had talked about it already some time ago.)

Yes, Lord.

do you Love Me?

Very much. You know I do.

do you desire that others love Me too?

Yes, this is my wish now.

work then with Me and write down all that I tell you; yes, Vassula?

I just wanted to say that this is like a miracle, being able to be guided in this way, Lord.

(Peace Message.)

I willed it, Vassula; I have chosen you to show the world that I need neither authority nor holiness;

I have chosen a mere child, helpless and sinful with no authority and knowing no one in power, to manifest through this weak instrument, with My grace, My Peace and Love I have for you all;

I want to convey to this dark world My Message, thus showing My effusions to the world; for My Mercy is ineffable and My affection beyond any human understanding;

Heaven above with all its Glory, reigns forever in peace and love and I shall see that on earth too all peace and love prevails evil;[2] My peace will cover the earth like mist, spreading from the heights to the depths and from one end of the globe to the other end;

I come to proclaim My Message to you all and turn you away from your evil doings; My word will be like a cedar, spreading out its branches like arms, healing your wickedness, feeding your misery and delivering you from evil; I

---

[1] In this dark world of today.

[2] Thy Will be done on earth as it is in Heaven...

come once more to enlighten this dark world and revive this flickering flame about to extinct and cover you with My Peace;[1]

I love them Vassula, o this love I have for them! have I not sacrificed Myself as a Lamb for them, to liberate them? I suffered for them;

My beloved ones, was My Blood shed in vain? I have poured out my Blood that your sins may be immersed in It and that you may be purified; I have bathed you in the torrents of My Blood to conquer evil and deliver you;

I am among you all; but, nevertheless, Satan is escorting you, for he has found means to seduce you and make you fall into his impious nets;

I, God, cannot see you heading into perdition, I am here to untangle you from his vices;

It is thus I stand before you, that you may know who your Saviour is; I come once more with My Heart in My Hand, offering it to you; will you refuse it? will you refuse My Peace? I come to call those who conform My children into bloodshed; I want them to hear My call, for My word will come like a hammer, shattering the rock,[2] penetrating every heart;

I ask you, have you forgotten your God, or is He of little account in your eyes? have you no fear of Me? I weary with your lofty aims! I have taught you to love Me but also to fear[3] Me, for I am the Almighty;

so what have you done? you are gnawing down your own graves, by having sown seeds of wickedness, dispersing them around the world, reaping them now and feeding yourselves upon its fruit of evil; learn that My whole Kingdom reigns in Peace, the whole of My creation was created in peace and love; My eyes have grown tired watching you slaughtering one another;

I care for you, for I am your Father who loves you; behold, I come with all My Sovereignty; I, who am your God, I come to you offering you My Heart; here, take It, all of It is yours; My Heart rends and lacerates, feel It; all of It is but one big wound .... you have torn the Heart of your God; you have pierced it through again and again;

leaders of war, will I have to come and tread on you showing you My power? will I have to reveal myself with wrath? My chalice of Mercy has brimmed over and My chalice of Justice is full! I, who breathed in you Life and consecrated you, I, God of all creation, who bathed you in My Holiness, come to you with My Peace, exhorting you to convert yourselves and live in My Peace;

I will cover the entire universe with My Peace letting it reign over you; for I am Peace and Love and All Wisdom; My appeal is addressed to all nations; they must know that peace reigns in My Kingdom; I come in spite of their wickedness to bless them and shine on them for they are My beloved sons and daughters;

listen to this Heart your God is offering you, a Heart you have forgotten and know no more, a Heart who loves you and seeks you out to impart life;

cease to do evil! cease rebelling against Me! are you afraid of My Law? My Law is not a Law of rebellion, My law is a law of peace and love, follow My given Law, respond to It and salvation will be yours; your weakness is to ignore My Law, bigoted by your own, thus leading mankind into destruction, antagonising your neighbours; your laws are based on violence;

O children! have I implanted in your soul hatred? My Soul is the Source of Love and Life in Itself and from It came all into being;

---

[1] Through my mind, a thought passed, I was thinking: "But with those sort of people, it's not worth the trouble, they'll never listen".
[2] One day, suddenly God enlightened me to understand that rock is our hearts, our hearts covered with stone.
[3] To accept, respect.

Vassula, do no more; I love you; trust Me, let your love cover My Heart, unite; love and work with Me;

I will, Father. Help me be worthy so that I may be able to glorify you.

February 26, 1987

(Beatrice and I flew to Chittagong and from there crossed the river to find the village Diang where we could meet Raymond Dujarrier who is a French, semi-hermit, mystic, Catholic priest, but also Hindu, Moslem and Buddhist. All in one. To exchange a few ideas and show him the writings. He called them: Divine Revelations of the Heart. What he said corresponded very much to the idea of the revelations and their purpose: that they are not for me only but for the benefit of others. Our whole trip went on perfectly smooth as if someone had programmed it. I forgot to mention that the day before our departure for Diang I had a feeling of great distress and was asking myself why I am going to Diang, to show what, to show rubbish? The whole day passed in agony. Then early the same day of our departure the first words appeared: "A liar was guiding you, collect everything and burn it." I knew then that evil from the day before was trying to stop my trip. A few seconds after this message I felt God's presence and He wrote: "I will be with you till the end, we are united forever; let My Light shine on you child; I am Yahweh guiding you; glorify Me by loving Me;")

March 1, 1987

(Today, several times a day, Jesus told me, while I discerned Him around me: "never weary of writing;")

Vassula, I desire that My words be known by many; words that come directly from My lips, for all the revelations I breathed into you are from Me; I work in this way too; now and then I come and refresh all that has already been taught by Me; I am your Saviour, always near you, always ready to withdraw you from evil; I come hoping that My word will penetrate hearts and rest in them;

Vassula will you amend for others?

What does amend mean here exactly, Lord?

amend means to compensate for others, who give no response to My love; repair for others; all you do is love Me with all your heart and mind;

I love You! but I want to learn to love You without measure to be able to amend more.

come, I will teach you; have I ever been known not to keep My word? daughter, I am your Teacher and from Me you will learn everything; I will progress you;

I am unworthy of all what You give me, I know for a fact when I compare myself to the humble and the so dedicated people. I am not proud of myself for having been chosen as the most wretched person, and much worse than the next worst one, to be given this guidance. I know that I have not been chosen for my qualities. On the contrary, I have been chosen because of my wretchedness. You have confirmed it, Lord!

have My peace, Vassula; wretched you are, but I love you anyway; give Me all your wretchedness and My Mercy will consume it; feel loved by Me; come, lean on Me; hear Me; keep Me company; do not forget that I am your Holy Companion;

March 2, 1987

glory be to God the Father for delivering you from evil;

Who is it?

it is I, Jesus, why?

(Here I felt embarrassed. I still do not understand, who is the Father, and what is the difference between the Father and Jesus. If He refers to God the Father, then how could Jesus say He is also Father?)

listen Vassula, give your attention to Me; learn that God and I am One;[1] I am the Father and the Son;[2] now, do you understand? I am One, I am All in One, I am All in One,

You are all in one?!

I am;

And the Light?

I am the Light too; hear Me;

(Here I thought it would be difficult to understand and <u>write</u> down as also the question of Holy Spirit was in my mind too.)

let us try; the Holy Spirit comes from Me; do you understand now? all in One, the Holy Trinity is One;[3] you can call Me Father too;[4] Wisdom comes from Me, I am Wisdom too;
   it is I, Jesus; every time you doubt come to Me;

But I feel embarrassed to still have now and then doubts after having completed eleven copy books of revelations, anybody would not be like me, by now anybody would have turned into a saint!

every time you feel embarrassed I love you more; Vassula, come you are My beloved and I love resting in you;
   do you love Me?

---

[1] Triune God but one in the unity of essence.
[2] 'Anyone who has seen Me has seen the Father... I am in the Father and the Father is in Me' (Jn. 14:9-10).
[3] In substance.
[4] Is. 9:5: 'Eternal Father...'

You know I do, Lord, but at times I feel as cold as a stone! How ungrateful I must be!

every time you have this feeling it is I who uses your love to warm up other souls who are in need of warmth; souls who are cold toward Me, do you understand now?
   daughter write these words now:[5] "I, Yahweh, will cover you with My Love giving you all My Peace, proclaiming My Word to all nations for behold, within Me abideth Love, Peace, Mercy and Wisdom; I will establish My Kingdom on earth as it is in Heaven;"
   Vassula this is only part of My message; write the rest later on; come stay near Me;

March 3, 1987

it is I, Jesus;

Forgive me for all my sins.

I forgive you; come, I delight in you; do you remember the day I showed you My glory?

Yes!

do you wish to follow it up? yes?

(I felt insecure.)

Father, can I wait a little?

be it; I will later on ask you again; I would like to show you more of My glory so that you are able to describe to My children how My Kingdom is;
   as for My previous message; when I feel you are ready to write it down I shall let you know; Vassula, will you let Me use you today?

In which way, Lord?

---

[5] I understood that this is a continuation of the peace message (from February 19, 1987).

by using the essence of the love you have for Me; so love Me fervently, Vassula; I wish to save a very special soul from falling, she is one of My chosen ones; we can still save her, Vassula;

I will leave two pure drops of My Blood on your heart; these two drops will be enough to cover your entire heart and make you feel My sorrow;

What shall I do?

can you work with love, for love?

I will try, Lord.

unite with Me; we will restore her soul today; we will strengthen her;

I will teach you how I work for these are Heavenly works, all Holy works are from Me; Wisdom is instructing you; never forget this, you are My flower which I leave to grow in My Light; I will purify your soil and give you what you lack; I will come back and let you know about My special soul's heart; I love you; love Me Vassula, for so many depend on this love;

(Later on in the afternoon, I was attacked by evil, blaming me. I knew it was not God since I learned that He will never blame me.)

I bless you daughter; I will never blame you for what I, Yahweh, have given you;

I delight in you; I have chosen you to reveal My Face; meditate, My Vassula; feel, feel this love I have for you; shortly you will be seeing Me; yes, I will come;

Lord, when you take me I do not expect anything since I have done nothing and am incapable of doing anything. Again ending with the word 'unworthy'. Yet how I wish to be near You!

Vassula, feel My hand; My hand is trying ever so hard to get hold of you and keep you near Me; I am longing to shelter you; I love to take you thrusting you in the depths of My Heart and hide you there all for Myself; you seem to forget My words, have I not bound you to Me, for eternity? have we not been united by Me placing a wreath of love upon it?[1] My beloved, we are working together; I am your God and Leader;

My Lord, I am weak and need you. I need to be strengthened in everything so that I will be able to glorify You.

Vassula, watch My hands; place your hands in a way that your fingertips touch Mine;

(I saw like lightning coming out from His fingertips, like electricity.[2] I placed my hands and touched His fingertips. This was done in discernment and meditation.)

feel My Holiness; My Strength is penetrating through your fingertips; such works are Heavenly works; I bless you; lean on Me; you have now absorbed Me; keep your hands in Mine feeling My warmth;

(Later on:)

Vassula, hear Me, now we have saved her from falling, rejoice! I have used the essence of your love; we are working together, helping and healing souls; never weary, daughter, in healing them;

(I was again attacked by evil. They said, "Will you disappear from here.")

Vassula, come, approach Me; have My love; do you understand why they hate you? you are snatching from evil My beloved souls, bringing them back to Me;

Lord, what about all the love other people give you, does it help too?

---

[1] On our union.
[2] 'His brightness is like the day, rays flash from His Hands, that is where his Power lies hidden' (Hab. 3:4).

yes! all love is used for restoring and healing souls;

(Continuation of Peace message.)

My Kingdom will spread and keep growing with the love given;
I am telling you truly that all My sufferings will not be in vain; with tremendous Glory I will prevail all evil; I will enkindle every heart thus, outspreading My seeds of Love and Peace, uniting My children; over the entire universe My Light will be shed for thus is My Will;
honour Me, Vassula, by loving Me; kiss My hands;

(I have done it in discernment as well as on a picture.)

glorify Me always; I love you all; come, beloved, nearer to Me, for My love for you is more than you can ever imagine;

(I felt so much happiness from God. God was so happy!)

March 4, 1987

As I know myself so treacherous I fear I might one day, out of weakness, abandon You. The thought is awful. I can't see how this might happen but I don't want it to happen or You leave me either!

Vassula, I, Yahweh, love you; do I ever abandon you? we have bonds together and being bound to each other you will be unable of abandoning Me; see? I have taken care of our union; we will stay united till the end, you needing Me and loving Me fervently and I free reigning over you and loving you without restraint; never without the desire of delivering you to Me;

Did you say that, My God?

I have said it;

are you going to ask Me your question?

I don't dare!

why? do not fear Me;

(I knew that He knew but I did not want it on paper.)

Please God!

come, let us learn; I am the Almighty and I know what is best for your soul; if one of you asks Me a question or a favour I <u>will</u> answer; My answer will be the best in which the soul can be nourished; it is like I would select from all fruits the ideal fruit which could give best results for her;
have you heard how many times I can forgive?

Yes, Lord, but some books say that although You do not want to answer them (in a supernatural way) You do, but disliking it, and You are <u>angry</u>.

I, Yahweh, tell you this, My way of thinking is not your way of thinking and My ways are not your ways;[1] Vassula, I am a God Most Merciful, a Loving Holy Father to you; I know your needs and weaknesses; My love to you all is a jealous love; come, come nearer to Me; I, Yahweh, take all opportunities to reach you;

My Father, when I am with You I feel so loved from You and my love to You but grows. Yet, I am afraid to fail You since I am full of sin.

Vassula, do I not know all this? you are a pinch of dust where upon if I blow on it you will disappear; I know how frail you are for after all you are but a passing shadow on earth; yet in your nothingness and in your wretchedness My eyes never leave you; I look upon your weaknesses

---
[1] Meaning that this theory is wrong.

with Compassion and Love; do not fear, for I will strengthen you; your sins I take and give you My forgiveness; Vassula, do no more today; I will call you tomorrow; have My Peace;

March 5, 1987

peace be with you;
Vassula, do you love Me?

I love you, Yahweh, my God, with all my heart, and near You I wish to stay.

I love you too; I will never abandon you;
Vassula, I am King and Sovereign of Peace and Love; before you I am, revealing My Holy Face to you all; this is the beginning of My call of Peace and Love; daughter, I will instruct you more with Wisdom; I am well pleased with you; delight Me, hearing My calls and writing them down; weary not writing; come, all will not be in vain;

Yes, My Lord.

I give you My blessings; come, lean on Me; glorify Me by loving Me, daughter; seek Me always; deny Me never; amend for others; fulfil My word; have My everlasting Peace;

(Later:)

Vassula, stay near Me; I will remind you that as a Spouse I will provide for you with great abundance all that you lack; I love you; every word I say, will be written; we will work together; weary not writing;

(I read St. Michael's prayer to Him. St. Michael answered me.)

with God's power, I, St. Michael, will cast into hell Satan and all other evil spirits that ruin the souls;

(I then read The Memorare of St. Bernard.)

beloved, daughter, I will help you; have My everlasting Peace; I am near you until the end; fulfil the Message, Vassula; fulfil God's word; lean on your Holy Father for He is Most Powerful; love Him and glorify Him, will you do all this? stay near us; I love you;

March 6, 1987

Vassula it is I, Jesus, your Saviour, are you hungry?

In fact, Jesus, I am right now.

always be, be hungry for My Bread; come, My Bread is free and when you eat from Me you will be filled;

Jesus, I was talking about earthly bread ...

I know, Vassula, but which would you prefer to have?

Both, Jesus.

your bread will only satisfy you for a while, but when you eat from My Bread you will be filled; anyone who eats from My Bread will live forever;[1]
I will feed you Vassula;

I love you, Jesus.

O daughter, how I long to hear these words from every lip! "I love you Jesus"; do you want to feel My Heart? look at Me, before you I stand;

(I looked at His Heart. All His Breast was alight.)

My Heart is ablaze with fervent love, My Heart wants to consume you in Its love, My Heart wants to entice you and forever be Mine! come, daughter, cry out for love, cry out for peace, be united to the end with Me; come, let us revive the others;

---
[1] Jn. 6:48-51.

love Me with all your soul and with all your mind to be able to glorify Me, beloved;

Jesus, loving You is painful, because one wants to be with You, I mean rid of the body and be near You. That is why it is painful to love.

I suffer too because of My Great Love for all of you; I cruelly suffered because of love; I still suffer when I do not get any response to the Love I have for you; can you imagine how I feel? beloved, I need souls who truly love Me; souls who could amend for those who ignore Me; tell them, let them know how it feels to love someone, having laid out My life out of love, and yet get no response, no love!

weary not of bearing My Cross of Peace and Love; bearing it for Me rests My weary Soul; I need to rest, beloved;

Jesus, I will do what You want and try to understand what You are telling me.

(In the evening, my soul was heavy and sad.)

March 7, 1987

Vassula, I Jesus love you; beloved, I have rested; come, I am pleased; believe Me, I feel rested! let us work with love and amend; come, I will teach you to amend; I am the Elixir of Life, I am the Resurrection;

Jesus, how I wish that every soul loved you! It must be awful not to get a response to a love so Great as Yours!

Vassula, My wish is already implanted in your soul; daughter, fill Me with joy and learn to say "let us go and work, let us do this or that," use the word us, we are united forever! delight Me by saying "Father, may your will be done," refuse Me nothing;

daughter, today you will follow Me in the dark dominion of My foe to see how those souls who refused Me suffer;

Jesus, are they lost?

those in hell are, but those in purgatory are saved[1] with love by My beloved ones who make prayers and amend; do not fear for My Light protects you and I am with you;

(I saw myself underground. It looked like an underground cave, dark; lit only by fire. It was damp and the ground sticky. I saw several souls in a row. They were tied and only their heads shown, faces of agony. It was very noisy, it sounded like iron machines at work. Lots of clamouring, hammerings, shrieks, it was very busy. In front of those heads was someone standing his hand outstretch and inside his palm was lava his arm waved from right to left, pouring (splashing) the hot lava across those faces which were swelled up from burns. Suddenly this man who I understood was Satan noticed our presence, and turned around.

(Satan speaks:) "Look at her!" and he spat on the ground with disgust and fury, at the sight of Jesus' presence and mine, "miserable worm, look at her we even have worms nowadays. coming to suck out our blood, go and f--- off." He said to me: "Look," and he threw hot lava again across those faces. I heard them cry out "Oh let us die ..." Then Satan, who looked exactly like a mad-man, fuming with rage called out: "Creatures of the earth hear me to meeee you will come!" I just thought that although he was menacing he was a fool to believe that in the end he would win. He must have read my thoughts of contempt and very menacingly said: "I am not a fool!" then he with a malicious laugh and with irony said, to those poor souls: "Have you heard, she called me a fool," then with sarcasm ... "Dear beloved souls I will make you pay for her sayings."

---

[1] Lifted in Paradise.

He was ready to take new lava to throw. I turned to Jesus in despair, asking Him to do something! To stop him! Jesus replied:)

I will stop him;

(The minute S. had lifted his arm to throw the lava it gave him great pain and he screeched with pain; cursing Jesus; then to me, "Witch, goooo, yes, go, leave us!" Voices from souls, found at the <u>gates</u> of hell were crying: "Save us, save us." [1] *Then someone came forward, I understood it was one of Satan's adepts and he (S.) asked him: "Are you on your duty? Are you doing what I have asked you to do? Hurt her, destroy her, discourage her." I knew S. was referring me. He wanted this demon to discourage me meeting Jesus, by giving the wrong word, or destroying the message I get. I asked Jesus if we could leave. He said:)*

come let us leave; I want you to write all this down; I will edit for you; be near Me beloved – I want My children to understand that their souls live and that evil exists; all that is written in My Blessed Word is not a myth; Satan exists and seeks to ruin your souls; I suffer to see you slumbering and unaware of his existence; I come giving you warnings, giving you signs, but how many of you will read My warnings like fairy-tales?

beloved, I am your Saviour; do not deny My word, turn to Me and feel the pangs of love I have for you; why, why are you so willing to thrust yourselves at Satan's feet?

O come all of you who believe no more in Me; come to Me all who have forsaken Me; come and behold, for this is the time to listen; all you who wound My Soul arise, revive, and see My Light; do not fear Me, I have forgiven you; I will take your sins and My Blood will wash them; I will condone your weakness and forgive you; come and absorb the dew of righteousness, restoring your souls which are heading for perdition; I come to look for you, I come in search of My lost sheep; will I, as the Good Shepherd, see you lost and remain indifferent?

Vassula, are you willing to pray for all those in perdition?

Now, Jesus?

yes, now;

I wouldn't know what to say, Lord.

I will teach you; listen to Me and repeat after Me,

"O Holy Father,
by Thy Power and with Thy Mercy,
I implore You,
gather all your sheep,
forgive them and let them return
to Your Beloved Home,
look upon them as your children
and with Thy Hand bless them,
amen"

come in My Heart, Vassula, for therein is profound Peace;

March 8, 1987

Vassula, beloved one, I want to remind you again that I am not favouring you from My other children; for your merits are none, and your worthiness even less in My eyes; but I love you even so; I gave you this Grace for this is My will; be My bearer and through you I will manifest Myself;

do not think that I am contradicting Myself; My love for you is boundless and you are My beloved one since I chose you; do not think for one minute, that because I point out your weaknesses I love you less, I am your Holy Father who knows you and if I do not point out your mistakes then who will? you are My frail

---

[1] Souls at the gates of hell, in a very low purgatory can be 'lifted' by our prayers, saving them to less torment.

flower which I form, letting you sip My Strength that you may grow, Vassula;

I want to remind you that the Revelations I am breathing in you are not just for your own benefit, they are meant for others too, who are in desperate need of My Bread; I come to feed all of you who are hungry; My Message is one of Peace and Love and to remind you of your foundations and who created you;

I come to tell you that My Body is My Church; yes, My Church which fills the whole creation; I come to show this world My Mercy;

you, Vassula, were one among those multitudes who wounded Me, who never responded to My Love, embittering Me; what is more embittering than receiving no response to a Love so thirsty and so great as Mine?

instead, in your wilderness you sought after daily material pleasures, symbolising them as gods, idolising them, alienating yourself even further from Me, embittering Me and wounding My Heart, a Heart of a living God so unsought and so unloved by you, a God completely forgotten; daughter, was I that far away from you?

come, come and feel My Heart, My Heart is crying out for you all; My sons, My daughters come .... come nearer to Me, turn to Me, allow Me to hold you, let Me thrust you deep inside My Heart and let It engulf you, giving you profound Peace;

come and enter My Spiritual World of Peace and Love;

come to Me and eat from My Body for My bread is pure and will purify you; My Body cries out for you; come and see Me, I who spend day and night at the Tabernacle, waiting for you to feed you; do not dread or fear Me, do not disown Me; why refuse Me a place in your heart?

come and get to know Me and you will love Me; for how could you love someone you do not know, or know only imperfectly? endeavour to know Me well and you will love Me fervently;

Vassula, you had gone astray and thus detached yourself from Me; you turned away from the Truth, transforming good into evil and being attached more to evil rather than good;

come then all those who still are evading Me and bring forth your sins, that I may pardon them; come and eat from Me, come and empty your hearts to Me and let Me fill them up with Love;

I know you are weak but allow Me to act in all of you; give Me your consent, beloved ones; let Me uproot all your iniquities, casting them away and sow in you My seed of Peace and Love; let Me purify you; Vassula, do no more, I will continue later on;

do not forget My Presence; remember, always, us, we;

I will remember. I will try, Lord.

let us go;

Let us.

(Continuation:)

come and get to know Me, I am not beyond reach; we walk side by side, you live in Me and I in you; we are never parted, never;

come and derive from My Infinite Goodness and let your inclemency dissolve in My Purity;

O daughter, in spite of having many of My beloved children made holy by Baptism there are only very few who know Me as I am; they forget to look upon Me as a loving Father, many of them leave Me, thinking that I am beyond reach; many of them think of Me in their own manner, attributing permanent feelings of despicable inclinations; some think of Me only in fear others doubt of My Infinite Love;[1]

(Here I was interrupted: the photograph I ordered of the 'Holy Shroud' arrived. I

---

[1] This message continues on March 18, 1987.

contemplated it and came back to writing while I was looking at it.)

remember, I am still suffering; Vassula, how embittered I am; why, why are so many of My sheep scattered; look at them, was it in vain My sacrifice; daughter, how displeased I am, how utterly shattered My Soul is; I suffer;

feed My sheep; weary not of writing;

No, Lord, I will not weary.

I will give you the Strength you need; come, let us work; let us continue; I am your Teacher; fill Me with joy and do not forget My Presence;

Vassula, you felt my Presence; indeed, I was sitting at the corner of your bed; let Me edit[1] what I wrote; "it is I, Jesus, I am sitting now, but at this very instant I will arise since you too will arise;"

(He hardly finished writing when the door knocked urgently and I jumped up. I stood there quite perplexed. Jesus was emphasising His Presence to me that evening very much. It was so much (like some other times) that I took a piece of paper to check and he wrote the above paragraph. (At the door was my bearer telling me something.))

I love you; weary not writing; giving Me this freedom[2] is what I desire;

Jesus, You are Wonderful!

be always cheerful when I am cheerful; follow Me;

you will grieve Me if you forget My Presence; never forget My Presence, never!

But Lord, it is difficult, sometimes I have to drive my car, I have to concentrate on the road, I converse with friends on trivial subjects, I help my son in his homework, so how could I constantly have Your Presence in my mind, it's almost impossible!

Vassula, My flower, when you are in that way you only have to remember the virtues, by being humble, devout, gentle, graceful, truthful, loving; yes, being virtuous is remembering Me; come, let us go;

I wish to make it known to you that I do approach in a supernatural way giving My Messages; do not forget that I am God of Mercy and in spite of your wretchedness and the indifference you had towards Me, I love you; I gave you this charism so that you learn directly from My lips; Vassula, resting in your heart feels good;

(Later on:)

(Again, the wave of doubt covered me.)

come, suffering purifies you; lean on Me, accept to suffer; amend, amend, amend for others; come, let us revive all My children;

(There, I became quite distressed!)

But, my God, I am helpless, how could I do anything?

(He said very softly:)

will I ever abandon you? use My grains and sow them into fields, yielding the fruits of Peace and Love; let My Word be known to all; I will be with you all the time;

Suppose they refuse It and put it aside, doubting about It? Suppose they think it's no good, suppose they do not believe it's You!

hear Me, My Vassula, why are you fearing? all of My creation was done by My Hand, have you forgotten that I am Omnipotent? all My creation obeys My

---

[1] Jesus uses my language; for we know from St Teresa of Avila that 'God adapts Himself' to His chosen one's language.
[2] Of using me.

Will; little one, I am the Most High; do Glorify Me; be like a flower needing My Light to live;

March 17, 1987

Vassula, will you bear My Cross now?

I do, according to Your will, Jesus.

feel; feel how heavy It is; I need to rest; follow Me, come nearer to Me, I will unburden My Precious Cross on you;

(Later on that day, I felt unspeakably distressed. Melancholic and now needing to be comforted, but not finding it.)

you have felt My immense burden on you; never refuse My Cross; My burden is heavy;
    Vassula seek not why I elevate you to Me;[1] leave Me free to do with you whatsoever I want to until I come and deliver you; beloved, your guidance has its martyrdom, by seeking to find the truth in it and not finding it, it martyrs you; suffer for Me, suffering purifies your soul; immolate yourself to Me and do not seek to find;[2] just believe;
    leave Me free to act in you, and through you manifest My Word thus healing My children; believe in My Redemptive Love;
    My Cross is heavy, yes, I will come many more times entrusting you with It; You are My bride, My beloved and My flower; by bearing It for Me you relieve Me; within My revelations I breathe into you, there are embittering passions of sorrows, pains and sufferings which flow out from the very depths of My Soul; come and listen one more time to My Heart and feel how It lacerates; feel how It seeks you all!

(Then as if He could not take it any longer, with a cry which came out from that sorrowful Soul, from Its depths it came, like as if It was close to death from sorrow.)

creation! which My Father created by His own Hand, why, why do you give Me so much sorrow!!

(Then He turned to me, his face and tone very grave, saying:)

have you ever thought of Me before I came to you?

(Guilt.)

No, I haven't.

(Still grave.)

would you have come to Me if I had not sought and found you?

No, I don't think so. (More guilt.)

now you love Me;

Yes, my Lord, I do.

My guidance has changed you, has it not?

Yes, it has.[3]

will you muster My children and feed them?

(I felt helpless.)

My God, how could I, with what means?!

(I want to please Him, showing my thanks, but I can't.)

trust Me; let Me guide you, Vassula; let Me muster My children; I know you are helpless; I know you are weak; you see, you cannot do anything without Me; now,

---

[1] God reminds me to accept what is happening to me.
[2] I was trying to discover whether this is a real guidance.

[3] There I really felt that I am nothing and it was not for my merits He approached me since in the very beginning I almost rejected Him!

will you let Me use you as My instrument until I have completed My Message?

Yes, as long as the Message will be from You, Jesus.

I am Jesus, never doubt; weary not of writing; every word My lips utter, will make you feel My wounds; I drag you down with Me in the dark dominion of My foe showing you how souls suffer;[1] I outpour on you all My sufferings that wound Me profoundly; My priest, for My priest you are, you will walk with Me; never will I abandon you; together we will share My Cross; together we will suffer; together we will strive; you will take your rest in Me and I in you;

March 18, 1987

I have taught you to love Me and recognise Me; I showed you My heavenly works, pouring out all the mysteries of My Heart, and showing you My ineffable Mercy, purifying you to be the source of My revelations and showing the world My Grace; indeed, I have bestowed upon you all My insatiable love showing My children how much I can love them;[2] nevertheless, reminding you that you are not any different than the rest of them and that you are not to keep this guidance hidden;

I want My effusions to cover this world, for this is My will; Vassula, allow Me to act in you as I please;

come now and console Me, yes, by loving Me; I am Yahweh and it is on Me you are leaning and it is to Me you are coming to and meditating; you are invoking <u>Me</u> in your prayers, so do not worry since you are worshipping Me and no one else;[3]

---

[1] When He showed me Hell.
[2] I'm like a sample.
[3] For those times that I worry that these writings are maybe not from God.

My wish is that all My children return to Me;

daughter, I have brought you up for this message; will you fulfil My word, Vassula? are you willing to continue working for Me?

Yes, my Lord, as long as I recognise it's Yahweh.

little one, I am Yahweh! have My peace, little one, and grow; never weary writing; allow Me to use you until the end of My message;

little one, who is your father?

(I was surprised at the question.)

You are.

(Message to the world.)

I am; you are My seed, you are Mine;

My children have turned away from Me and their hearts are frozen with egoism; they have forgotten Me; I want to ask them; why do you repel Me, what have I done that displeased you? have I insinuated ever to you that I am angry towards you? why are you dreading to face Me? beloved, I will not blame you for your sins; I forgive you now; I will not shut the door in your face; I tell you truly that I can forgive a million times and with My arms open I stand before you, asking you to come to Me and feel this love I have to give you; let Me enkindle your heart; come and get to know Me; come, all you who avoid Me and fear Me; all you who do not know Me; come nearer to Me and you will understand that I am a God full of Love, full of pity and full of Mercy;

do not reject Me, before you even know Me; My superabundant love offers you an efficacious grace to know and choose between good and evil; I have given you freedom to choose, but I have also given you qualities to make out of you superior beings; I have given you gifts; use your gifts I bestowed on you and with your intellect and the heart I have given you understand and come forward, acknowledging Me and get to know Me better;

I have enlightened your hearts to enable you to love; I it is, who has given you this grace; would you accept this grace?

(I remembered myself of before.)

But Lord, some had no chance in knowing You, no one taught them, its not really their fault is it? So how could they possibly think even of You?

Vassula, how true!

daughter, My Church needs to be renewed; I have come to consolidate My Church; otherwise multitudes are bound to be lost; Vassula, I will come back giving a message to My devout ones; let Me complete My desires about My children who turned away from Me; I am the Source of Love and from this Source flows this Infinite Love which covers all creation; all I ask of you is a return of Love;

many of you believe I am a God who is quick to anger, and so fear Me; you fear to approach Me; others believe I am beyond reach and only enjoying My glory, never caring for you, and My eyes turned only upon My devout ones, thus making an image of a God full of predilection; did you not know that the weaker and the more wretched you are the more I seek you and love you?

I am Holy, but I also want you to understand that I desire to become intimate with you and have Me as your Holy companion;

do you know of the parable of the prodigal son, Vassula?

Yes, some of it.

he had sinned, but how did his father receive him?

With great joy?

more than that, he received him with great love, and celebrated this event;

grieve Me not, My beloved ones, and come back to Me; I will not refuse you; I will welcome you in My embrace; return to Me without fear;

March 19, 1987

I am here; it is I, Jesus;

Vassula, elevate yourself to Me; I want you to be perfect; delight Me and become perfect; are you willing to be perfect?

(I was speechless.)

I want you to be; I am asking you, Vassula;

But Lord, to be perfect is quite impossible. As I am, to be close to being good is already something for me.

Vassula, I will teach you to be perfect; I tell you truly that it is not impossible, but you must let Me mould you; abandon yourself completely to Me and I will form you into what I desire you to be;

Jesus I don't think I can ever be. I'm difficult to mould, it will be like trying to mould a rock.

Vassula, ah Vassula, do you not trust Me? I am God and I can mould even the rocks into any shape I want; do you know why I have chosen you?

Yes, Lord.

here is still one more reason; I chose you because you are weak, and your weakness charms Me; child, come and feel My Heart, My Heart desires to be loved; come and feel My Heart with your mind; Vassula, are you ready? feel Me;

(I was petrified.)

grieve Me not, come and feel Me; you are not feeling Me;[1]

No, I have not felt you; I had not the courage to do it.

will you tell me your problem?

It's getting worse now.

why?

(I felt embarrassed because I felt so unworthy.)

My embarrassment. I feel embarrassed to face You.

Vassula, why? grieve Me not and tell Me your problem;

I felt embarrassed to touch Your Heart. It's like I saw myself as a leper coming to touch someone whole. who am I to approach You!

every time you feel embarrassed I love you more;[2] daughter, since we are united for eternity and you are Mine, I will allow Myself to penetrate deep inside your heart; marrying Me glorifies Me and purifies you; we are united;

Yes Lord, but look to <u>what</u> You are united!

I love you, come and lean on Me now; Vassula, feel My Heart;

(Later on:)

(I felt His Heart, which was very warm, and palpitating with the desire to be loved.)

you need not feel embarrassed feeling My Heart, I am Your God who asks you this; allow Me to use you like I wish; allow Me to kiss you;

(I got suspicious, thinking it's evil trying to make me fall in sin.)

I am the Lord Jesus Christ; do not fear;

(I was still careful. Even though I had not felt evil around, still I was suspicious.)

do not fear;

(I could not 'free' myself, again this 'leper' feeling came on me. I did not move.)

do you know how much I love you?

Yes I do, Jesus.

why then do you refuse My kiss?[3]

Because I'm not worthy of a kiss from You.

Vassula, have I not told you before not to refuse Me anything? and what have you answered Me?

That I'll never refuse You anything.

Yes, why then refuse My kiss; Vassula, never refuse Me; if I ask you something it is out of love, allow Me to kiss you, allow Me to do it! will you let Me now? come to Me and feel My kiss, a heavenly kiss on your forehead, are you ready?[4]
 I love you;

---

[1] In the sense of sensing His Love.
[2] I understood later on that He felt pleased that I realised my unworthiness.
[3] Much later on, after a few years only, when I got to know Jesus more, I understood that Jesus was teaching me to be intimate with Him, like St Gertrude and others.
[4] Jesus kissed my forehead. He left me in an ecstatic state of mind. How can I explain it. For the following <u>two days</u> I felt hollow, transparent, like clear glass, He gave such a <u>tremendous</u> feeling of peace of the soul; my breathing seemed to go through my lungs and fill into my entire body, thus having this feeling of being air.

March 20, 1987

Vassula, let Me tell you something; love Me till the end for the end will be sweet and I will be with you;

How much You must have suffered!

My sufferings were not in vain; I have liberated you from evil;

I wish You could be happy sometimes.

I am happy when I am among My beloved ones;

Do they make you happy?

yes, they uplift My sorrows;

It's a pity that we are not two thousand years back to be with You.

I am still among you, daughter;

Jesus, since you kissed me (yesterday evening) and all day today I feel 'dissolved' in You, like I'm transparent and tremendously peaceful! It's like I am hollow ...

Vassula, I am Peace; I will always give you My Peace; integrate your whole being in Me and I will dissolve you within Me; ah Vassula, come always within Me and feel My Peace;
  are you still willing to let Me form you?

Yes; Jesus, always.

yes, leave Me free to do whatsoever I want with you; I will mould you into a pure and devout being, solely for My interests; you are going to withstand trials with My Strength solely for My interests; My word will be like a rivulet, flowing, then rushing, until it pours out and turns into an ocean, an ocean of Peace and Love;

(Later:)

Vassula, why do you never praise Me? I am the Lord who saved you from darkness; realise who you are; among the most wretched ones, you are by far the worst of them;

(I sighed.)

I love you anyway; praise Me, Vassula, for liberating you;

(I was thinking what to say. I hesitated.)

say;

My God, I love You
and it is through
Your abundant love and mercy
that You showed me Your Light;
blessed be Your Name,
amen;

(I repeated His words.)

March 21, 1987

it is I, Jesus; Vassula, will you train, beloved? discerning Me with your mind?[1] Vassula, look at Me;

(I did.)

yes, correct;

Have You placed Your hands on the desk?

I have;

Now You've crossed Your arms?

I have;

Now You've lifted one arm and Your hand reached Your cheek and Your forefinger on

---

[1] Jesus wanted me to use the gift of discernment of spirits that He gave me.

Your cheek, the other arm stayed where it is? Like You are thinking?

correct! I am emphasising My presence; Vassula, look at Me;

(You have a book? which You took out from Your mantle from the left side with Your right hand?)

I have a book;

(It's not very big.)

exactly, you are discerning well, Vassula; look inside and read what it says;

(I try, but I am not very good at it.)

It says...

My altar is you;

I can't Jesus, I can't figure out the rest!

try again, My altar upon which I will...

(I can't see. I think I'm reading wrong!)

little one, what would you do without Me? you must elevate more your soul to Me; Vassula, I will help you; leave yourself entirely to Me, never be discouraged; I will come back with My book later on;

(I did feel discouraged, believing I disappointed Him for not raising high enough my soul. I went as far as to think He will exchange me for another soul. That His patience has limits!)

Vassula, you must never ever believe that I will exchange you; will you believe Me? come, we will try next time; try and discern Me more with your mind as you did now; Vassula, let your entire being penetrate in Me and dissolve within Me; completely;

love Me and amend for others; elevate, I will teach you to elevate your soul; let us go;

March 22, 1987

serenity is what I love; you will work with serenity and not haste; I have come back with My book;

What is in that book too?

I have written in it a few names of souls; souls who are to revive My Flame, the Flame of Love; will you read where I point out for you?

Yes, Lord, I have been worried about that little book which I couldn't read.

I know,

(I can see its cover is soft and gold.)

yes, its cover is golden; look inside it and read, "I will make of you My altar, upon which I will place My burning desires of My Heart, My Flame will live within you; be drawing from My Heart and fill your heart; I, the Lord, will keep My Flame ablaze for ever and ever;" will you kiss My book now, daughter?

(I did.)

I will tell you;

(I had a question.)

it is a spiritual guidance for My chosen souls; now you know;

(Later on, the wave of uncertainty and doubt covered me.)

Vassula, do not fear; it is I, Jesus; listen, beloved, all the guidances have their sufferings too; in yours is the uncertainty which makes you suffer; have I not said that suffering purifies your soul? accept it, and leave Me free to do what is best for you; let Me act in you; are you willing?

I'll do it if it's You, Jesus.

I am Jesus, Your Saviour! we will suffer together, we will strive together; here, lean on me; come, let us go and read together;

(Later:)

I am here; live for Me; glorify Me by loving Me; come, all is for My interests of Love and Peace; deny Me never; evil will always try and interfere to stop My designs but I will prevail so rely on Me;

But, Lord, can I complain about some things?

feel free with Me, Vassula;

I want to tell You what is bothering me, probably everything I say or think is wrong so whatever I do will be wrong. It's true I have no real support, by that I mean I am here, writing messages I receive from You. Now, others apparently had the same as I. Other guidances or messages that came from You to other people, but these people were mostly in monasteries or convents; they were surrounded by religious, priests, bishops, etc. when this supernatural approach was happening to them, they were watched carefully, followed closely, then it was easy to pass the writings to the Superiors and from there to the bishop and then to the Pope. They all accepted it as coming from You.

I might be wrong, but it seemed easier for them to accept it from one of their circle whom they knew well and so it was edited; at least parts of it. They were approved.[1] Then here I am, I have approached priests. They happen to be Catholic, for me, as a Greek Orthodox by baptism, it does not matter what they are, even if I was Catholic and the priests would be Protestant I am not selecting; we are all Christians. Several priests know about it now. Each one's reaction differs from the other like night and day. One of them to this day says it's Evil, in other words I'm possessed, since I'm possessed by a spirit; but I know it's You God Almighty. Having read a little he made up his mind and does not want to ever change it. When he'll understand I'm not possessed, he'll bring up that it's my subconscious. Anything but You, then the reaction of another one was, "yes continue writing because it's divine and from God", so, he believes it's God's words; but is too busy to ask or even to follow to find out the 'suite'. This is what amazes me, if he believes God is trying to express a message, why then not bother more and find out what it is?

A third priest was informed and listened dutifully looking now and then at his watch then, said, good, go on, it's marvellous, continue writing, I asked him to come any time again and talk about it. I never saw him again. Then another priest was informed, and he said, only reading a page or two, "I don't want to give any opinion, but we Catholics are warned that evil acts in the same way too;[2] not that I'm saying it's evil but we are told to be careful." Fair enough I said, but then since everybody agrees on one thing, and that is: that it is supernatural, why then not take it more seriously, to understand and clarify it?

After all they are people who seek God, the first one who said it's EVIL then told me, that God gives messages and there are many, many books with those messages all over the world, and it is very common; there are so many guidances in the supernatural way, so it is very common, but mostly in their circle.

Another priest said they are called Divine Revelations of the Heart and they are from God; then he gave an address of one prof. mystic whom I can find and talk with. I know, that if I was 'one of them' I'd have it easier. It's just that I'm out of their circle and my appearance too clashes.

---

[1] And thus relieved for the Word can lay heavy.

[2] Maybe, but for how long? Until masses return to God? Because masses already have and it's the beginning...

I am Jesus; Vassula, lean on Me and rest; era, O era have you given credits before even glimpsing on My words? are you seemingly glorifying Me and by defending Me unwillingly deriding Me?

Vassula, I love you; lean on Me, beloved;

Lord there are still other things, when I tell You or give You my feelings of doubt, I'm pretty sure I wound You, since I'm doubting, and if I'm not doubting, and it is not You in the guidance, I'm wounding You, because I'm doing this, so whatever I'm doing, I wound You, if I believe or not believe it's you, whatever I think, I hurt you; and this makes me sad since I want to be the last one that would wound You! I suffer for this too.

O daughter, grieve not; never believe that I am wounded from love; eating from Me is all you do; I am Jesus, Jesus Christ, and it is My bread you are eating; soul, O beloved soul do not afflict yourself anymore; believe Me, beloved one, and feel loved by Me;

Forgive me for being so weak ...

I forgive you fully; feel how much I love you; your weakness is what attracts Me most, your ineffable weakness! your wretchedness is beyond words; O come to Me here inside My Heart let your soul entirely annihilate within Me; be My heaven, I love you; have now My Peace;

March 23, 1987

remember I am One, the Holy Trinity is One;[1] I want that our union be perfect; discern Me carefully; yes, you have seen well, I have with Me two rings;

They are silver-white? and very shiny!

they are out of pure white gold;

---
[1] In the unity of essence.

(There I thought evil was misguiding me, how could this be?)

listen Vassula, it is I, Jesus; do not fear; beloved, come, I have brought you this ring; I want you to wear it now; discern Me;

But is this possible?

yes, I am blessing our union!

beloved, this act is a spiritual heavenly act; your soul is united to Me, I tell you truly; believe Me, I will sanctify our marriage;

allow Me to place this ring on your finger; I love you; feel Me; I love you and I bless you;

Jesus placed the other ring on His finger.

see? what can you discern more?

(I can see a ribbon joining two 'circles'.)

this I shall place on our heads; we are now joined; I am crowning our union;

Jesus many will blame this as fantasy!!

why; many come to Me and marry Me, glorifying Me, and I so much rejoice to be united to them! Vassula, I have risen you from the dead; I shed My Light on you; I looked after you, and soothed you; leave Me free to continue My works on you daughter; be like soft plaster willing to be shaped up as I wish; leave yourself free in My hands and do not resist Me;

Lord, I'm so happy, too happy that I fear I might be wrong!

no, you have well discerned; I love you to the extent that I am well prepared to fetch you right away; I am longing to deliver you and have you near Me, but I have created you for this Message;

Lord, I'm fearing that I might have misdiscerned and that I have profaned You by thinking that You gave me a ring and joined us; though I was pretty sure about it.

My bride, My wretched bride, why are you fearing Me? grieve Me not and approach Me; I love you; lean on Me and remember, I it is who sanctified our marriage; do not worry, it is I Jesus, leave your fears and approach Me; I felt your hand;[1]

(I had been looking at His picture (big format) of the Holy Shroud while writing, and unconsciously with my mind I had pushed gently His hair (left side) placing it behind, away from His cheek. I was surprised at the immediate reaction.)

Have you felt my hand, really?

I have; Vassula do you realise I am God?

I'm sorry I did this.

do not be; be intimate with Me, just like you are; come, give Me your hand and I will keep it in Mine;

March 26, 1987

(Here below God gave me a vision.)

delight Me, Vassula, and understand that I God am One; I will dearly wish to show you more of My glory; child, do you know how Heaven was created?

By You, through You.

yes, I have measured every width, height and depth and all dimensions are perfect; every little living creature comes from Me and is truly Mine; all Life comes from Me, My Breath is Life; do you wish to learn more about My Heavenly Works?

Yes, Lord.

then let us have a walk in My Glory;

(I found myself walking with God's Presence in a beautiful garden, very colourful, plenty of bright light, but not from a normal sun. While walking I noticed an enormous <u>ball of light</u> almost touching the horizon. It was like a big Sun; but one could look at it without having the eyes burnt.)

how do you feel, daughter?

It's beautiful, it's all strange!

what can you see?

This sort of 'Sun'.

yes, it is My Holy Abode; and what can you see around that Light?

First it appeared to me that it was spots which moved around It, but then they turned out to be little angels encircling It. They appeared to be millions of them.

they are cherubims encircling My Glory; what else do you see?

Some steps going inside the 'Sun'?

let us enter this Light, are you ready? take off your shoes for we are entering on holy ground; we are now inside the Light;

(I thought by entering It I would find myself in very bright light, but no, everything was of blue colour, but what struck me most is the silence and the feeling of Peace and Holiness. It was amazing! Inside all was a circle!)

yes, it is a circle;

(The 'wall' around was <u>no</u> wall, but living things, they were angels, a wall of angels and closing like a dome the 'ceiling' made by angels ... all blue, they were millions, billions, one stuck to the other, they were tall angels, one on top of another, stuck all together, forming a solid wall.)

---
[1] Jesus said this very quickly.

My seraphs are guarding this Holy place and are worshipping Me incessantly; can you hear them? "Holy of Holies, Holy is our God Most High,"

How many are they, Lord?

thousands, My child; who is this with the gold sword and so beautiful?

I don't know.

(I saw someone like an angel which differed from the others, because he was in 'normal' colour, dressed in a long white robe, golden hair to the shoulders, and he held in his hand a beautiful gold sword, glittering, and his robe was of the purest of whites.)

Vassula, the sword is My Word; My Word is pure; It pierces and illuminates;

(Suddenly the 'dome' opened like a flower.)

behold, little one, try to discern; I am near you helping you; you will see above you now the Holy Battle that is to come; O daughter, keep a vigilant look around you and be aware that evil exists; can you see anything?

(I saw, when this 'wall' opened like a flower, horses with black velvety fierce eyes. The image went further away, and I saw a battle.)

My army will combat Satan and his followers, including all those that tried to destroy My Law; remember that I am the Alpha and the Omega, the First and the Last; My Word is everlasting; now what can you see?

A reptile like a big snake which was thrown down from the horse.

this dragon under the lance of My Saint[1] will be conquered; when this will be done all his followers will fall too; Vassula, you will come now to see My Hall of Judgement;

(I saw a big hall, but no one yet there. Suddenly in one corner I saw a group (souls) it was the clatter of chains that made me look. They seemed haggard, beyond description and spotted with charcoal or some black spots. They seemed scared, uncertain as to where they were. They did not see us. They seemed to be surprised by their surroundings.)

listen to the trumpets; they are My angels announcing Me; give Me your hand for you are My little visitor; yes, every angel falls prostrate before Me; have you seen this multitude of souls, they have just arrived from underground; [2] these are tormented souls who have been released, they were at Satan's gates;

Who released them?

I did, with My heavenly works, and all who amend and love Me; you see why I want you to love Me? the deeper you love Me the better chance they have to be lifted and come to Me; do you want to know what will become of these souls?

Yes Lord, what happens now?

let Me tell you, I will baptise them with My Holy Spirit and free them completely, for not until they would be baptised by the Holy Spirit would they be able to share My Kingdom;

You mean these were not baptised?

they were not;

Would they want to?

yes, they want; come, I will explain; let us sit; what you saw was only an image of

---

[1] Saint Michael.

[2] Purgatory, at Satan's gates (very low).

them; they were not really in My Hall; souls are not judged until the end;

Where were these souls if they were not in Your Hall?

these souls were in Hades;[1] by being in Hades they are helpless; when you choose Me and desire to follow Me, you are saved, but if you fail to recognise Me, because of this obduracy you will fall; where you will go, will be endless martyrdom;[2]
  I must warn you all, not that it has not been said before, but if anyone blasphemes the Holy Spirit they will never be forgiven, for this is My Law;
  lower your eyes before Me, child;

(I did.)

let Me bless you; I forgive your sins; say these words,

"May the Lord and God Almighty
be Blessed,
May His Kingdom
reign in eternal Glory,
May His Holy Name be Glorified,
May His Word
penetrate and rest in each heart;
amen;"

Vassula, do no more today; rest; I will dictate tomorrow My message...

(I felt God suddenly embittered.)

...about those who represent Me but are not giving Me enough love nor draw from My Infinite Love either, daughter;
  come, keep Me company; I need to rest;[3] come nearer to Me, share My sorrow;

My God, I'll do as you want, but also do not forget that there are many who love You

---

[1] In Greek: Purgatory.
[2] In Hell.
[3] To be consoled in a loving heart.

dearly and do not forget their sacrifices showing their love for You.

yes, they uplift My sorrows, and soothe My wounds, but I need larger amounts of souls like these, ready to amend and diffuse My Infinite Love, spreading it like mist; I desire that they open their hearts and receive Me; I will fill their hearts with My Love and when their hearts will overflow with Love, they will be able to diffuse it and feed My lambs;
  beloved, will you let Me rest in you?

Yes, My God, do.

will you rest in Me?

Yes, My God, I will.

come then; I love you;

I love You too, My God.

March 27, 1987

Vassula, I love you;

I love you too, Jesus.

how I long for all My priests to be holy since they represent Me; I wish them to become pure, holy, humble and merciful; I want them to allow Me to pour into their heart the superabundant Love of Mine; I want them to draw more from the Riches of My Heart and fill their heart, impregnating it so that it overflows, thus diffusing It all over the world; it is necessary that they seek to understand My lambs and love them, healing them; but to be able to do all this, they must learn to love Me as much as I have loved them; they must learn to love My children as I love them; they must honour My Church;
  I desire love; Vassula, tell them, let them know that My lips are parched and thirst for love; <u>what use are sacrifices and</u>

rituals to Me, when their hearts are petrified and arid?

I desire to fertilise this wilderness with Integrity; I need warmth, I need a living flame, purity, zeal and an ardent love; allow yourselves to draw from this Infinite Love and fill up your hearts; all I ask from you is faithfulness, purity and love; come, come and repent to Me, come and change your lives; I will exalt you and you will receive Me; I want to remind you of My ways;

I have given you so many messages and signs, signs that you ignore; have you forgotten My words? do not be surprised at the weak instruments I use to manifest My words; why, I could take any one of these stones and change them into devout followers of Mine!

some of you will be seeking for proofs, that it is I, Jesus, who gives you this Message; have I not said, that I will pour out My Spirit on all mankind and that My sons and daughters will all prophesy, that I will display portents in heaven and on earth? My ways are not your ways and My signs, are not your signs;

I am revealing My Face again, but how many of you would believe? I groan with pain, I stifle, I suffocate to watch My seed filled with dead words; fidelity...is this what you call yourselves to be when your hearts are dead?

come, come and absorb from My Heart; I ask you solemnly to repent and amend; love Me purely and honour My Holy Eucharist; yes, all you who deem yourselves just and pious, come and change your hearts; open your hearts and receive Me and when you do, I will unveil your eyes and open your hearing;

Vassula, I will dictate to you tomorrow; you may rest, beloved; have you discerned Me while I was editing?

Yes, Lord, You were at the back of my right arm? Were You there?

I was, yes; yes, now I am facing you, Vassula; yes, feel My Presence as you do; fear not, I will be near you;

come let us rest in each other;

March 30, 1987

it is I, Jesus Christ;

all revelations are from Me; sip from Me; a flower is growing near Me, sipping from Me; My flower, sip while you grow, absorb from Me; come, I love you;

Jesus, I don't mean to use the language I am using talking to You. It sounds very disrespectful. It's my daily language but I don't know another. Reading now books of religious, nuns, the way they talk with You is very different. Maybe they have been taught? I don't mean to sound vulgar; perhaps my heart speaks.

Vassula, I forgive your ignorance; I will teach you, you are learning; you are realising how wretched you are; nevertheless, I love you; wretchedness attracts Me since I can offer you My Mercy; I have chosen you to show the world My clemency;

I'm not proud (I probably represent most of our 'modern' world ...) that You chose me because of my bad qualities, and not of merits. I feel like Juda ...

lo;[1] Vassula you are not like Judas; you are helpless, ignorant and wretched beyond words; you are My beloved whom I sanctified; I took care of our union since you were unable to; My desire is to form you; I united you to Me, asking you to be My bride;

Jesus, I learned that really nuns do get 'married' to You.

yes, they come to Me and become My brides; I delight in them! you were

---
[1] Lo = 'no', in Hebrew.

unaware that you could be My bride and be united to Me so I have taken care of our union, see? I sanctified our marriage placing a ring on your finger; work with Me and remember that I am Holy; never forget th

April 3, 1987

I am watching you; remember we are united; I am Yahweh and I love you,

I love you too, Lord!

eat from Me; I love all of you; I have said that My Kingdom on earth will be as it is in Heaven; I will uproot all evil and I will reinforce My devout followers; I am Yahweh and My word stands secure; do not fear little one, for I it is who leads; I am the Most High; I will offer My Bread[1] to all mankind thus appeasing their hunger, but I want a return of love from them; I thirst for love; tell them, let them know how My Lips are parched from thirst;

(I had discerned Him, His presence was clear. His lips were dry, cracked, with blisters. He had difficulty talking, as His mouth was dry and His tongue could hardly articulate. He seemed to have come from a desert where for days He was without water. It was a pitiful image.)

April 4, 1987

(While going around in Switzerland, I watched people and how they live. Many, like everywhere have daily problems, some more than others. Many seem so unhappy and struggling. This I never noticed before God's approach to me.)

yes, Vassula, I want you to see all, I want you to watch and hear everything they say; I grieve to hear and watch My lambs; why have they forgotten Me, when I am their Consoler; I can console them, they can turn to Me;

(Here I was wondering if it was Yahweh or Jesus.)

Vassula, I am One, I am One![2] Vassula, I am God who gave you life; I established My Word; I came on earth in flesh; I am One; bless you Vassula; the Holy Trinity is in One; I am One;[3]

(I was just thinking to learn by asking priests about this.)

with Me you will learn;

(Later on:)

daughter, when you will understand how indifferent the world has become towards Me, you will understand My bitterness; My chalice of Mercy is full and My chalice of Justice is full too; they are grieving Me, embittering Me, creating revolutions,[4] rebelling against Me and My Law; I am the same Living God, but My people have grown fearless, they challenge Me, they provoke Me! creating them was a delight for Me, why are they rebelling against Me? whom have they to turn to? I suffer; where do they believe they are heading to? My Body is weary and injured,[5] My Body needs to rest and be soothed;

Are you referring to the Church, Lord?

yes, My Body is the Church; Vassula, I wish to consolidate My Church; I wish to unite all My priests, like an army, an army of salvation; My sheep are scattered, all priests should unite;

My God, I personally am baptised as Greek-Orthodox, whom are you referring

---

[1] His Word: His Message.
[2] One in substance.
[3] One in substance.
[4] I think religious revolutions.
[5] The Church.

to My Lord, to Catholics or Protestants, or sects? or other religions? If I dare ask You this it's because it's existing.

O Vassula, Vassula, I am One; I God am One; My children are all created by My Hand, why are all My children dispersed? I desire Unity,[1] I want My children to unite; I am One God and they must understand that the Holy Trinity is all in One! the Holy Spirit, the Holy Father and Jesus Christ the Son, all three are in One;[2] Vassula cling to Me, learn from Me;

My God, what about the Light?

I am the Light, I am One;[3]

April 5, 1987

Vassula, I love you infinitely; I will let you feel My love by letting you feel My Heart;

I placed my hand on His chest and felt His Heart throbbing.

each beat of My Heart is a call to a soul; I long for My beloved to hear Me and approach Me; today I have taken the essence of your love to Me, to use it for healing a soul, Vassula;

I had felt it ...

creature, live in My Light;[4]

I love You, Lord.

woman, live in Me;[5]

Teach me to love You more.

---

[1] Unity. I do not dare to think out loud about what God's desires are!! I understood...
[2] One God.
[3] One God.
[4] The Lord's tone was strict.
[5] The Lord's tone became milder.

beloved, come, let Me hide you in My Heart;[6] work with Me, never weary of writing; do not forget My Presence;

April 6, 1987

(Two weeks before Easter.)

Vassula, prepare yourself for My torments; devote yourself to Me; you will feel My pains; I am preparing you for My Crucifixion; I will suffer, but you will share My sufferings, beloved, you will feel My anguish and My wounds; will you suffer with Me?[7] come let us rest in each other;

April 7, 1987

(I felt as if the whole guidance is pressing on me, and that I am alone with God's Word heavily on me, and not having anywhere to unload it, I don't know what to do? I felt helpless beyond description, and alone, alone with this weight on me.)

Vassula, do I ever abandon you? I am God; lean on Me, trust Me;

I should, yes, but there are times it's beyond me. I can't help it. I feel responsible.

My child, have patience, trust in Me, come to Me I will comfort you;

I love you, Father, beyond words.

(I felt how He was so ready to console me.)

I love you daughter;
My sufferings I will make you feel; when My Crucifixion comes nearer, I will come to you leaving you My nails and thorned crown; I will give you My Cross; beloved, share with Me My sufferings; your soul will feel the anguish I had, your

---

[6] The Lord's tone became very tender full of love.
[7] I will do Your will.

hands and feet the excruciating pains I felt; Vassula, I love you and since you are My bride I wish to share all I have with you, believe Me, you will be with Me; Vassula, have no fear for I, Jesus, am with you;

come, you will understand in phases how I work; have My peace; beloved, I have prepared a place for you;

April 8, 1987

(Today I have a few things to do, but I could not resist writing to God, so I quickly asked Jesus: "One word, Lord, just one word.")

one word, Vassula? LOVE

I love You!

(I meant by "one word" a short sentence or so ....)

April 9, 1987

(While in Switzerland I was wondering where would my home would be one day. We're still looking around. Roaming, roaming, roaming.)

feel My presence,

(I saw Jesus pointing at His Heart.)

your home is here ... straight in the middle of My Heart; daughter, glorify Me by drawing souls to Me;

(My older sister for the first time learned about this Message. She read the last five copies. The influence of this was to make up a family quarrel of eight years with our first cousin. They are good friends again. I never uttered a word. Then she left, for Rhodos, where she lives.

That first night she talked to her husband, he was more shocked than her. They read together notebooks 5 and 6, that evening. Then they went to sleep, But he couldn't. He started to pray and ask God to forgive his sins. Then a miracle happened. God gave him the same vision I saw! The one of the beautiful garden and that 'sun' all round, guarded with millions of angels. God made him penetrate, like I did, inside that round light, and when he felt God's presence so close, he started to shiver and weep. He woke up my sister telling her. She was amazed. They couldn't wait until next morning to tell me of this.

– Then in buying now the book of Enoch, which I always wanted, before I started to read it I opened it at page 102. Just like that, and what do I read? The same vision Enoch had as I had, the bright round Light, guarded by thousands of angels! [1] *It was too much to be of a coincidence; because this vision I saw while in Bangladesh on March 26. Then on April 11, 1987 when I was in Paris, while searching for books in a library I stumbled on a book called Metanoia and what made me look at it was its cover. The picture of the cover was exactly my vision, Enoch's, and my brother in law's. The round light with the angels guarding it. After my sister left I wrote again letting God take my hand. God gave then Strato a written message.)*

I love My lambs; unite My lambs; whoever reads My Message will be eating My Bread; whoever will get a sign from Me will be those whom I wish to illuminate with My grace;[2] draw My sign;

ΙΧθΥΣ ><> ichthis

Vassula, start summarising the guidance and rewrite My Message; I will guide you, illuminating you; all that is repeated was for your education; you needed it;

---

[1] Much later on, in 1996, a friend of mine sent me a picture of the vision that Saint Hildegard had and it was the same.
[2] God made me understand that all those who read His Messages and do get illuminated (an attraction to God again) is enough sign that it's He who feeds them and the Message is from Him.

My Message is to be called Peace and Love;[1]

(It's terrible, I'm too realistic, too sceptic. I can't help feeling again today doubtful that this is happening. Why, why is it that they believe so fully and constant, and I so inconsistent? I, who know very well that I can't handle my hand, and know how powerless I become when God takes possession of my hand, how he can throw the pencil off my hand, and how he can move the pencil without me much touching it. It's happening to me, He has given me so many proofs, and look, waves of doubt, still! And then many times thinking that I might be misguiding everybody! There are so many in this guidance I can't count! and it's not even published ...)

beloved, I am Yahweh; give Me your weaknesses and let My Strength annihilate them;

(What patience God must have, with me, to stand me ... I think the main reason why I have doubts is because of me, because I know myself, I compare myself to those who got a supernatural approach to God and had received Messages, how good they were and how devoted. That is what strikes me, it's like comparing night with day. I admit one positive thing though, at least I love God deeply, and no one can tell me that this is my imagination or like one priest told me that even that the devil can put in your brain... If I was weak and listened to all what I hear I would have cracked up. Today I heard from a lady (who just started Freud) that all this could be in my subconscious, a love complex for God. Rubbish. To her, if we do have a love for God, it means we are psychologically sick? But her theory or Freud's does not affect me a bit; firstly, God warned me of these theories already that I will be accused of, also I do not particularly like Freud since he was an atheist, even Jung left him! For Freud we appear to be only material!)

---

[1] With time Jesus is illuminating me that the Ecclesiastical Editions are also meant for Hebrews and Muslims!

My child, people always judged in human ways; I am a God full of Mercy and Love, but so little understood;

But Lord, You have chosen a 'no good one', that's what brings doubts to me!

you are My daughter too! I love even the most wretched among you;

April 10, 1987

remember My Crucifixion lasted for hours; I suffered many hours; all of My Blood was shed; I love you; come and console Me by loving Me;

(Jesus was feeling sad, and was longing to be consoled. He constantly reminding me of His crucifixion these days and giving me images of it. Sometimes I feel His Presence so full that I think I could touch Him solidly, I could so to say feel the air moving when He moves producing it!)

April 16, 1987

(Easter Thursday)

Vassula, I was present in My Church; I walked before My Cross; I paused a few seconds in front of you;[2] My daughter all these years I had been waiting for you to be in My so beloved Church;[3]

---

[2] Strangely enough while the Procession of the Cross was going on, we had to move to give space to the priest who carried the Holy Cross (about two meters long) and the church boys with big candles following; because of the dimness the priest was not looking where he was going and went straight on me; realising it he stood for a few seconds in front of me, trying to see his way again; my cousin who was with me noticed this incident immediately. My heart raced as I could not back more, I faced the huge Cross and as behind me the crowd had lit candles I couldn't move!

[3] I had not been in that Church since the baptism of my eldest son I think, fifteen years!

Lord and Saviour You have indeed searched for me and <u>found me and brought me to You and Your Church</u>. It has been years .... You've been waiting years!!

I remained before My Cross and everyone who came to worship Me I blessed in turn;

(The Holy Cross had been placed in the middle of the Church and so everybody went by turn kissing It.)

April 17, 1987

(At the end of Holy Mass on Good Friday, the priest distributes the flowers that covered Jesus' tomb. He gives bunches to people. I received just three flowers in my hand; I understood this as a sign from God to remind me of the problem I had understanding the Holy Trinity.

Two days went by and I did not write which I missed terribly as when I write like in meditation I contact and <u>feel</u> God very much.)

My God, it's been a long time!

how long;

Two days!

two days, Vassula? and I, who waited years for you, what shall I say then?

I'm speechless. Jesus, I'm sorry to have wounded You. Forgive me.

come, I forgive you; all I wish from My beloved souls is to let Me arrest their heart for just a few minutes and let me pour into it My superabundant Love;

(Jesus said this in such tenderness and love. Whenever God approaches me to give me an important long message the devil or his adepts attack me. I do not feel him physically but the only thing he is allowed to do in this guidance is manifest himself by writing, thus insulting me and cursing me.[1] Since I was taught by God to know the difference and recognise his words I usually avoid him to finish his word even, which infuriates him. If it escapes my notice God blocks my hand and it cannot write. This paper is from my note book. These attacks are always stronger when God's important message is about to be written. I have realised now the pattern ... so I don't give up although I do feel hopeless at times.)

April 23, 1987

(Sometimes I wonder what freedom is, before God's call I was free too. I had my family life in harmony and having really no responsibility no cares, such as this message which <u>crushes</u> me and weighs on me, but then I was aloof from God. Suddenly, God held me ... In the beginning I did not like it, since I had no love for Him, but in a short time only (three months) after preaching to me He taught me to love Him. Now after eight months the whole Message is almost completed.[2] It's weighing on me and I'm looking for somewhere where I can unload It, it is so <u>very heavy</u>!! What <u>is</u> freedom? The weight was intolerable.)

I, the Lord, will let you know what freedom is, write;

freedom is when your soul detaches itself from earthly solicitudes and flies towards Me, to Me; I, God, came and liberated you; you are free now; when you were attached to the world, Vassula, you were a prisoner to all its temptations, but your soul now like a dove has been freed; you were caged, beloved; caged; let your soul fly out freely, let it feel this freedom I have given to all of My souls but how many of them refuse this grace I offered;

---

[1] In a way it is a good sign, for he shows he exists, and that this revelation annoys him, to say the least.
[2] So I thought...

do not let yourself be caught again; tied and caged, I have liberated you; while I was passing, I saw you in your cage, withering away slowly and dying; Vassula, how could My Heart see this and not redeem you? I came and broke your cage but you were unable to use your wings, for such were your injuries, so I carried you to My abode, healing you tenderly letting you fly again, and now My Heart so much rejoices to see My little dove flying freely and be where she should have been from the very beginning;[1]

I, the Lord, freed you; I have restored you; I have liberated you from your misery; My eyes never leave you from their sight; I watch My dove flying freely knowing all the time that you will always return to Me, for you recognise your Saviour and Master; your soul needs My warmth and you know that your abode now is in the middle of My Heart where I always desired you to be; you belong to Me now and I am your Master who loves you;

(The thought of going to Switzerland came to me, I fear that I might change there ...)

Vassula, I will not let you soil yourself again; do not fear, I will always be near you cleaning you; I have My reasons for you to be there;

(I was trying to think God's reasons. Then I asked.)

I want My seeds to be sown in Europe; be My sower, Vassula; live, Vassula, among people who wound Me; let your eyes see everything and watch what My creation has become; let your heart feel how little I count for them; let your ears hear how they profane Me and wound Me; will your soul not revolt? will you not cry out for Me when you will see and understand how My people have forgotten Me?

---

[1] Jesus was saying this with such happiness in Him, breathing deeply.

Vassula, your soul will be exposed in wickedness, in indifference, in the depths of iniquities and in the vile depths of sin of the world; as a dove flying above them you will watch the world, seeing with bitterness every action;

you will be My sacrifice, you will be My target; like hunters after their game they will hunt you and pull out their weapons pursuing you; they will rate you at a high cost for whosoever could destroy you;

Lord! What will happen to me?

I will tell you this, daughter; all will not be in vain; shadows on earth fade out and pass away; clay will always wash away with the first drops of rain, but your soul will never pass away; I, the Lord, remind you what your answer was to My question, I had asked you once; "whose house is more important, your house or My House?" you answered correctly that My House is more important;

I did.

I will always keep you in My Heart; I love you,

I love you too.

let us go, do not forget My Presence!

April 26, 1987

let Me tell you, beloved, that I have drawn My designs before you were born; we will be working always together; are you willing to?

I am willing to, if You accept me, in my incapacity, My God.

I love you; Vassula, I will help you;
earlier last week you were ravaged and attacked by evil; nevertheless I have

written with you every word I wanted to; I covered you;

Was this when the devil cursed me?

yes, while he was cursing you infamously, I was blessing you; I protected you;

(Later on:)

let Me tell you, Vassula, that the least you are the more I will be; allow Me to act in you and do My will in you; be nothing; feel nothing and let Me be everything so that My word reaches the ends of the world and My Works of Peace and Love entice every heart;
    allow Me to remind you of your misery, so that by reminding you, it will prevent you from becoming elated, by all the graces I have given you; be My pure altar... fisherman of men, spread My Net of Peace and Love all over the world, have It pulled and let Me delight at Its catch! when I was in flesh on earth, I taught a small group of men to become fishermen of men; I left them in the world to spread My Word to all mankind; I, the Lord Jesus, will instruct you and show you how this work was done;

(What can I say? How could I do anything, let alone such a mission; I feel that the message is getting heavier by the day. I do want to please God but with what means. I can only see an Alp in front of me and the revelation heavy on me.)

I am bearing My Cross together with you; yes, It is indeed heavy, do not weary though; I, the Lord, am helping you; keep close to Me I will not forsake you;

Still, it's so much.

(Jesus is encouraging me to continue.)

Vassula have I not helped you this far? so why would I abandon you; lean entirely on Me; trust Me; what I have commenced and blessed, I will finish;

April 27, 1987

Vassula, I am the Lord standing in front of you;

(Jesus was there smiling and making me feel His appearance. He was holding with His two hands His mantle, pulling it open showing me His Heart. His chest was lit.)

enter in My Heart, penetrate and let It engulf you, let My Heart enrapture your heart, inflaming it, leaving it ablaze radiating My Peace and Love; come, let us be together; allow Me to be your Holy Companion; are you willing, daughter?

(I feel unable to approach Him. Who am I to approach Him? I realised how unworthy I am. How could one even allow oneself to dare talk to God, we who are a bunch of ungrateful sinners, let alone ask Him favours, even less having 'conversation' with Him! We are so lousy and unworthy that it makes me feel sick. I feel like taking a tape over my mouth. And in His presence where I was, I put a veil between Him and me out of respect, with my mind, for His presence.)

daughter, what have you done? [1] why daughter, why?

To respect You, Lord.

I want you to eat;

(I saw in His hand Bread.)

take My Bread, little one, you will have to take away this veil to take My Bread, come;
    I will take away the separation ...here take My Bread, approach;

(I did; I took from His hand His Bread.)

do you realise how delighted I am feeding you?

---

[1] Jesus appeared shocked.

(Jesus was full of Love and happy.)

Can you feel My happiness, Vassula? bring forth your weaknesses and your wretchedness that I may annihilate them in My Strength and My Mercy; little dove, fly freely but always return to Me and have My Bread, I love you;

I love You too, Lord.

(After this for a whole day I felt His love on me, what can I call it? 'Ecstatic state'? By being in that way I felt His Presence even more than usual.)

(Later on:)

you have seen My Holy Sanctuary where we penetrated and I let your eyes see how My Holy Sanctuary is guarded by My Seraphims; today I will show you what I have inside My Holy Sanctuary; can you see this strong Ray shed on My Holy Writings?

Yes, Lord!

they are My Holiest Writings written before I created you; My Holy Book holds the secrets and keys to My Heavens and the whole of My Creation; near My Holy Book I have placed two archangels guarding ardently My Holy Writings; come, I will show you more of My Glory, little one;

(God took me in a place where I felt uneasy.)

do you see this mountain of fire?

(It looked beautiful but menacing.)

from its side flow two of its rivers, they are all out of fire;

(It looked like flowing lava but clearer red.)

I the Lord shall part, on the day of My Judgement, the evil souls from the good souls; then, all the followers of Satan shall be cast in those two rivers of fire and thus punished, before the very eyes of the just; Vassula, I will let your eyes see more of My Heavens, for there are several more behind My Holy Sanctuary; creature, My Will will be done, for I am God, Yahweh Sabaoth, let Me free to act in you; we will work together with love, until I will establish My Works and when I do, I will come with My Holy Book again and will let you read in it a passage which you will write, thus sealing My Message of Peace and Love;

(In the middle of the night I was woken up by Jesus' loud cry that came from the Cross. It was full of anguish, suffering, pain, sorrowful, and bitter. It sounded like a very strong moan! Dragging.)

April 29, 1987

(Next morning.)

I am the Lord Jesus; you heard My cry, it was I; It woke you up,[1] I cried out from My Cross, It was My last loud cry I gave when I was in flesh, a cry full of sufferings, pains, and bitterness resounding from the depths of My Soul, piercing the heights in Heaven; It shook the earth's foundations and tore in half the hearts of those who loved Me, as it ripped the veil in the Temple; It aroused devout followers of Mine, as It aroused the dead from their graves, overthrowing the earth that covered them, as It overthrew Evil;
 Great thunder shook the very Heavens above and every angel trembling fell prostrate and worshipped Me in total silence; My Mother, standing nearby, on hearing My cry, fell to the ground on her knees and covered Her face weeping, carrying that last cry with Her to the day of Her dormition; She suffered ...

---
[1] It woke you up, is symbolic?

I am embittered; suffering still from many iniquities of the world; wickedness, lawlessness and egoism; My Cry is growing louder every day; I was left alone on My Cross, alone to bear the sins of the world on My shoulders, alone to suffer, alone to die, shedding My Blood which covered the entire world, redeeming you My beloved ones;

that same Cry is now on earth like an echo of the past, am I living in the shadows of the past? was My Sacrifice in vain? how can you not hear then My Cry from the Cross? why do you shut your ears and dispel It?

Lord, for whom is this message?

for all those who have ears to hear My Cry;

(I felt very touched knowing how much He suffered all alone, and is still suffering.)

My God, I accept to be as You wish me to be in Your message of April 23, your sacrifice, your target. Let me bear Your Cross for You and let me give You rest. Let me comfort You. I'm not alone. Like I said before, I'm with You![1]

I love you little dove, I indulged you with all My graces; allow Me to use you for My own interests and My own glory; retain nothing for yourself and look upon My own interests only; glorify Me, work for Me, add to your sufferings, My sufferings;

I wish the whole world praised Your Name and its voice reached You.

unity will strengthen My Church; Unity will glorify Me; Vassula, love Me;

Teach me to love you as You want, Lord.

I will; I will not abandon you; do not weary bearing My Cross; I am near you sharing It, beloved;

(In Paris during Easter:
When the Archimandrite said to me on looking at the Message: "It is a miracle." I also thought how wonderful, how beautiful that God gives us a Message, but on the other hand how terrible, terrible because it shows a sad God, a suffering God; God gives a Message in agony, unhappy and abandoned by many. It is a sad Message.)

Am I learning at all, Jesus? Not that I ask to satisfy myself but to know at least where I stand. I mean if I progress at all!

Vassula, I, Jesus, am before you and you are indeed growing; I raised you from the dead and I fed you; you are eating My Bread; My Light shines upon you, I am your Teacher and you are learning from Wisdom;

Jesus, many times you remind me to stay small and remain nothing, now You tell me that I'm growing?

Yes, you must grow in spirit, in love, in humbleness, in humility, in faithfulness; <u>let all the virtues grow in you</u>; nevertheless, becoming nothing in vanity, in wickedness and all the repugnant and detestable practices in My eyes; I want you to become perfect;

April 30, 1987

Jesus, today I will ask You if You are willing to give a special message for a person who is dying?

dying?[2] she is not dying, her soul will be freed, she will be liberated and will live! she will come to Me; her soul will be free;
write and tell her how I am seeking every soul; how I am feeding hungered

---

[1] I take back what I said on April 7, 1987. I take back.

[2] Jesus seemed a bit astonished at my words.

souls; how My Bread gives eternal life; how I restore the sick; let her know that I am the Elixir of Life and the Resurrection;

(Jesus gave me a message for this person, in a separate paper.)

May 1, 1987

I, God, will give you enough strength to enable you to accomplish My Works; deny Me never; do not seek your own interests, but My own; leave Me free to use you and descend on earth through you manifesting My Word, until I come to deliver you;

Vassula, I will predict your end; all of My chosen souls never feared this hour; I will reveal to you five more of My mysteries, come now and kiss My five wounds;

(I did. First His Hands, then His feet, then His side. Nevertheless I do not yet understand what Jesus means by five mysteries coinciding with His five wounds. But I know that when the time is right, He will let me know. So I learned not to ask.)

Vassula I will tell you My secrets when you grow a little bit more;[1] beseech My favours and I will grant them,

*My God and Father
I will ask You one thing
which has a few clauses;
and that is only
for Your interests and glory:
May Your Message
reach the ends of the world
and draw many hearts to You.
May Your will be done
and Your Holy Name glorified.
May Evil lose its grip
and be crushed for ever.
This is what I wish now,*

*and every time You will hear
my voice for a request
it will be none other
than for Your Glory.
Any favour asked from me
will be for Your Glory.
Any cry of help from me
will be for Your own interests,
and nothing for me.
All the strength I will ask
will be for Your interests,
God Almighty.*

little one, place your feet into My footprints and follow Me;
it is I, Jesus,

Jesus?

I am; beloved, call Me Spouse and Father too; I love you; come let us work;[2] love Me fervently and amend for others who wound Me;

My God, I was thinking, how could I be like a dove flying above the 'wicked world' if I myself am wicked with sin, being in the same state as all the rest. I will be unable to 'see all' as You said, and 'hear everything', for I'm no better than the ones that wound You ...

Vassula, be in Me; endeavour to attain purity; draw from My Purity which I offer; draw, sip from Me, absorb Me; I am Infinite Wealth and every soul can draw from Me;

Having given me <u>so</u> many graces I might become vain, and evil can tempt me easily!

I will always remind you of your wretchedness and the shadows of your past; I will remind you of how you denied Me and rejected My great Love, when I approached you, and of how I found you dead, lying among the dead in darkness and of how out of Mercy and Love I revived you, lifting you to My breast;

---

[1] During the years, I've learned to penetrate into His five Wounds by the power of the Holy Spirit. These were the five mysteries.

[2] Jesus said all this in such grace and serenity that only God can talk in this way.

come, let us pray, say:

"My Father, lead me wherever
Your will wishes me to go
allow me to live in Your Light
and warm my heart,
that it may glow, giving warmth
on those who approach me,
blessed be Your Name,
for giving me all these graces
in spite of my nothingness,
blessed be Your Name,
for the Good You have done to me
and the Mercy You have shown me,
lifting me near Your Heart, amen;"

let us repeat;
remember that all the graces I am giving you are for My own interests; retain nothing for yourself; glorify Me sharing My happiness;

I wish that I will be able to glorify You and that the world may praise Your Name and their prayers reach You rising like incense, their praises resounding in Heaven at Your door like a knock.

Love will conquer evil;
love Me with all your soul and mind; let Me be everything; I, the Lord, will provide you till the end;

Then take me, even though I am nothing, and do as You wish with me. I am Yours.

come, let Me rejoice always hearing these words of total surrender; I love you daughter;

I love You, Father.

May 2, 1987

I am Jesus,

Jesus, I sense that You are about to give me an important message; according to the pattern. Evil attacking me to discourage my writing.

I have a message for those who love Me,[1] and immolate their souls for Me; I wish to encourage them giving them Strength;
I, the Word, will manifest My words through this weak instrument; I will descend on earth through this Message, letting My Light shine on you all;
I bless you, beloved of My Soul; I love you! I have within Me in the depths of My Intimate Soul, a Living and Inexhaustible Flame; I am Purity and Devotion and an abyss of Wealth; My beloved; come and draw from Me, saturating your hearts come and sip from Me; come and penetrate into My open Wounds; come and immerse your souls in My Blood! drink from My Living Fountain so that you will be able to submerge, irrigating this desolate wilderness, healing My lambs;
draw from this Living Flame and let It engulf your hearts! I love you to a degree your minds can never grasp; come; do not weary bearing My Holy Cross for I am with you, bearing It with you; follow Me and keep close to Me, place your feet into My footprints, do not weary of striving and suffering, glorify Me and let your voices rise in Heaven like the sweet smell of incense;
praise Me; let Me rejoice, let Me delight in you; let Me delight in your love for Me; fill up your heart from this Infinite Love and let It flow out on My lambs, healing them;
let every living creature on earth feel My warmth; let every cold and petrified heart melt and dissolve in My Purity, integrating in My Body and becoming one with Me! let every shadow of the past, revive into a living soul, full of Integrity, Peace, and Love; make an Eden of my creation!
unite! unite and be one, for I, God, am One; unity brings strength, <u>unite</u>; be My devout sowers, sowing My seeds of Peace and Love;

---

[1] All priests, religious, sisters, brothers, all those who love Him truly.

I have created grains that will yield into a heaven on earth, for My Kingdom on earth will be as in Heaven; take My grains which lie in My Heart, purified by My Blood, and scatter them all over; I am bearing those seeds, beloved, and I desire that you enter into My Heart and draw them; seek unity;

I will heal My flowers, I will fragrance them, I will flourish them, I will embellish My garden, I will irrigate your hearts, I will revive you;

Creation! I love you! I will shine on you and let My warm Rays dissolve those heavy dark thunder clouds, scattering them away, dispersing them; My Light will pierce them and all darkness and evil that laid heavily upon you will disappear; this darkness that brought you only weakness, wretchedness and wickedness;

My Warm Rays will revive all My flowers and I will pour from Heaven My dew of Righteousness, Holiness, Purity, Integrity, Peace and Love; I am your Devout Keeper with a vigilant eye on you, remember I am the Light of this world; I am the Word;

peace be with you all; glorify Me; lean on Me; strive and do not weary bearing My Cross, healing My children;

My Vassula, never weary of writing; I love you; Wisdom will instruct you;

I Love You, Lord. May Your will be done.

May 5, 1987

(When I feel God's love on me (us) my mind almost reels! When He makes me dissolve in His Body and His Body annihilates mine it is then that I feel like air, like truly I am spirit without flesh! Ecstatic state? Even these words cannot describe fully the state His Love can bring me to. His grace and goodness are impossible to describe, there are no words to describe such greatness and splendour of His Holiness. And to know how I, before His approach, rejected Him!)

Vassula, come to Me; My five Wounds are open; Vassula, penetrate into My Wounds and feel My pain; come, let My Blood sanctify you in My Wounds, glorify Me; I will guide you, daughter; freely I give, so give freely too; I the Lord will return with My Holy Book;

(Jesus had a small book with Him.)

discern and read where I point, "betrothed, blessed of My Soul, daughter of Mine; feed My lambs; scatter My grains, let them yield a rich harvest, reap it and give My Bread freely; I am the Bread of Life; feed My sheep, I am always with you till the end of times;"[1]

My God, thank You for Your Guidance. I sound arid with these naked words but I have to put them on paper. May Your Name be Blessed forever and ever!

I love you; I will not forsake you; we will work together; do not weary writing; now I have sealed My Message of Peace and Love, I will guide you, Vassula; come to Me;

I shall follow You, Lord. I love You.

leave Me free to act in you,

Lord, may Your will be done.

I will instruct you with Wisdom;

(Later on:)

(Yesterday after the end of God's Message I felt God in me and I in Him so very much, I felt I could not separate ever.)

My companion, I love you; Vassula, give Me everything, give Me all you have;

I have given You my love. I have given You myself. I have detached my feelings from

---
[1] The contents of the book revealed my mission. The Apostolate.

earth. I have surrendered. Can I give You anything more?

daughter, I love to hear you surrendering; let Me be your Captor;

(I could feel Jesus this evening so strongly that I could see distinctly His Face which was not easy the other times. This evening He seemed so very intense, fervid, eager, like someone who comes determined with fervour to convince someone who is lukewarm.)

will you kiss My Wounds?

(I did, in a 'mystic' way. Then I asked Jesus to sit at the chair nearby me. Immediately I felt 'mystically' again that He did. He faced me and stretched His arm on the table reaching me on my copy-book. Jesus imprints in my mind these impressions.)

flower of Mine, devote yourself entirely to Me, are you ready to hear Me?

Yes, Jesus.

betrothed, blessed of My Soul, freely I gave, so freely give; unite with Me, be one with Me; look into My eyes;

(I did.)

Jesus, what can I do more?

love Me,

But I love You, I said it many times, and You know I mean it. My soul longs for You. You wanted me to be detached, and I became detached.

do I, Vassula, not long for you?[1] do I, as your God not suffer too?[2] beloved, live in Me and I in you, you in Me and Me in you, us;

―――――――――
[1] That is where I understood what it meant that "The soul longs for its God, and its God longs for its soul."
[2] From being separated by being in flesh the soul.

adapt in Me, unite;

But You have united us, Jesus. You said You did!

I have;

(I suddenly felt physically exhausted, so I asked permission to go.)

Shall we go, Jesus?

daughter, why?

I'm exhausted, Jesus.

beloved, I want you to stay, will you stay?

(It was the first time Jesus insisted.)

I will stay then ...

torn is My Heart when I am left alone,

But You are with me, we are together...

I am with you now, but you do forget Me many times; leave Me free and let My Divine Hands mould you as I wish; I will form you to My image; let Me free to work in you; I am Jesus and Jesus means Saviour, daughter; I love you to jealousy; I want you all Mine; I want everything you do to be for Me; I do not tolerate rivals; I want you to worship Me and live for Me;

breathe for Me, love for Me, eat for Me, smile for Me, immolate yourself for Me; everything you will do, do it for Me; I want to consume you, I want to inflame you desiring <u>Me</u> only; adorn Me with your petals, My flower; crown Me with your love; remove My thorned crown and replace it with your soft petals; fragrance Me with your fragrance, love <u>Me</u> and Me only;

I have laid out My life for you out of Sublime Love; would you not do the same for Me your Spouse? betrothed, rejoice your Spouse, make Me happy! bind yourself to Me with eternal bonds; live for

Me and Me alone; be My Sacrifice, be My Target, be My Net; creature, do you love Me?

How can I not love You, My God? I do!

say it, say it many times; let Me hear it, I love hearing it; say it a thousand times a day and every morning after you rest in Me, face Me and tell Me, "My Lord, I love you;"

Jesus, I love You, but why are You becoming stern?[1]

(Maybe I am not doing enough.)

come, do not misunderstand Me! it's Love talking, it's Love's desires, it's Love's flame, it's Love's jealous love; I cannot stand rivals; lean on your Holy Father, Spouse, Companion and God; come, let us rest in each other; love Me, daughter, with a jealous love too;[2]

May 6, 1987

(My message to God before His message of May 6, 1987 –
I am learning what God means by surrendering completely. Being detached. Leave everything and follow Him. His Words are symbolic, they are not material. Surrender, I have by loving Him first and beyond everything else and the feeling I would like Him to use me. Being detached, yes, to the extent of being detached from my body, meaning that I realise I have a soul that wants, desires to detach itself from the body to join Him, and follow Him only.
– Suffer; yes, suffering because of not being with Him, of being still material on earth, of having the feeling of being a widow here. – Suffer; to know that I have to follow daily life, material life. It is indeed a burden to be rubbed constantly with a balm of Technology and Science, with disbelievers, with sceptics, with people who think you are losing foot because of age. Suffer; to have to follow their programs. Suffer; to hide one's feeling when I only feel I want to dissociate from the world and be alone, with God. Just He and me and no one else and nothing else around me to distract me.
Even this that I wrote I asked God to help me write down my feelings, since I am unable to express myself, and so He did, whispering the right words in My ear! He wants me to be among mankind; one more cross to carry. My body aches.)

Mine too; all you feel I feel; daughter, bless Me,

I bless You, my beloved God.

(Later, still feeling dissolved in God:)

I love you, see? love will suffer, love binds, love offers abundant fidelity, love has no restraint to sacrifice;
Vassula, the hours are fleeing, your time is near; offer yourself, grow in humility, eat from My hand; My beloved, I will unbind your chains and your soul will fly to Me very soon;

I love you, My God ...

May 7, 1987

I love you, it is I, your Spouse,
My flower, I will purify you; I will continue saturating you, reviving you with My Light and feeding you with My Strength; Vassula, I will honour you by letting you wear My thorned crown;

Jesus, how can You trust me?

I love you; by wearing My crown you will understand the mockery I received, for soon you too will be mocked upon; do not forget, I will suffer as much as you will

---
[1] Here, I meant, demanding. Jesus was demanding out of His fervent love.
[2] The word rival means everything else that we put BEFORE God. We must put God first.

suffer, for I am in you and you in Me; I have united Myself to you, we are one; come now, beloved, we will continue My Works; I will give you enough Strength till the end;

(In this message, I understood later on, Jesus prepares me. I will be mocked and laughed upon. At least He is with me, we will share the mockeries together. Once thrust out in the world for my apostolate, the mockery and persecutions will start.)

Jesus, do you know I have not even managed to reach a hundred times saying, "I love You", and You asked me to say it a thousand times!

Vassula, ah Vassula, do you not know that every act done with love is telling Me "I love you"; you are showing Me your love in that way too;
    everything you do in your life you do it to Me;
    come; embellish! flourish! radiate! fragrance! adorn Me with wreaths of love; let every one of your petals replace a thorn from My thorned crown; the more petals the less thorns piercing Me; I love you; love Me; teach others to love Me; show them My appeal;

With Your help I am showing them. I can't do much.

love Me and heal My Wounds; let the tears shed for Me be a soothing balm to My Wounds; Vassula, wreaths are not made only for funerals – they are also made for brides; allow Me to place a wreath upon you in August;

May 8, 1987

Jesus today I have lots of work at home, but two words from You will make me happy!

just two? love Me;

May 9, 1987

I was thinking when I just watched a documentary about the 'Fatima Miracle', how even with that, many people were sceptical, calling it all sorts of things, like Mass Hypnosis etc. In the old times this sort of miracle would have been believed and written in the Holy Bible, but nowadays, years have to go by before being accepted. I'm fearing that Your message will not be counted that it's from You, since there will be no physical proof or prediction in it. Every high authority, IF it comes that far, will not even pay attention to Your appeal, and I know that Your Cup of Justice is at its full now! The world is offending You very much. They will not listen.

is there a higher authority than your God?

No, My God, none, but if they do not listen? Some of them might think it is propaganda for the Church; I mean those who are in high authority and anti-church. They might think that all this was made up! Made up by the Church!

Vassula, I am the Most High and all authority will come from Me;

And if they do not believe?

I will not write down what will happen if they will not listen from their obduracy; are you fearing Me, little one?

(God must have felt in me a fear that passed through me; at the same time when He was writing the word 'happen', I felt a pang of sadness in God's Heart.)

I am, from Your wrath!

I will endure and forgive your sins, but I will not endure your hatred against Me; I am your Creator and your breath comes from Me; I hold the whole of My creation in My Hand;

I loathe paganism;[1]
Vassula, let Me guide you; come, My child, rest in Me;

(Later:)

your sigh, betrothed, is like a million words of love to Me; yes, I am talking about your sigh you gave Me this morning;

(It's true, this morning I just thought of Jesus with love. I wanted to tell Him so much, but I could not find even the right words. I gave a sigh only; but He seemed to understand a lot from my sigh.)

Vassula, love Me blindly and let Me use you as I wish; be utterly nothing so that in being nothing I can be everything and thus complete My Works; creating you was a delight for Me;

My God, I fear to disappoint You by being unfaithful to You. I don't know even if I was at all faithful to start with, so why am I saying about keeping faithful if I don't know that I have ever been at all faithful?

from all eternity I knew you to be weak and wretched, but I love you; I have taken My measures so that you remain faithfully Mine; have you imagined that I have not known all this? I knew everything, and that is precisely why I chose you; I told you that your ineffable weakness and misery attracts Me; come, this guidance will restore My honour, I rejoice at how it will remedy your injustices;
Vassula, crown Me with tender words!

My words, Lord? What possible value have they got to such a Majestic Presence?

every tender and loving word coming even from you becomes divine in My Presence; it becomes great in My Ears;

---

[1] Atheism.

never weary of writing, My little instrument; everything you do comes from Me; I suspend you with My Strength and I call you when I wish; I love you, love your Lord too;

(I felt again that His Greatness annihilated me completely, it was like plunging in the deepest ocean. A wonderful feeling, of wanting to be possessed by God and being pleased to be!)

May 10, 1987

Vassula do you remember when I fed My people with manna? I threw it from Heaven, it came from My stores in Heaven; do you know that it is I who lifted the seas so that My people could cross to the Sinai?

Yes, Lord.

I am Omnipotent, little one; I am the One who installs together this guidance to feed many; I have, Vassula, communicated with you all this time! see?

My God, and still I'm fearing that this is done by my subconscious ...

let Me tell you instantly that you would never have done all this work on your own! do you believe in miracles?

Yes, I do.

consider this as a miracle then, I love you;

I love You, Father. How could I explain to people when they ask me how do I see You. I feel Your Presence very much, and it's no fancy.

tell them that you see Me with the eyes of your soul;

Sometimes, Jesus, I think I'm imagining You and want to turn my eyes away from

You (the vision) to convince myself it's not You ...

in doing this you offend Me, Vassula; I have given you this grace,[1] accept My gift, accept what I give you!

Lord, sometimes and especially in Bangladesh with the heat I feel exhausted, I wish I could do more work. Sometimes I wish I was like an amoeba, split in several pieces!

I give you enough strength to complete My Works; Luke once said; "I will never exhaust since I am working for the Lord, for the Lord Himself is my strength"; little one I have led you as a father would lead his little child by the hand to school; estimate what you have earned with Me?

I have indeed earned a lot. Since I never practised religion, nor had a Bible in the house since school time, and not having been to church since the baptism of my first son (15 years ago). You taught me many things. Not that I now consider myself as a scholar, but at least You taught me who You are and how much You love us, and of how to love You.

I have given you fruit from My own garden; I wish to fill up your stores with My fruit;

(I asked Him something which I don't wish to write down.)

I know Vassula, let it be like I wish it to be;

(I could not help but produce a smile to my ears, it felt so good to have a small 'chit-chat' in this way with Jesus. I felt Him like I was talking to a good friend, I couldn't help smiling. I was almost giggling, I was happy.)

I am cheerful too;

(Yes, He was, it was marvellous!)

Vassula do you know how I delight and enjoy these moments, these moments where you talk to Me as a companion? Vassula, we still have work to be done; be blessed, I will give you a sign of My Presence, beloved;

Jesus, what sign, I mean, where?

in your house; I will prove to you that I am present;

I love You, Jesus. I wish I could please You.

altar! keep drawing from Me and keeping My Flame in you ardently ablaze;

May 13, 1987

(Yesterday, May 12, in the evening while passing the staircase level I was stopped by this intense odour of incense. The smell reached up to the second floor. I was surprised. I went and asked my son if he had lit a mosquito coil (although it did not smell at all like a coil, but pure church incense). He said, no. I left this incident aside and got busy with other things. One hour later I wanted to go in the study where I usually write to fetch a pencil, and while I entered the study again this intense beautiful odour of incense passed me by, it bathed me entirely! I left that particular spot to see if it smelled elsewhere, no, there was no odour elsewhere except again where I the second time smelled it, again it was there covering me.)

O beloved, when I covered you with My odour I blessed you at the same time;

Oh Jesus, was that You?

Yes, you felt My Presence; this was My sign,[2] the incense comes from Me;

---

[1] To have intellectual visions as well as imaginary visions.

[2] Jesus predicted the day before that He will give me a sign of His Presence.

If only I was sure that evening!

I will give you more signs of My Presence, My flower; be alert though;

> Jesus, my Love,
> my Breath, my Life, my Joy,
> my Sigh, my Rest,
> my Holy Companion,
> my Saviour, my Sight,
> my Everything, I love You!

Vassula, love Me fervently; annihilate into My Body; adorn Me with tender words, loving words; let My pains diminish; soothe My Wounds by imbuing them with loving words;

(I discovered by reading today St. Teresa that odours do exist. If they are from the devil they have a horrible stench so she says. Strangely enough this was like another proof to me given today to show me that the incense odour did come from Jesus. I was very happy!)

May 14, 1987

(Today what joy; in reading the life of St. Teresa of Avila who had visions, I fell upon a vision she describes of hell and I was very pleased to find that her description fitted in my description of hell that God gave me, she explains it this way: "dark and closely confined; the ground seemed to be <u>full of water</u> which looked like <u>filthy, evil-smelling mud</u>" ... etc. yes, the whole thing looked like a grotto, low-ceiling ... my description is on March 7, 1987.)

May 15, 1987

come, surrender; I delight to hear you surrendering for in surrendering it rejoices My Heart, little one! ask Me to use you ...

Father, if I am of any use to You, use me then!

I love you; come, do you wish to write?

I will write if it is Your wish.

do write then;
   let it be known that I, Yahweh, willed to enlighten you; your only recourse is Me; My Heart is an abyss of Forgiveness and Mercy; little one, as I have enlightened you, so will I enlighten those who turn to Me;
   – Vassula come,[1] be closer to Me, Will you receive Me...

(Silence from my part.)

grieve Me not;

(Silence.)

be with Me, purify yourself; love Me;

(Silence.)

grieve Me not, beloved...

(Silence.)

will you receive Me? ... fill Me with joy and be with Me; love Me, I love you; come to Me more often; receive Me more often; I love you; will you pray with Me?[2] wound Me not,

(I consented.)

> Beloved Father,
> purify me with Your Son's Blood,
> Father,
> purify Me with your Son's Body,
> Beloved Father,
> hold away the evil spirit
> that now tempts me,
> amen;

(As Jesus was writing it, I was saying it. I suddenly realised, it was like I woke up after Jesus' prayer. I realised what was

---

[1] Jesus was now speaking to me.
[2] Here I felt like saying: "Oh no, not again!"

happening from the beginning of the message of today. Jesus was calling me to Holy Communion but I was pretending I did not understand. I even felt like answering, no. I was hurting Him and yet I was reluctant to reply, I made Him say it explicitly. Jesus ran to my rescue, I felt I was about to fall. Just after His prayer (He prayed together with me), I realised that I had an evil spirit pulling on me. Strange feeling I had when I felt the evil spirit release his grip on me when the words came "Beloved Father, hold away the evil spirit that now tempts me".

Jesus had put so much force on my hand, my hand felt very heavy, and at the same time I felt His enormous and most powerful strength sustaining me; like a most powerful Giant. After the prayer it was like I woke up.)

come nearer to Me; sanctify yourself; I love you and I will sustain your falls; I will not see you lost; a flower needs to be watered and fertilised to maintain its beauty; I am your Devout Keeper;

I love you;

I love You too.

(Jesus had seen the evil spirit pulling on me, I did not realise it, while the evil spirit was pulling I felt silly. Jesus was very quick to rescue me. Only when the evil spirit's grip released, I realised my close fall! I can't believe what happened!)

May 16, 1987

(Last night coming back from a dinner, I went up the stairs and a great odour of incense penetrated my nose again. I understood.)

Vassula, when you smell incense it is I, Jesus Christ, I wish you to feel my Presence; Vassula, I love you to distraction and beyond measure, alas! this Love which overflows my Heart, this ardent Flame of Love burning, is so little understood, so few come to draw from It ... so few ...

Jesus, many people don't know how to approach You, I'm so sure of that.

they can come and talk to Me; I hear them; I can enjoy for hours any conversation; it brings Me so much joy when they would count Me among their friends;

Last night, a man told me that all women desire to be Magdalenes.

lo, not all;

Well, those that love you probably do then.

I want them to;

Jesus, I think we will have to rush.

where to?

Downstairs, check the oven.[1]

come then, let us go;

Jesus when before Your approach I heard of You like a myth, I never realised how You are REAL. In my eyes, You were so far away. A story in a book!

I know Vassula, I know, for many I am still a myth; find Me in Gethsemane next time we meet; I will reveal to you My anguishes, My sufferings and fears of that night; come, allow Me to rest in you, daughter;

(Next day:)

come, find Me where I have told you;
O Gethsemane! what have you to unfold but fears, anguishes, betrayals and abandonments! Gethsemane you have depleted men from courage, you have

---

[1] I'd forgotten the oven which was lit.

suspended in your still air My agonies for all eternity;

Gethsemane, what have you to declare that was undeclared? you have witnessed in the stillness of Holiness, the betrayal of your God, you have witnessed Me;

the hour had come, Scriptures were to be fulfilled;

daughter, I know that many souls believe in Me as though I was but a myth; they believe that I existed only in the past; for many I am but a passing shadow now eclipsed with time and evolution; very few realise that I existed in flesh on earth and exist now among you;

I Am All what came to pass and is to pass; I know their fears, I know their anguishes, I know their weaknesses, <u>have I not witnessed all these frailties in Gethsemane?</u>

daughter, when Love prayed in Gethsemane, a thousand devils were shaken, fearing demons took flight; the hour had come: Love was glorifying Love;

O Gethsemane, witness of the Betrayed, witness of the Forlorned, arise, witness and testify; daughter, Judas betrayed Me, but how many more like Judas are betraying Me still; I knew instantly that his kiss would spread among many and for generations to come; this same kiss will be given to Me over and over again, renewing My sorrow, rending My Heart;

Vassula, come let Me be consoled, let Me rest in your heart;

(Next day:)

Vassula, will you write?

Yes, Jesus, if it's what You wish.

love Me, daughter, in My torments of Gethsemane; I was deceived by one of My own, one of My beloved ones; and today, I still receive indignities, recollecting My agonies of the past; My Heart swelled and filled with bitterness;

(I had problems and I lacked confidence to continue suddenly.)

Jesus?

I am;
little one, write; My sweat of agony poured out of Me like big drops of blood;

(I suddenly thought of the time I was almost tempted by the evil spirit ... and felt ashamed.)

weakness attracts Me, for I can give you My Strength, come bring Me your love, lean on Me,

(I leaned.)

Yes!

(Jesus was glad.)

here, eat from Me, fill your heart from My Heart; love Me, think of Me, be Mine, entirely Mine; adore Me and Me only; I am calling you to receive Me, yes, in the little white Host ... come and drink Me; purify! I love you and I will see that you receive Me, do not deny Me ever! desire Me and Me only;

I will be waiting for you at the Tabernacle; you will see Me, like I have taught you, with the eyes of your soul;

Jesus, it's my fault to have interrupted You. Do you wish to continue?

I do; hear Me, the soil absorbed those drops but today the soil dryer than ever needs irrigation, it desires peace and is thirsty for love;

(Suddenly Jesus stopped.)

grieve Me not, but will you pray again with Me? love Me Vassula; come,

"O Father,
fulfil what must be fulfilled;
may Your words penetrate,
bless and purify
the hearts of Your children;
Father, do as Your Heart desires
and may Your will be done,
amen;"

are you willing to continue working for Me?

I will continue working for God if it's His Will to do so.

it is My Will;

Then I will continue working. Do not forget my incapacity though!

lean entirely on Me, your Jesus; I know how helpless you are; I wanted to have but a mere child who would have to depend entirely on Me;

Jesus?

I am;

Is Your message of Gethsemane finished?

no; I will continue; My children have to be revived and shown that I am among them; with My Message, which I blessed, they would see Me and feel Me; many will return to Me, I, who long for My beloved ones;

Jesus, how can I do anything?

Vassula; will a father not help his child cross the road when it needs his help? so I will help you till the end;

I don't know if I am doing right by distributing Your message, am I doing wrong?

no, you are giving My Bread as I gave It to you; My Bread must be given freely!

May 17, 1987

(I read St. Michael's prayer.)

read the next one;

(I read The Memorare of St. Bernard (St Mary) being worried about something: when My friends read the messages and start thinking again of God, some returning to God and some being happy with hope unfortunately sometimes what happens in their delight is that they would talk about it to a priest friend, and he would warn them not to believe it's God. In fact, I realised myself that out of the four priests here knowing the writings, two discouraged me and two encouraged me. I would have liked though that those that discouraged me and discourage others, I would have liked them to decide after having read from A – Z. Then if they still thought it nothing they should tell me why and explain it. How could one give an opinion without following it and discussing with me not more than once!)

fill up your heart with God's Flame; I love you;

Beloved Mother, I fear that God's message might be trampled by people who are not even following it up or reading it!

fear not, child,

I'm distressed!

I know, will you acknowledge, Vassula, the Works of Jesus?

I do ...

Vassula, I have prayed for you, agapi mou, be patient; lean on Jesus;

(I prayed to Jesus.)

lean on Me,

I'm fearing for Your message to be crushed, by those who have not read it even.

do not fear, love Me; to purify your soul glorifies Me, come, let us go; remember, us, we ... grieve not;

(Jesus led me yesterday to Sunday Mass. I can't follow the Mass properly, as all the rest, since I've never been taught the songs and procedure. I'm always one step behind the others, but I know Jesus is there and is talking to me. The bread felt consoling.)

May 18, 1987

(I've been at 6.30 to Holy Communion as Jesus asked me. In the middle of it Jesus started talking to me. I received the Bread and in my mouth it felt like a lacerated piece of flesh[1] which had been ripped off from scourging. Funny how I felt it yesterday different; and today different. It seemed like Jesus was giving me different impressions.)

Jesus?

I am;
love Me, come close to Me; I will give you different impressions every time you receive Me; Vassula, I grieve when you are distant to Me;

(It's true. Sometimes when 'the wave' of doubt covers me, I refuse to talk to Him or see Him, saying to myself that it's not Him, and I avoid His image, avoid talking with Him, avoid all what He's taught me. I'm trying to convince myself that my imagination played tricks.)

you are grieving Me, beloved; you are offending Me when you block Me out and seem so far away; understand that the devil is behind all this; he is desperate and wants you to believe that you are only imagining all the graces I have given you; he wants you to forget all My Heavenly teachings; he wants to drag you back to him;

when you seem so far from Me, I fear, I fear for you; when a shepherd sees one from his flock wander away would he just sit? a good shepherd would rush to it, pick it up and bring it back;

when I see you wandering away, I will not wait; I will rush to you and fetch you; I will draw you closer to Me; little one, I will cover you with my cloak when you are cold; I will feed you, lift you close to my Heart when distressed; what will I not do for you;

Jesus?

I am;

Why all these graces for me? Why?

let Me free to give to whom I please;

But I don't want to be different from others!

Vassula, you will be receiving Me, let Me use you; have I not told you that I will liberate you?

I don't understand.

I wish to liberate many souls from their chains, chains of evil; I am using you as an instrument; do not misunderstand My Works; My appeal is not for you only; My appeal of Peace and Love is for all humanity!

Yes Lord, but I feel a bit uncomfortable when friends know about this. I mean I feel uncomfortable when some of them look and say, "You are privileged." I feel awful.

feel awful, daughter, for being chosen because of your wretchedness; I have not chosen you because of your merits; I have told you already before, that your merits are none and what comes out of the Lord's mouth is but the Truth; come often and repent to Me; remember I do not

---

[1] Jesus was showing me that Holy Communion was not just plain bread that we are taking, but that indeed it is Christ's Body we receive.

favour you more than the rest of My children;

I know, Jesus. I know that's why I feel embarrassed for You giving me this grace, to call You anytime I wish.

Vassula, Vassula, I give even to the most wretched; let your friends see how My Heart is an abyss of Mercy and Forgiveness; let them see how I raise even the dead; let them see how I love even those that denied Me;

Jesus?

I am, beloved;

I don't know what to say.

say that you love Me;

I love You and You know it.

I love you, daughter; yes, in spite of your wretchedness; remember, talk to Me; I am your Spouse; share with Me, smile at Me when you see Me;

Yes, Jesus. I feel that my very presence offends You. And I know I'm repeating myself. How can you stand me ...

I love you;

I love You too.

feel Me; look into My eyes;[1] yes, remember, daughter, that I am your Holy Father; let us go now;

May 19, 1987

Jesus?

I am; Vassula, remember this guidance is from Me;

---
[1] I looked at Him; His Eyes were grave but FULL of love...

Do You know, Jesus, what I long for?

I know daughter,

I sometimes wish that this grace You have given me to meet You in this way, and the grace You have given me to see You with the eyes of my soul, could have been just for me alone, You and me, me and You, and I would have felt so marvellous, nothing to worry about, showing no one our secret.

(I sighed.)

daughter, I have asked you whether you wanted to work for Me and your answer pleased Me; let Me remind you that you are My beloved soul through whom I will manifest Myself and desires, for this is My Will;

But My God, without offending You, Your Word can lay heavy if it's not unloaded. What can I do?

beloved, will I not help you, I am the Lord;
"brothers, read My Message, fill Me with joy and remember My Works, believe in My Infinite Wealth and Mercy!"
Vassula, follow Me, I will lead you; little one, I will give you My Strength, never leave My Hand;

My God ... what do you want from me ...

Vassula, I want love, love, love; My Body aches from lack of love, My Lips are parched for thirst of love; I want to use you, little one, as My instrument for My guidance;

My Lord, may Your will be done, may You fulfil Your desires.

beloved, lean on Me, listen to My Voice, never feel alone for I, God, am with you;

(I felt somewhat consoled.)

Lord, shall we start the day?

come, I will; lean entirely on Me; I am guiding you;

May 19, 1987

(Babette came. She talked to Jesus, the three of us were together. Babette did not need to ask her question aloud. Her mere thought passing through her mind was instantly answered, with His own handwriting. Jesus by this is stimulating us about His <u>real</u> Presence and He <u>is</u> calling us to become more intimate with Him and remember His Presence, loving Him.)

May 19, 1987

I must admit that I was impressed, Jesus meeting Babette in this way ...

lean on Me;

Jesus, my friend asked me to ask You, why don't You come to us again? Just like before, in flesh? So that people change.

ah, Vassula ... I will be coming back; every dawn that breaks is closer to My coming to you Vassula, do you know what that means?

Tell me Lord.

Love will return again, Love will be among you once more, Love will bring you Peace again; My Kingdom on earth will be as it is in Heaven; love will glorify Love; I am soon with you, My beloved; pray for the time is near;
   will you, little one, still work for Me?

I wish to hear Your name.

I am Love;

Yes, I shall work for Love; in my incapacity, depending on You entirely.

I know you are lost without Me, beloved; you are My flower which needs My Light;

I'm so happy!

O daughter, I love you to distraction! lean entirely on Me; I will augment your knowledge of discernment;

My Lord! Are You augmenting my feelings to feel You and see You and hear You?

I am, you will feel Me and will be able to discern Me more;

My God! Why all these graces upon me? I've done nothing to merit anything!

I know but I love you, do not forget though who you are;

Please help in reminding me, Lord.

I will prevent you from becoming elated by all My given graces, by reminding you of your wretchedness; I will remind you that all the graces you are receiving from Me, are for My own Glory; every grace you receive from Me will be for My own interests and not for your own; so draw from My Heart and fill up yours; I want My altar to be constantly ablaze; live for Me, breathe for Me, be My own for all eternity;

(I will for God.)

My God?

I am, love Me and look after my own interests;

Lord! ... (I sighed.) I, a zero, and You know it, Lord. Do not trust me, please.

let Me act in you freely;
   come, I will satisfy your question; <u>Love will return among you as Love</u>; we will pray together,

"O Heavenly Father,
Father of Love,
come to us, delivering us from evil,
Father love us and allow us
to abide in Your Light,
do as your Heart desires,
may Your Name be glorified,
amen"

allow Me to use you,

Permit me and let me hear Your name again.

I am Jesus Christ, beloved, Son of God; all I ask from you, Vassula, is love and to share My Cross of Peace and Love together with Me;

Yes, Lord.

daughter, never leave My Hand; love Me, daughter;

*Teach me to love You the way You desire us to love You. If you want, let me love You the most in the world.
You are smiling!*

I am so happy! do you wish to do this for Me?

Yes!

beloved, with Me you will learn; are you willing to suffer for Me too?

For the Lord, yes, if He wants it that way too ...

then all will be done according to My will;

(You know what's good for the soul so I will depend on God.)

I am God; come now in that special place I have for you in My Heart and remain in there;

May 20, 1987

(Sometimes I surprise myself, why do I get this urge to meet Jesus in this way? Why and how and for what am I keen in writing, hearing His messages? For all these months it's something that has become indispensable.)

I love you; it is I, Jesus, who gives you this urge to meet Me; Vassula, love Me always; I will tell you, sister, My desires;

(Jesus was so tender, a sad look was on His face.)

I wish to unite all My priests; I desire from them to love Me more; I want from them purity, zeal, faithfulness; priests must understand that unity reinforces love, unity establishes love;
for how long will discord reign among them? love is unity; My love unites them to Me; My Church is weak with their discordances My desire is Unity; I wish that My Church becomes one;

But Lord, if You say there is discord, someone will have to give in. How will they know?

they must pray for enlightenment; they should come to Me and draw from My Heart;

Whom are You referring to, Jesus? When You talk about them and they?

all My Church; I desire them to unite and become one; My Church has weakened because of this distinction; It has weakened enormously;

My Lord, to me this sounds like a new message.

I will enlighten you, Vassula, by showing you, in small phases, the way I work;

First, the teachings to me...

yes,

...then training, then the Ecclesiastical Editions, of Peace and Love, then guidance of Peace and Love with messages?

yes, Vassula, and now My desires, My desires of uniting My Church; how can a body function if one or two of its members are disabled or injured or dismembered? would it have the same capacity and strength as one which is whole?

My Church is My Body; how can My Body function if they disable It? daughter, draw My sign,

ΙΧΘΥΣ ><>

this was the sign of the first Christians; love was one; love was united;

Jesus, I know that Easter is in different dates. Can You tell me which is the right date? Ours or theirs? (Please give it to me on a separate paper.)

Vassula, take a paper then;

Thank You, Jesus. (Jesus gave me the correct date for Easter.)

come now let us join in prayer; a prayer to the Father for Unity:

"Father,
I come to You and ask You
to enlighten Your sheep,
enlighten them to find
Peace and Love in Unity,
amen"

unite My sheep, Vassula!

Jesus, who am I to unite and know anything about priests and their discussions and what is going on? Who am I to tell them on a piece of paper what is written and to tell them that it is You who wrote it?

Jesus, You are giving me messages, You are telling me Your desires of Your Heart. Lord wouldn't it have been easier to have given everything to someone of the Church, in the Church already, someone who has access to all the high authorities, someone of renowned purity and trustworthy? Lord, You have indeed picked up on one who is crippled and discouraged by half of the priests who know about the writings, they are half of them disinterested to follow-up. I am tired of wanting to show them, since I know it bores them and annoys them. What to do?

this, Vassula, is what your shoulders bear; this is My Cross on you; I will share It with you, never weary;

Lord, how will Your message reach the right ears? I'm an outsider.

It will; It is like a rivulet flowing, slowly becoming wider; from flowing it will start rushing, then gushing; the rivulet will turn into a vast ocean; Vassula, lean on Me when you are weary; I love you and will help you to bear with Me My Cross; beloved, never feel abandoned;

I felt that Jesus will always lift me when I stumble. He made me understand that I can always lean on Him to regain my strength.

Vassula, I will lead you;

May 23, 1987

(Yesterday I did not meet Jesus in writing. But His Presence was made felt by Him. His words too. He was talking to me at the same time as my husband or friends. It was as if He was pulling me by one arm and the others[1] by the other arm.)

Jesus?

---

[1] The world.

I am; to have faith is also a grace, beloved; talk to Me, I am your Spouse;

(I told Him something. He answered me.)

let Me do whatsoever I want to with you; Vassula, I am God and by now you must have understood that by having you elevated to Me and having taught you to love Me and by letting you meet Me in this way, I want something out of you;

you were taught to write by My given grace; this grace was given to you to enable Me to use you; I have bestowed upon you many graces, so that you may glorify Me;

I have united you to Me; I have taken you as my bride; I and you are one now; do you not see clearer, daughter? I love you all and I have approached you for My own interests;

My God,

I am;

(I reminded him of something.)

Vassula, I fulfil always My goals;

I know, I know, I wish You could tell me clearer.

daughter, I love you far beyond your understanding; I know you are ineffably weak; I know that without Me you are totally insufficient; unable to move; do not worry, I will lift you like a father would lift his invalid child; I will take care of you, I will supply you; I will see that all My Works will be fulfilled; remember, I have trained you to be My bearer; I will not see you leave without having accomplished your mission; I love you; love Me and Me only; I do not want rivals, worship Me for I am your God;

Vassula, to wait upon your God is to serve Him; serve Me; come, be one with Me; in your ignorance, daughter, I accept you; I have indeed around Me loyal servants, they are My beloved of My Soul; they are of great esteem in My eyes, I entrust them with My Works, they honour My Name by serving Me fervently, worshipping Me, immolating their soul for Me, and with great grace bless My Word; I love them and I look upon them lovingly; withhold not your question;

Why did You choose me since I'm no good and only create...[1]

wretchedness attracts Me; altogether you are nothing, nothing at all! but by being nothing I am everything you are not, for what have I as rival? I find no rival within you since you are nothing; such is My delight in you daughter;

I can't understand.

no, you cannot understand but does it matter, does it really matter, I am Sovereign of all creation; you are all Mine, and you little one, you without the slightest interest, attracts Me; <u>littleness holds My attention; nothingness infatuates</u>[2] <u>Me</u>; Vassula, one day you will fully understand My Words; were you to serve Me, I would reveal in you nothing but passion;

Passion.

yes, passion; will...

(I, through weakness, stopped Him from writing His question. I heard it though ... nothing can stop Him from letting me hear what He wants to say.)

I can abide in you even in your awesome weakness; love Me, Vassula; do not fear Me; I am Love and I am very fond of you; I will never ask of you anything that can harm you; I am Love and Master of Love; child, in spite of your incessant doubts

---

[1] He did not let me finish.
[2] I had never heard this word in my life before.

and failures, I have chosen you to be My altar; since I know your incapacity to draw from My Flame, I will pour Myself My burning desires in you, thus keeping My Flame ablaze; beloved, come, you are My flower which needs My Light; live under My Light, I do not want to see you perish;

Lord, You attract me too. You know that ...

does that amaze you? your wretchedness is attracted by My Mercy; your ineffable weakness by My Strength; your nothingness by everything I am; live for Me;

(I told Him my desire.)

earn your desire, Vassula,

(I saw Jesus trying to show His desire.)

Vassula, come, come closer to Me, Vassula,

(I was hesitating.)

again I ask you to want but Me only; Vassula, do not deny Me! listen to My Heartbeats, can you resist Me?

How can I resist God?

(Yet I'm trying to, for I don't know how I'll end up.)

I love You, My God.

come then to Me, have no desires for yourself; do you want to see Me there?

(In my mind passed a famous picture of Jesus in a famous place, I don't know why.)

If it's Your wish, Lord. But do not answer me, do as You wish though.

daughter, all your work, let it be for My glory; My desires should be your desires too, I will write My desires and lead you;

It is about unity?

Yes, Unity of My Church; I want My Body strengthened; unity will strengthen My Church;
 will you remember My Presence? come then, let us go;

May 24, 1987

I am with you;

Do you want me to serve You?[1]

I do, I want it very much; Vassula, come, I will show you how and where you can serve Me; remember everything I have taught you;

(Teachings, mystic teachings so that my faculties are all alert, so that by being aware I will hear Him and feel Him all the more.)

have My Peace; listen to My Voice;

I wish I could hear You crystal clear ...

Vassula, you will hear Me well enough to write everything that My Heart contains, all that My Heart desires; beloved, free yourself to be able to serve Me and wait upon Me; do you know what 'free' means Vassula? I will tell you; have confidence;

(I felt that what He taught me would not work, and I might fail Him.)

free is to detach your soul from worldly solicitudes; free your soul and love Me and My Works; serve Me in this way, detach yourself;

I will have difficulties, My Lord!

lo;[1]

---

[1] I asked this because this is what God had asked me and I through weakness and fear stopped Him from writing it.

Yes, My Lord, I can see difficulties.

Io, Io, stay near Me;

I fear to disappoint and fail Your desires.

fear not, sister; beloved, love me;

(I felt Him and loved Him.)

love for love; love Me as now; work and serve Me as now; be as you are; I need servants who are able to serve Me where love is needed most; work hard though for where you are, you are among evil, unbelievers, you are in the vile depths of sin; you are going to serve your God where darkness prevails; you will have no rest; you will serve Me where every good is deformed into evil, yes; serve Me among wretchedness, among wickedness and the iniquities of the world; serve Me among Godless people, among those that mock Me, among those that pierce My Heart; serve Me among My scourgers, among My condemnors; serve Me among those that recrucify Me and spit on Me; O Vassula, how I suffer! come and console Me;

My God, come! come among those that love You, go to them, at least for a while go and You are loved there. Rest in their heart, forget; can't You forget for a while at least?

(Jesus seemed SO distressed!!)

Vassula, forget? how could I forget; how, when repeatedly they are recrucifying Me?[2] five of My Wounds are left open for all who want to penetrate in them;

(Jesus leaned on me. I felt distressed; He seemed comfortless, worn out.)

Vassula, come, you are my little flower, I want smooth and soft petals from you to replace My thorns;

---

[1] That is: No.
[2] He dictated so quick I could hardly follow.

Jesus let those who love You unburden You, let those who love You rest You and replace You in Your recrucifixion.

(I didn't know how to console such distress.)

beloved, those that love Me strive and suffer with Me; they share My Cross, they rest Me, but they are few; I need more souls to unite with Me and bear My sufferings; flower, love Me, never refuse Me,

Jesus?

I am;

Will You help me love You more?

I will, beloved;

(I feel speechless. What can I say; if any one knew how painful it was to see Him so hurt! It was like He was dying all over again. How can one comfort one who is dying from wounds? And to tell Him what? That it will be all right? When one knows He is injured to death!)

May 25, 1987

(I start to realise how much easier it is to meet God with this grace He has given me if I come without the slightest doubt or disbelief, feeling Him, seeing Him, and letting Him write. I start to understand. Full faith makes all the demons flee and they feel at loss, with no power. They fear and are exasperated! When I come hesitant, doubtful, they feel strong and attack me in writing their insults. Full faith and an open heart for God can make the mountains move! I feel Him like an electric sense in me; wonderful and I never want to leave Him or this instant of God's finger on me ... I want it to last forever!)

love me, love Me, feel Me, feel My insatiable love for you; I thirst for your love; I require more love from you, Vassula; hear my Heartbeats;

(Jesus was passionate.)

I bear no rivals, none at all; if I see or meet rivals I will ravage them; nothing will replace Me, I will stay Master; depart glorifying Me; tonight I will purify you by My Heavenly Works for Peace and Love;[1] pray, beloved, blessed one; unite My Church by drawing My sign which I gave you, draw now;

ΙΧθΥΣ ✺

with Blessed sign I, the Lord, will show you the way to Me; believe, believe, believe; flourish and help others, flourish to bring back Love, flourish to bring peace,[2]

I love you Vassula; Vassula grieve not, My beloved; blessed one, come to Me your Father your Spouse your God, will I ever abandon you? from love I will take you, from My elate and insatiable love I will free you; pray with Me,

> "Heavenly Father,
> may I glorify You,
> redeem Your children from evil,
> may they be in Your Light,
> may their hearts open
> and with Your Mercy receive You,
> amen"

Vassula will you realise fully My Presence and kiss My Wounds?

Yes, Lord Jesus.

(I discerned Him and saw Him again in full glory. Seeing Him with the eyes of my soul, I saw He was this time beautiful, with a beautiful crown on His Head. He came to me as a King.)

Lord, give me Your right Hand.

---

[1] Jesus means in the mystic way.
[2] I was distressed.

(I kissed His right Hand.)

I love you;

(I kissed His hands, feet and side wound.)

I love You, Lord.

to guide you was a delight for Me,

(I felt...I cannot find the words.)

come with Me, I will show you something;

(I saw from His breast which was lit, sparks.)

every spark, which leaves My Heart and touches your heart, will inflame your heart and consume it; My spark enkindles you; draw from My Heart; I will one day inflame entirely your heart, letting My Flame enwrap your heart, engulfing it;

What will happen to me if by just a spark only I feel this way?

(It was like Jesus was taking pleasure knowing now He has conquered me.)

yes, I delight to have prevailed and conquered your love; when My Flame will enwrap your heart entirely you will never ever be separated from Me; you will be My bride in heaven; I have created you for Myself;

But then why am I here? I don't understand.

no, you cannot understand Vassula, but one day you will;
time is a rival for Me, when you look at your watch and I am with you;

(I had offended Him because I looked at my watch.)

come daughter, take My Hand and let us go; come we have so much work;

This work or the other (housework)?

both; daughter everywhere you go, I am;[1] altar, My Flame should stay ablaze forever; annihilate in Me;

May 26, 1987

Jesus, a friend of mine said, "We never see Jesus happy or giving us a big smile in all the pictures representing Him, why?" I told her that I saw You happy many times, and I will not forget that broad smile You gave me, all Your face was smiling that morning; that morning You told me You had rested in my heart.

Vassula, I smile in pure souls; I smile and delight in lowly men, I delight in holy men;

Jesus, my God, I don't understand why I love someone I have never seen or met in my physical state, how and why do I love You?

ah Vassula! loving Me .... everything coming from Me is Love; I created you to love Me, I created you out of Love, your soul thirsts for love;
 but how few are those that understand and accept this grace;

May 27, 1987

Your whole guidance is easy to understand, Lord. It is not a complicated language.

loftiness wearies Me; learn to be humble, simple, modest, just like Me!
 Vassula, if you wish Me to be your Father, I will treat you as My child; if you wish Me to be your Bridegroom, I will treat you as My Bride; if you rebel against Me, I will treat you as a Judge; I am your Saviour; favour Me above everything and all; never deny Me; come often and drink and eat Me; I delight in you;

May 28, 1987

Lord, You want me as Your sacrifice, You said?

Vassula, yes, be My sacrifice;

My God; I really do not know quite what sacrifice could mean. It can vary, but I understand that it contains suffering of some sort. Since You ask me to be one for You let it be. But, to be a sacrifice for God, one has to have some value, to glorify God. Since I know I am a speck of dust and chosen because I'm the most wretched, what sort of decent sacrifice would I be? So even to be a sacrifice for God one has to be in a state that would honour Him, that the 'sacrifice' is of some sort of esteem to be able to take place and honour God. Even that, my God, I am unable to give, unless You make me decent to be Your sacrifice, and thus become valid.

Vassula, do you remember when I came and asked you to love Me? do you remember when an angel came to stir you unexpectedly?[2] that is the way I come, so be alert, do not sleep; I came to you unexpectedly and asked for love; I wished you to honour Me, I wanted to capture your love and be your Master reigning over you; I wanted you to need Me; how I yearned for your love, "lama sabachthani?" I came to you, but you denied Me;

(When I knew that it was Him I did deny Him.)

Vassula, I have detached you, but I will detach you even more; have My Peace;
 beloved, amend, amend, amend;
 I raised you from the dead to be able to unite My Church;

---

[1] I longed as never before for God. I thirst for God.

[2] The first time my hand wrote. It was sudden.

(I sighed.)

let me show you the way; in spite of your doubts, I will unfold to you My Heart's desires; never weary writing; I will work in you, lean entirely on Me;

Jesus, someone mentioned some time ago to me that you will give no more signs, You said it to the Pharisees; he said this when I said that this guidance (message) is from You.

Vassula, when I said this to the Pharisees I meant My miracles of the time I was in flesh and among them; condemning Me now, for it is to condemn My Heavenly Works, shows how arid and closed their hearts have become; My signs will never end; My Presence will be felt in the world and I will continue to show Myself in signs;

believe, believe O men of little faith, do not distort My Word, for what have you to say about Fatima; are you dreading to believe that I am the One who gave you this sign? O men of little faith, what would you not declare rather than accept that Heaven's signs are from Me! love My Works, accept My Works; believe, believe in Me, I, who am Infinite Wealth and Mercy; My signs are so that all men see that Love has not forgotten you; Love has not withdrawn and glories in His Glory; Love is among you, never leaving you;

May 29, 1987

beloved, repent; creature, bless Me; believe in what you ask;

(I had asked Him to forgive me my sins but I realised it came from my lips only when God said "believe in what you ask.")

I forgive them; love Me, honouring Me; love Me, glorifying Me;

(I asked Him again and blessed Him.)

I am God, creature, be at My Stations; desire Me only at every Station; I stand at every Station; I will be at the Stations of My Cross and I want you there; I want you to kneel at My Stations;

Lord, I don't know what You mean! What stations?[1]

I will wait for you there; inspect what I demand from you, inspect;

I will purify you to enable you to be My sacrifice; desire Me, satisfy My insatiable thirst; satisfy My burning Flame of Love; satisfy Me your God; by giving Me full faith I will lift your veil entirely to see Me without constraint; surely you have heard of My beauty from others who saw Me before you? believe, believe entirely; come closer to your Father and I will lift entirely your veil; daughter, have I not brought you into My Hall?

Yes, Lord.

then have faith in Me; do not let men drive you away from Me; I have given you this gift so use it to reach Me; do not fear Love, I am Omnipotent; believe in My Omnipotence; daughter, I desired you to be in My Hall, so how much <u>more</u> will I not desire you to remain;

My God, maybe we'll lose each other from my own fault.

have you forgotten our links? I am your Spouse and you are living in My House; I am feeding you; I envelop you with My Light; I watch over your frailty, I treat you like a child because of your misery, what will I not do for you! are You happy with Me, Vassula?

Yes Lord, may You be Blessed forever for it is You who gives me happiness, You are my smile.

---

[1] We Orthodox do not say the Stations of the Cross.

love Me in spite of your doubts;

Lord?

come, you are weak but I will strengthen you; I want you strong for My Message;[1] would you wish Me to unveil your eyes completely and see Me clearer?

I would, if it is Your wish too.

you need a few more steps towards Me, you are almost there! I will unveil your eyes and you will behold in front of you, your Saviour! five of My Wounds will be open so that you penetrate into them; I will let you taste My sorrows; I long for that moment;
 fill Me with loving words; Vassula you are bonded to Me, yet, have you not felt more free? smile at Me when you feel My Presence and see Me; I am fully aware of your capacity and wisdom; I know I have with Me a nothing, a nothing at all; come, do not misunderstand Me, will I have a nothing or would I rather have a rival of some sort? I will of course choose a nothing to send on earth My words and My desires, without the slightest negation;

Lord, You have given me so much I feel very much in debt!

have you got anything to give Me, Vassula?

(I'm hesitating, what can I give?)

surely you have just a bit of something! even if you have nothing to give Me, I love you;

Maybe I have something to give You?

have you asked yourself whether I wanted it or not? I am self sufficient, I suffice by Myself;

Would You want me to give You something anyway?

I do;

But then whatever I give You will be no good in Your eyes!

why?

Because You are Perfect.

I will receive it and even if it is evil I will turn it into good! I am Divinity;

Have I then anything good to offer You?

you have; but all that is good comes from Me; I have given it to you, everything good <u>is</u> from Me;

(I'm a bit disappointed, I can't please Him.)

Then I have nothing of my<u>self</u> to give You.

no; I have given you all that you have and is good;

Maybe a good painting, offering it to You![2]

your paintings, Vassula? have I not bestowed upon you this gift of art? has this also not come from Me?

What then can I offer You?

love; worship Me; worship Me; <u>offer Me your will</u> in surrendering to Me, this is the most beautiful thing you can offer Me;

You know, Lord, that I love You, and also that I surrendered!

I enjoy hearing it, little one!

---

[1] The real apostolate had not begun.

[2] My own hand-made paintings.

May 29, 1987

(I felt suddenly His Cross on me, I thought I would never manage.)

lift! lift My Cross! strive with Me! together ... together ... I love you, lift My Cross! I must rest now in you;

(Later on: before meeting the charismatic group.)

will you feed My lambs? hold My Hand I will lead you, guarding you;

(That evening I smelled incense again.)

never doubt of My Presence;

(I asked Jesus to help unblind and take away the evil spirits which surround the young man who refuses to accept God. (A case known to me while in the charismatic group.))

fill Me with joy and summon Me for everything you want; Vassula remind him of His Brother; I am his Brother who loves him, who cares for him; remind him of My existence; I love him to distraction; I died for him; will you do this for Me little one? believe in My Redemptive Love;

May 31, 1987

(Sunday.)

Vassula, come and receive Me,[1] I will be there, delight Me, come and see Me! say you are Mine, let Me hear it!

I'm Yours, Jesus, and I love You.

for years, Vassula, I was waiting for these words! love Me now that you are Mine;

Teach me to love You as You wish.l

trust Me, I will;

(Later on:)

(It still amazes me how my hand moves ...)

Do You know that Jesus?

I do, but am I not Omnipotent? Vassula, be peaceful, be calm, be serene, like Me;

(I was interrupted while writing twice by my son, coming in, slamming the door, etc. I felt upset! Too much noise.)

love Me, answer Me!

I love You, I love You, Lord!

never replace Me; have Me first, face Me first and remain facing Me for ever; be like a mirror, a reflexion of Myself, never seek others but Me, never seek your old habits of your earlier life; I am Holy and Lord, I and you are one now and I mean to keep you just for Myself and for eternity; humble yourself, learn from Me, desire Me only; breathe for Me; do not turn left or right now, keep going straight, beloved, allow Me to use you, hold on to Me, enrapture Me with your simplicity in words, simplicity infatuates Me, say to Me your words, let Me hear them again, tell Me, "I love you Jesus, you are my joy, my breathe, my rest, my sight, my smile,"

daughter, were you given time to think and meditate you would please Me furthermore; <u>you will from now on seek Me in silence, love Me in absolute silence, pray in silence, enter My Spiritual World in silence;</u>[2] reward Me now, I love you; honour Me by giving yourself to Me, do not displease Me, be Mine beloved, speak!

How in silence, Lord?

---

[1] Call to Holy Communion.

[2] The unceasing prayer.

in silence looking at Me, I want you to stay still, without having interferences of any sort, seek Me in silence;

Without interferences at all?

none at all; desire stillness;

Jesus, how could I possibly find this stillness in a family, it is almost impossible!

I will give it to you; I pity you, Vassula! My remnant, My myrrh, My love, what will I not do for you! My Heart fills with compassion for your misery, and your falls; I the Lord will help you - never feel abandoned or unloved;
  do you know how I felt that time you felt so unloved?

Where?

in My Church;[1]

No, Lord.

I felt crucified all over again, bruised, scourged, spat upon, nailed again; Vassula, how I love you! help Me revive My Church; help Me by letting Me use you; courage, daughter, courage;

---

[1] After I had been told that sometimes Jesus <u>does refuse</u> people and He can shut the door to them. (In an argument I had with a priest, giving me to read a passage from the Bible about the Canaanite women whom He refused. But in the end, He did not refuse her, He had only challenged her to show her faith – but that, I did not know, and the one who showed me this passage did not let me read till the end.) I had gone to Church taking Holy Communion, so I felt according to our agreement that I had taken something not permitted, breaking all the laws of the Catholic Church; and that I took something without permission, thus being very evil. The following Sunday I went to Church, I stood near the door, so that I'm half out (since I felt unwanted) and since I believed I was evil and that God was very angry with me, I did not go forward with the others for Communion, fearing I would make things worse if I did.

Jesus, I didn't know that all this would hurt You, I mean my feeling of being unloved!

no, you did not know either that I never refuse anybody who comes to Me; I am Love and Love is for everyone, no matter how evil you can be;

June 1, 1987

Vassula, both My Hands have wounds, both My Feet have wounds, My side is open, wide open showing My Heart; they are recrucifying Me;

Lord,

they are damaging My Church;

Lord, is it so very bad?

it is, evil has blinded them; love is missing among them; they are not sincere, they have distorted My Word, they have lamed even My Body; My cup of Justice is full do not let it brim over! I want them to stop smothering My Body; I, Jesus, am Love; I want them to stop throwing venomous arrows at each other; harmony among them will restore part of the damage; truthfulness will unmask evil, why all these ceremonies when in truth they have nothing to offer Me? I need purity, love, fidelity, humbleness, holiness;
  seek in Me all that <u>I</u> desire and I will give it to you; seek <u>My</u> interests and not yours; glorify <u>Me</u>, honour <u>Me</u>; words are not enough, deeds of Love and cooperation will revive My Body; brothers! love one another, O beloved how much will I have to restore!
  come daughter, rest in Me; peace upon you;

June 2, 1987

meet Me later on and I will give you preliminary advices; Vassula, design,

(head) **| | |**

unite those lines,

(figure)

to unite you must all bend; you must be all willing to bend by softening;

I understood. He gave me a clear and simple vision of three iron rods; they were upright, close to each other. He said, "How could their heads[1] meet, unless they all bend?" (Bend in humility e Love.)

– Later on in the morning I went out. The more I was thinking of this vision the bigger the 'mountain' appeared. I was stifling ...

Jesus?

I am; courage, up pupil! lift! lift My Cross beloved, up now! grieve not; together ... together ...
My Vassula, together we will strive, lean on Me when you are weary and let Me lean on you when I am weary,
meet Me, let Me accomplish My desires, be like soft wax and let My Hand engrave on you My words; be willing, do not fear! I love you beloved, O come! Love will not hurt you;

(I'm fearing this work.)

come, let us pray,

"O Father,
be with me until the end,
I am weak;
give me Your Strength
to glorify You,
amen"

beloved, come, leave your fears and hear Me; wait upon your God; <u>I want to unite My Church</u>;
Vassula, I have trained you to receive Me, beloved, courage!

I need Your courage, I have none.

I will encourage you and will reinforce your love to Me, all for My Glory;
Vassula, will you write down My words, sip from Me; do not seek comfort, be poor, be like Me when I was in flesh on earth; be plain so that we both feel the contrast and the grandeurs of those that scourge Me, let Me feel the contrast! be drawing from My Heart, embellish My Church, draw from My Heart and you will understand, My little girl;

(I think there I mean that I start to realise what work this is. That's why I'm fearing: Jesus is starting to <u>dig in</u> the Church ...)

June 3, 1987

(I was attacked 'in writing' by evil again. It was like cats which jumped on my back, I was "fed up" with them, it seemed like "all hell broke loose"; they annoyed me so I said to one of them: "In the name of Jesus Christ leave and be thrown in fire." It left. There were several of these and one by one was treated the same way as the first one with the same words. Jesus told me: "Ask in My Name and it shall be done, but you must have faith in what you ask, work in this way, pray and ask, pray in My Name; work in My Name, ask in My Name, revive My Name, be My reflection, synchronise with Me, lift your head towards Me, believe in what you ask;"

He told me that the demons fear me, I'm a menace to them. Later on I realised where I was, I felt my feet in wet and slimy mud, and in a flash I recognised the surroundings of hell. It was just a flash. I

---

[1] Heads: later on, I understood that heads means also authority; leaders.

then understood why so much evil interference was there today in writing. Jesus said when I asked about this: "Could it have been anywhere else?" *We were together passing at the gates [1] of hell, healing souls, wrenching them away from Satan's gates.* "Vassula, allow Me to use you in this way too; This is part of your work too;")

June 4, 1987

(Today God lifted me in His Palm, made me feel so small. He asked me to look at Him. I did, and saw a Beautiful Smiling Giant!)

Vassula, look at Me, look at My Face;

(He was smiling in beauty! I felt like a tiny spot in His Palm.)

does it matter to Me? does it matter to Me if you are but a speck of dust, feel how I love you!

(He was Beautiful, and all this is Beautiful!)

I am Beautiful; Vassula, when you think of Me, think of Me as I was on earth with men's features, your image; think of Me in that way;

But Lord, how do You really look? How and what are Your features?

I am Everything; I am the Alpha and the Omega; I am the Eternal, I am the Elixir; love Me;
remain in Me; <u>never fear Me</u>; let this fear, which was wrongly taught by men, be replaced by love; live in Me without fear; fear Me only if you rebel against Me; I am Love; tell them, tell them what an abyss of Love My Heart is!

June 5, 1987

Vassula, find Me in My Stations; be blessed; we will work together;

(I have not gone to His Stations yet. I will, I'm waiting for the priest, as he has been asked by Jesus to be with me.)

June 6, 1987

Jesus?

I am; to look into God's Face is to have seen Love;

I was looking at His picture, the Holy Shroud.

do you want Me to dominate you entirely, Vassula?

Yes, my God, I would if it is Your wish.

leave Me free then, never obstruct Me, live for Me;

Lord, how do I obstruct You, tell me so that there are no obstructions.

sins obstruct Me, sins, Vassula; will you really let Me act in you as I wish?

Yes, my God, forbid me from sinning, forgive my sins, act as You wish in me, do not consider my cowardice, pay no attention to it, drag me if You must, feel free with me. Do Your work. I do not want to be the cause of any delay, I do not want to be a hindrance to Your works. So pay no attention to my weakness, do as You please.

daughter, I am pleased with your words; come, I will continue My Works; leave Me free to do My Will; come let Me clarify how I work; I have given you many graces, Vassula, but I want you to acknowledge My graces, delight Me and believe in Me more;

---

[1] Lowest purgatory closest to hell.

I'm fearing that if I displease You, You might take away these graces ...

why should I withdraw My graces?

Because if I don't improve and don't follow in time You might take them away.

no, never!

To me it seems right, to take away if one does not please You.

it seems right in your eyes, child; until I come to deliver you, I will feed you; I will never withhold My food; I, who longed for you for years, I waited for years to press you close to My Heart, loving you, would I now pull away My food from you? come, lean on Me as much as you wish, remember, I am love, I give freely and I do not take away what I give; I will always remind you of My ways;

June 7, 1987

Vassula, yes, look into My Face; to have seen Me, consoles Me; tell them, that it takes so little, to console Me; come and praise Me, loving Me;

(I had the picture of the Holy Shroud in front of me; and I was looking at it, when Jesus wrote that message.)

June 8, 1987

Vassula, I would like to establish My Works,

What should I do?

I will guide you; I will guide you even further, depend on Me, have My Peace;

June 9, 1987

(Last evening I saw God's Face in the sky. The sky was a Beauty! It was like a painted picture from a skilled artist. I recognised God's Beauty in there. It was obvious.)

yes, Vassula, see Me in My Creation; recognise Me and love Me;

June 10, 1987

(Dhaka, Bangladesh)

(Yesterday was the final packing for our departure, lots of work!)

Lord, I was thinking of a theory which is called, "Christ Consciousness", I think it means "our good inner-self"; maybe this is how the writings come?

Vassula, have I not told you that we are united, we are one, beloved, call it: "true life in God"; live for Me;
    here is what I want you to write;

(I was wondering by a feeling what would God write now ...)

My desires, little one;

(God made me read a part of Scriptures.)

yes, elevate, hear Me, will you see Me in My Church? Vassula, come to Me;

Which Church, Lord, which do You mean?

all are My Churches they are all Mine, they all belong to Me and Me only, I am the Church, I am the Head of the Church;

But the way You said it, Jesus, it was like you wanted me to go to a special one. That's how I understood and heard You!

you can come to Me anytime in any Church, do not make any distinction like the others; they all belong to Me;[1] I am One God and have One Body, a Body which they have lamed; millstones have damaged My Body;

My God, You seem so upset!!

upset? O Vassula, why, why have they cruelly dismembered Me?

(God is very upset. He reminds me of the time He went and overturned all the money-makers' tables in the Temple in Jerusalem. So far I <u>never</u> heard or saw Him SO UPSET!)

Vassula;

Jesus?

I am;

Is that You really so upset?

O yes, it is Me; O yes, I finally can place My words on you; Vassula, charism is not given to you for your interests, it is given to you so that My Words be engraved on you;

I have never felt You so upset before! Are You?

I am; My Body aches; It has been torn apart;

My God! but what can I do? I'm helpless!

do I not know all this, Vassula? I shall use you till the end; never fear Me daughter; uniting My Church will be the Glory of My Body; have My Peace, beloved;

Yes Lord, I won't look left or right or behind, I will look straight ahead.

yes, understand how I work; be still like now, be willing to please Me, be one with Me;

Lord, suppose the ones You want them to listen, do not? Then?

now you are a step ahead of Me! child, walk with Me; together, yes follow Me, trust Me; come I will guide you;

(I was suddenly taken by surprise, I heard the dog bark, (unusual) then my bedroom door opened and I recognised in front of me the thief who entered three nights ago in our room stealing money, and who fled. There he was, again. I ordered him out. He turned around and left, then I gave the alarm. I knew that God was definitely trying to tell me something.)

Vassula, I am reminding you of something; when the brigand[2] entered your room, did you expect him?

No!

so will I come too; sudden; no one recognised him either, because no one expected him to be there;

(Jesus meant the ten packers and the office men who saw him but did not believe he was a thief. I have a feeling that this last sentence is very important and hides much more than it says. The word "recognised" is very deep too.)

did it remind you of something else? let Me tell you, he had sinned, but those who passed judgment on him, breaking the rod on his back, were they not in sin too?

I do not know what You are trying to make me understand. Yes, we are all sinners.

Vassula, will I see all this and keep silent?

---

[1] The Church never divided itself, but people divided it and divided themselves.

[2] God used the right word as later we found out that he belonged to a group. Brigands are groups of thieves.

Are You defending the thief, Lord?

no, Vassula, I do not ...[1] name Me one man who has not sinned;

(I can't think of any.)

big sins, small sins, all are sins, to sin is to grieve Me; Vassula, I am witnessing so many sins; Love is suffering; Love grieves, grieves; ...creation! My creation, return to Love...
daughter, imbue Me with love; amend, beloved, amend;

June 11, 1987

(By now most of our furniture gone I have to look for chairs to sit to write, the house is still messy after the packers left, heaps of papers here and there shoes, bottles, papers, belts on all desks. Yet in all this, moving, among the buffets we had to prepare for farewells (one of 80 people, another 30) God's hand did not release a bit, I always found time for Him to write two - three hours daily. He gives me incredible strength and don't feel the least tired, I'm in total peace, His Peace.)

Vassula, beloved of My Soul, stay near Me, face Me, let My finger touch your heart; My child, if you knew how much I love you; I will guide you till the end; sacrifice more for Me; – will you suffer for Me?

Yes Lord, do as You please.

(He had previously asked this, but I had hesitated, fearing. Now He asked again.)

Vassula, I am so happy! will you sacrifice yourself for Me like a lamb?

Do as You please, Lord.

---

[1] Jesus was silent for a while.

all will not be in vain, all will be for Peace and Love; My thirst is great Vassula; I will lead you into arid lands, where your eyes will behold what you have never seen; I will lead you with Heavenly Force, right into the very depths of My Bleeding Body; I will point out to you with My finger all the sacerdotal sinners who are the thorns of My Body; I will not spare them; I am worn out, My Wounds are wider than ever, My Blood is gushing out; I am being recrucified by My own, My own Sacerdotal souls!

My God, You give me so much pain, why would they do that to You? Why?

Vassula, they know not what they are doing; beloved, strive with your God, be willing to face My sufferings and share them with Me;

I will, to console You; remember those who love You!

they are the beloved ones of My Soul; I need more of these souls, immolating their hearts for Me; I love them, I trust them, they eat from Me; they are My sacrifice, they are the smooth petals, which replace My thorns; they are My myrrh;
Vassula, do not fear; we will penetrate deeper still where darkness prevails; I will lead you;

(Later on my soul started to feel God's bitterness. Every thing, every food or drink which came into my mouth tasted bitter. He made me drink from His chalice. I then had problems in breathing, my soul and body ached.)

June 15, 1987

(Yesterday I flew to Hong Kong (for our holiday). While in transit in Bangkok, something happened. I sat to read at the transit hall at the end of a row of chairs. Suddenly in front of my feet an Arab threw

a carpet, totally ignoring me, with two others behind him, and fell to the ground worshipping God. With quite a loud voice attracting much attention. I felt awkward, as no one was sitting around me. I felt I was disturbing as I was just in front of them. I didn't move. Their voices rose higher and someone took a picture of the whole awkward scene, from behind me.

Later on God told me: "this man said his prayers loud enough; enough to attract a lot of attention, he was heard in transit, but in that hall only, the walls heard him, My Heart never heard a thing, all the words remained on his lips; nevertheless, I heard your voice in spite that no one heard you and no one knew what you were telling me, but it came from your heart not from your lips;"

I did not want to write this down because of fear of discrimination, but God told me, "what have you to fear, I am the Truth, and does this not also happen with Christians too?"

Today we made a tour with a bus in the town and outskirts, suddenly instead of these tall buildings, I saw huge Black Crosses,[1] I thought it was my imagination but I heard God's voice saying: "no, it is not your imagination; they are My Crosses;" When seeing "Consumers' Paradise", I thought that if I had to live in it I would die, it would be torture for me; and to think that a year ago I thought it was Paradise!

God does not want to spare me from saying this too. At our tour bus the guide showed us a super-villa of the richest man in Hong Kong. He told us there are two millionaires very well known by name in all Hong Kong; God's Voice came in my ears saying: "But I know not who they are; they belong to the world;")

their riches are worldly riches; they have nothing in My Kingdom;

(God took over to write this Himself.)

beloved, I am giving you signs; be alert, Vassula, believe what you hear from Me;

I'm thinking of the Arab.

holiness was missing from him; even you could see it;

(Later on:)

O Vassula, do I not deserve more respect?

(I feared this, I had no opportunity to be with God writing so I took my chance in the hotel room with my son around and husband. T.V. was on, I blocked my ears with a 'Walkman'. I had nowhere to go!)

I justly withdraw all your facilities;

Why, Lord?

why? so that I teach you to desire your God; wait until we are alone;

Forgive me ...

I forgive you; so Vassula, work while you are suspended;

How, Lord?

allow Me to whisper in your ear all My desires; Vassula, desire Me; use the graces I have bestowed on you; remember it is not only My Hand, using your hand; I opened your ear, I showed you how to see Me and how to feel Me, so use the other graces too; I love you;

Jesus?

I am, Vassula;

We are together in this way again.

yes, but not for long; reserve Me not for later, merely because you do not pursue your lifestyle of before; have Me locked in your heart, child;

Lord, will I have bigger trials?

---

[1] I remembered the words "arid lands".

O yes, you will face many more severe trials;

(I sighed.)

trust Me; I will be near you; you are My sacrifice are you not? why would I have you then among evil? I offer you to them, to be among wickedness;

But I am also wicked. What's the difference? I'm like them.

are you, why then do you want to come to Me, at home?

Because I love You.

I fashioned you like Me to enable you to draw others to Me, I will detach you still more from earthly solicitudes; wait and you shall see; Vassula, yes;

(I just saw Him in front of me.)

love Me; come, take My Hand as you did yesterday;

(Later on:)

Vassula write the word aids,

AIDS?

Yes, replace it by the word Justice;[1] My Chalice of Mercy has brimmed over, and My Chalice of Justice is full, do not let It brim over! I have told you before that the world is offending Me, I am a God of Love but I am also known to be a God of Justice; I loathe atheism!

(Later on:)

beloved, you will penetrate into My Body, I will let you see My thorns and nails,

Lord, how will I see all this?

I will give you sight, so that you see; I will give you strength, to pull out My nails and thorns; recrucified I am,

But Lord, why have You let Yourself be recrucified?

Vassula, Vassula, taken by my own, neglected by My beloved,[2] come, honour Me, love Me!

I love You, I cling on You. When will this happen?

ah, Vassula, do not run in front of Me; come, all in good time,

But You know Lord that I'm an outsider, a nothing and not knowing what's going on where You are mentioning, then who would want to see my papers (Your writings). They will, if it reaches them, throw all the writings in my face laughing, they will probably throw it around me like confetti. After all, who am I? Nothing but a 'Professional Sinner'!

remember who is leading you! I am God, do you remember what you said to your friend, yes, the unbeliever? they were My words: you are like a mouse running away from a Giant; you are a speck of dust;

(True, a friend of ours, an unbeliever, received a message from God. He said to me later on: "In half a minute this message destroyed beliefs of 20 solid years. Why should I, a Professional Sinner, get such a message? But I will fight it. I will run away." I laughed! Then told him God's words.)

Vassula, trust Me,

Lord, I do, but it's me that's the problem. Why do You trust me? You should not. My Lord, I'm all good-will, yes, but as You

---

[1] Read Rm. 1:18-32.

[2] He said it in a very sad tone, like someone being betrayed by his best friend.

said, very weak. Don't trust me! I'm very sinful.

Vassula, you are ineffably weak; I knew this from all Eternity; but be nothing, I want you to be nothing, how else would I manifest Myself alone if we were two? let Me free always and I shall act in you; come lean on Me!

June 17, 1987

(Dhaka)

You make me aware of my wretchedness and that you approached me in spite of my wickedness and having absolutely no merits for such graces given to me. Comparing the saints, it's obvious. Do You understand then why the 'wave of doubt' comes? Just because of that; because of my unworthiness; remember, You taught me everything from scratch, and remember how I in the beginning denied You, knowing It's You? You see what I mean? When I have the 'wave of doubt' because of the reasons above, I know I'm offending You and hurting You. As You said once, "you hurt Me when you forget who saved you from darkness;". On the other hand my mind almost reels to understand, why You come to a soul like me given a mission of such importance, to someone who had to start from scratch in Scripture, a 150% sinner!
The more Your guidance goes on the more miracles it gives. Total atheists are bent, but You blessed It Lord, so I should not feel surprised. One after another unbeliever returns to You by reading It. People who told me: "You'll NEVER make me read one page of all this, I don't believe in anything but solids, money, business ...", these words ringing still in my ears, and to see now this man keener than his wife (who tried to convince him at first without success) wanting <u>all</u> the editions of Jesus' Guidance, saying that It gives him tremendous peace. I never spoke to him, since I am not good in 'parole'. It just happened: Jesus, of course. You're Wonderful!

it is I, Jesus, beloved Son of God; I have been sending you all these books so that you may believe in My Supernatural Works; I have been feeding you My Bread; never doubt of My Works; I wish you to learn the details of all My graces, so be alert to all new manifestations; all will come from Me;

(The Cross seemed to crush me again. 'The Cross' is the Message of God.)

Jesus?

I am, lift! lift! do not fall, I am near you to help you; lift My Cross, do not be like the Cyrenean; be willing; come, beloved, the way may be rough but I am always near you, sharing My Cross; Vassula, look at Me!

(I looked at Him. There He was holding the corner of the wall, in a most pitiful manner. He was wearing His Crown of Thorns and had on Him a cloth (half naked) soaked with Blood. He was covered with Sweat and Blood all over, more Blood than Flesh ... fresh from scourging.)

do I deserve this?

NO! My God!

honour Me daughter;

Who has done this to You Lord?

who? Souls, Vassula, it is them; replica of Sodom, replica means copy;

(Later on:)

daughter, <u>I desire unity in My Church!</u> <u>unity</u>!

Jesus was <u>insistent</u> and loudly He said these words.

June 18, 1987

Jesus?

I am; I will use you Vassula;

Use Me till the end, Lord.

beloved, tell them to give Me the freedom to act as I wish, that in their prayers and in all petitions to Me, they should add: "but not our will, let Yours be done;" learn from Me, honour Me;

June 19, 1987

Vassula, deeds, deeds, I want to see deeds; I delight to hear your loving words which are a balm to My Wounds, but I will delight furthermore to see deeds from you! come; I will remind you how I worked on earth while in flesh, and how I taught My disciples to work in the same manner;

Padre Pio worked like You.

he worked for Me; I gave him all those graces to honour Me and revive My Name; to work in My Name glorifies Me and purifies you; remember, I shine on everyone;

Including people like me?

yes, including souls like yours;

June 20, 1987

(Thailand)

how I was pleased to receive your light;

(St. Mary.)

adorn Us with love, have our peace;

(Very lovingly St. Mary said these words. I had lit a candle for St. Mary before doing the Stations of the Cross.)

June 21, 1987

Lord, why have so many people forgotten You?

O Vassula! My Body is maimed to the extent of paralysation; Vassula, introduce the light in My Stations, kneeling at every Station;

(I remain silent ...)

Vassula, I have spoken,

Lord, what can I do?

nothing, let Me do everything;

(Yes, but no one will do it since no one knows!)

to have faith is also a grace given by Me Vassula, have faith in Me!

(Later on:)

Now that You seduced me, what will become of me?

do you want to know? I will hurl you from My arms in this exile that My creation has become! you will live among them!

My God! Don't You love me anymore?

(I became quite distressed.)

It was wonderful being in Your Arms, and now You want me off!

O Vassula how could you say that![1]
My Heart rends and lacerates to see you among all this evil; understand My child that I am sacrificing you to be

---

[1] I felt a pang of pain in Him.

among Godless people; I suffer to have you out in exile; daughter, many will try and hurt you, I could bear now your sufferings,[1] but I would not bear, no, I would not bear to have them hurt you;

What would You do, Lord?

I would not by-stand;

But why have You cuddled me and seduced me so as to hurl me out? It's almost not fair!

(I was almost screaming!)

have I not said that you will be My sacrifice? I am using you; you are My net; yes, I am hurling you over to the world; you are to offer Me souls; for their salvation, I will redeem them; this will not go by without you suffering; the devil hates you and he would not hesitate to burn you, but he will not lay a hand on you; I do not allow him;

(It reminds me when I touched the other day the exhaust-pipe of the boat which just pulled us in. I put all my weight on that pipe, hot enough to fry an egg, with my left hand. I almost fainted with pain. Having burnt all my left palm, the impulse to put it in the sea was great, for relief, but I remembered never to put any burned flesh in cold water as it produces injuries. For ten minutes, my hand was still hot and red and <u>swollen</u>. But after half an hour everything was gone, no pain, no burns and it felt just like my other hand, in perfect condition again.)

child, I will not see you hurt; I love you and out of love I will choose <u>My</u> purifications for you; I will never allow any stain on you, understand what I mean;[2]

Lord, <u>anything</u> that will come from You I will love, if it's delights or if it's sufferings.

beloved, yes, make a heaven for Me in your heart; how I delight to hear this from you, child![3]

yes, and any suffering chosen by your own will, thinking it will please Me, will be a horror in My eyes; you will only be deceiving yourself; it will be for the devil, not for Me; reparations will be instructed by Me;

I love You and depend on You entirely.

by loving Me you glorify Me, yes;

(I heard Satan saying: "Those moments are martyrdom for me!" He could not bear my heart rejoicing in God's love to me and my love to Him. Loving each other.)

it is like sealing him with a red-hot Cross all over him;

June 23, 1987

Jesus, You have been my Teacher from the very start. But wouldn't I have someone like a Spiritual Director, as they say, to guide me a little? So far I have no one and those I approached either were not interested, or too busy, or horrified. No one told me: "My child, do this or that," in a gentle manner, and followed this up. The only one who definitely gave an order was to say: "Stop, this is not from God, so stop writing, at least for a few days and see what comes." I listened to him, I <u>did</u> stop, but Your Hand managed to write while I was doing my own notes, "I, God, love you, never forget this;" You took full possession of my hand. Then again in a few minutes "Never ever forget that I, God, love you;" It felt like someone who loved me visited me in prison, a surprise visit. It was wonderful!

---

[1] Being split: My soul in His Heart and my body in the world.
[2] It means any sufferings indulged by Satan will not be realised, but any sufferings that will come from God will be realised. Thus purifying the soul.
[3] God will choose Himself my sufferings.

My child, let Me be your Spiritual Director; am I not pleasing enough for you? I am Everything you lack; Vassula, delight Me by modifying My Stations, by simply adding the light and honour Me by kneeling at each of My Stations; I will give you more of My instructions all in good time;

Jesus, thank You for letting me meet David.

My child, narrate Me and ask him: will you let Me use you?

Lord, haven't You asked this already before? What do You exactly mean?

by this I mean, whether he will be willing to work for Me? My Cross is heavy, will you unburden Me for a while?

Yes, Lord.

come nearer;

June 26, 1987

(Bangkok)

(At 7.30 in the morning, I saw a coloured cloud, very attractive to the eye. Then five beams came out like a star. I said: "Look!" and a hand behind me pushed me forward. Another change came then, on one of the beams a candle appeared, I said again: "Look!" The hand behind me pressed me making me fall on my knees. I still did not bother to see who was doing this to me as I did not want to miss a single moment of the event. The five rays by now by their speed of turning around they produced a kind of lit ring; and suddenly from the very centre of that lit ring Jesus appeared; I said: "Look!" Again the hand behind me pushed me and now I had my hands on the ground. Suddenly hundreds of voices were worshipping Jesus. They were just saying: "J-e-s-u-s" all the time. Then Jesus' image left and instead a scene appeared. I again said: "Look!" and the hand pushed me flat to the ground, prostrated by now, only my head lifting to watch the last scene. I saw someone kneeling surrounded by five others; in front of this scene a very bright silver chalice. The five were doing something to the one kneeling in their midst. The words ANOINTING was heard by me. Then everything just disappeared.)

My God, I have not understood Your dream to me.

Wisdom will instruct you;

June 27, 1987

(So now I realise; I have been split. My body goes around, but without my soul in it. My soul – My God, You have taken it. I feel like a carcass. Detached totally. Has anybody experienced this? To think as long as you are awake and conscious of God only. Has anyone experienced an awareness of God for 24 hrs a day for every day and more than one year? And the minute my mind would start to forget my chin is taken by a Hand to turn my head and face Jesus' smiling Face. I surprise myself how I cope still with other things!)

Vassula, I have just taken your heart,[1] placing it in My Heart; I am Yahweh and I love you! cradle My Love; creature, stay in your Creator's grace;

How, how could I stay in Your grace?

you have to be holy;

How can I be holy?

by loving Me fervently;

Then, if it is Your will, help me be.

I will help you, have My blessings; I will never ask anything from you that would harm you, remember this always;

---

[1] This was said, as if my heart was nothing, very simply...

come, I will unveil My deepest and most intimate desires; allow Me to engrave them on you, little one;

June 30, 1987

(Dhaka)

(I rushed because Jesus was urging me to write.)

I called you!

(I felt and saw Jesus happy.)

yes, I am, I feel happy! come, let us work, I shall repeat My desires; Vassula, do not fear to show My Works;

Lord, I remind myself of this good friend of ours, Martha, the impulsive one. I'm impatient now like her. I want things to go quick, tomorrow, today, now, if possible, to have all Your desires ACCOMPLISHED NOW, thorns plucked and thrown away, lance drawn out from Your Heart now, and all what You desire!

Vassula do not rush;

(I felt His Hand caress my head.)

hear My desires again, I want to remind them of My Ways, I want them to stop throwing venomous arrows at one another, Vassula, was I a politician?

(Jesus surprised me with this question, He had a different tone in His Voice.)

Well, this time even I know you were not a politician ...

exactly, I was not a politician, Vassula; who do you say I was?

You are meaning while you were here in flesh, Lord?

yes,

The Beloved Son of God.

yes, you see, even you knew I was not a politician; Vassula, let Me see;

(Jesus is thinking with the usual position of His arms, one across His stomach and the other arm elbow on waist and forefinger on His cheek.)

have you ever felt through My whole guidance any trace of wickedness from My part?

No, not a trace, Lord. Never.

good;

What's this, Lord?

how have you felt Vassula?

(Jesus ignored my previous question.) I felt spoilt by You, loved extremely much, cuddled, forgiven.

go on;

I felt elated by Your love, peaceful, wonderful; I felt never happier than when I was with You, and with Your love showing me the way again. Teaching me LOVE, holiness, humility.

yes, you see Vassula there is no trace of political upheaval; none;

(Jesus made a gesture with His Hand showing, or emphasising "none".)

this is how I am, I am All Love and this is the way I would like My true, but <u>true</u> followers to be;
  – hear Me, I am the Church; do not <u>ever</u> forget this; have My Peace, Vassula;

I love You to folly and You know this now, Jesus.

beloved, My Heart will engulf you with its Flame of Love; allow Me to keep you in My Heart;

(I thought of the vision.)

the five rays come out of My five Wounds;

And the candle on one of the rays?

I wish to introduce the light;

At Your Stations?

yes;

Then I saw You.

yes, I was wearing My thorned crown remember?

Yes I do. But what was the last scene?

my anointing;

And why was I pushed to a prostrate position?

prostrated you should have been;

And the Chalice, Lord?

this is to purify yourselves and to honour My Holy Eucharist;

Thank you, Lord.

Vassula, deep in My Body I have the lance's point penetrating My Heart, it is there always; I want the lance removed; glorify My Body in establishing Peace, Unity and Love;

Beloved God, it's all too vague for me. I don't know the meaning of Your words.

remove the thorns that penetrated in My Head; Vassula, will you do this for Me; I will be before you always, heal My Body, soothen It; My Five Wounds are wide open, see? love Me, adorn Me, embellish Me, remind them of the first Christians who loved Me more than their own life;

Lord, more than photocopying and distributing Your message I can't do!

you will do much more than this; never forget who is leading you;

Yes, Lord; I depend on You.

July 3, 1987

Jesus?

I am;
beloved, inspirations come from Me, like dew drops come on leaves;
I have made a pact with you, to be faithful to you, I have taken My measures so that you too will remain faithful to Me, see?[1]
Vassula, for My sake, will you unite My Church? I am before you and it is I who will instruct you, just follow Me; I want all My Churches united; I want My sacerdotal souls to remember My Works of before and the simplicity My disciples had; the humbleness and the faithfulness the first Christians had; come, I will unveil My deepest and My most intimate desires of My Heart, allow Me to engrave them on you little one;

here I felt really hopeless. I feel God is desiring so many important things which He tells me, writing them down, and I am sitting on them, paralyzed. I feel I do not do what He wants since nothing is being changed, but how can it change if really no-one knows much about this. I feel I'm displeasing Him, disobeying, not doing what He desires most.

Jesus?

---
[1] Jesus made sure I'll not give him the slip knowing how weak I am ...

(Over a hundred people have copies of these revelations, but it's not enough!)

I am, live in peace; I will restore My Church; allow Me, Vassula, just to imprint My Words on you; I love you, glorify Me by loving Me; to unite My Church is My Work; you will be My bearer only, do you understand the difference?[1] even when I say: revive or unite My Church, Vassula, it is never directed straight at you; you will learn, have you not learned part of My Works with Me?

Yes, Lord, I have.

wait and you shall see;[2]
I have one question to ask you; why were you now not coming to Me for consolation?

yes, exactly, yes;

(In a flash of a few seconds Jesus gave me a vision and a whole story behind it. Like a parable. It was of a child and a mother. The mother had lost her child for years. Finally having found it she was so happy and was trying to teach her child to go to her for anything it wanted since she loved it and it belonged to her. The child had great problems getting adjusted again to someone who says it's its mother and who cares; it was used to swallow by itself its miseries having had no one to turn to. But now again it forgot that the mother is the one who could help it and console it. The vision was that of a tiny child in complete misery again, whining around the house, ignoring the mother. The mother seeing the child in its misery felt hurt, hurt to see her child miserable; hurt to see the child still not wanting to come and throw itself in her arms and showing that it needs affection from her. The mother's heart was utterly shattered to see her child in misery and ignoring her too, she who could do so much if it had confidence in her!
- The child was me; the mother, Jesus.
- And all this because I felt as if I'm not getting anywhere, the message on my back and not doing much. I decided to go and sleep on it to forget. So I went to bed and tried to sleep to forget, in the afternoon this was. I thought of Jesus but I felt too miserable to even face Him.)

beloved, I am your Consoler! lean your head on Me, allow Me to caress you and soothe your pain, allow Me to whisper in your ear My words; inside My Heart I have a place for you; spend no time elsewhere; come now in your place;[3]

I'm incapable ...

I will lift you and place you in there;

July 7, 1987

(Switzerland)

Vassula, you shall face severe trials,[4] do not forget My Presence, I am near you;
believing in My Heavenly Works is also a grace given by Me; My Works, in your eyes, appear quite unorthodox, but I am God and with whom could you compare Me to? and to what can you compare My Works to?
Vassula, when I see how so many of My sacerdotal souls deny my signs and My Works, how they treat those to whom I have given My graces and remind the world I am among you, I grieve ... they are unwillingly damaging My Body, **pono!** [5] they deny My Works, thus making deserts instead of making the land fertile!

---

[1] It took me years... (August 29, 1998, while re-reading).
[2] There was a long pause. He had my hand paused on the paper not saying anything before saying: "I have one question" etc.
[3] He said this in such tenderness that only God can speak in this manner ...
[4] The Lord is preparing me for my apostolate.
[5] Greek: meaning "I ache!"

Lord, if they deny Your works there must be reasons!

spiritually they are dead; they are deserts themselves and when they spot a flower in that great wilderness they made, they rush to it and trample on it, destroying it,

Why?

why? it is a misfit in their wilderness, they make sure that their desert stays arid! I find no holiness in them, none, what have they to offer Me?

Protection Lord! Protection not to distort Your Word!

no, they are not protecting Me, they are denying Me as God; they deny My Infinite Wealth, they deny My Omnipotency, they are comparing themselves to Me; do you know what they are doing? they are promoting atheism, they are multiplying My scourgers, they are increasing spiritual deafness, they are not defending Me, they are deriding Me! I have willed, in spite of their denials, to help them, so that in turn, they would help and feed My lambs;
 love Me Vassula, honour Me by never denying Me;

I will never deny You. I will never deny that <u>these</u> are Your Works Lord, even if I had to die!

My sweet myrrh, My remnant, My beloved, look after My interests; be My altar; remain little so that I work in you and act in you, come let us pray,

"Father of Mercy,
unite your sheep,
bring them together again,
let them realise their aridity,
forgive them, mould them into
what you desire them to be,
remind them of Your ways,
May all Glory be in Your Holy Name
for ever and ever, amen"

(I feel sad for God ...)

beloved, grieve for the world and what it has become; rest in Me;

July 8, 1987

Lord, a priest told me once that after You died and was buried Your body disintegrated into air and so they couldn't find You. In other words this priest denied Your resurrection.

Vassula, they are distorting My Word; I have risen, I have not disintegrated; My Body has risen;

Lord, are You talking to me in symbols or are You telling me that You actually arose in Body?

child, I have spoken literally to you, My Body has risen, tell them to stop distorting My Word to please human understanding;
 I am Omnipotent;

(Later:)

Lord, I am fearing that I might delay your plans.

how will you delay Me if I am the One who works?

With sins, obstructing.

I will ask you to repent often, I will point out your sins, I want you pure;

July 9, 1987

My God?

I am; Vassula, I have so many mysteries hidden from you! those few I revealed to you are 'seen'[1] in human eyes, thus not

---
[1] Understood.

comprehending them; either they will be placed aside, or will be given the wrong explanation; how could you possibly compare My works with human works; science cannot be compared with Heavenly Works, it is as if you want to compare Me with men!

true, My Works appear unorthodox to you, but what grieves Me most is to see My own sacerdotal souls doubting My Works, refusing to believe, thus remoting Me instead of promoting Me;

My creation has turned into a desert, dry, unfertile, thirsty for love; on what will My lambs feed upon when they have nothing to offer?

July 10, 1987

flower of Mine, integrate in My Body, to live in wilderness is hard, but I will always guide you to My Fountain where I will quench your thirst and give you rest and shelter; daughter, be My sacrifice, all will not be in vain; hold on to Me, you are not alone, we are together crossing this wilderness; allow Me to imprint on you My special command: "love your neighbour as yourself;"

But Lord, it's not new. You said this before.

are you following it? every ecclesiastical soul has yet to learn to obey My Command, let them draw from My Infinite Love and learn to love one another;

feel Me, all parts of My Body lacerate Vassula; I have not completed dictating you My desires and I still keep in store a bigger desire! Vassula you are beginning to feel it because I am enlightening you to sense what I desire; I love My creation boundlessly;

My God, if it is 'this' what You desire then indeed Your Kingdom on earth will be as it is in Heaven!

little by little you will understand,

Jesus?

(I felt helpless. I told Him something.)

I know, but have I not guided you so far? visions I will give you and you will write them down, be with your God who suffers too!

creation! My creation! today you deny Me as your God but tomorrow you will praise Me, worship Me and desire Me!

come, Vassula, never forget who I am; hold on to Me, call Me like yesterday[1] and I shall rush to you; I love you; honour Me by desiring Me and loving Me;

in such situations, most of you say that it was luck, forgetting Me! there is no such word as 'luck' in My vocabulary! it is I who helps you, creation;

July 11, 1987

repent!

I thank You for looking after me, My God.

(I repented.)

beloved, all is forgiven for such is My Mercy;

I will teach you to look before you make your next step; be alert; favour Me above all; flower, do not turn away your face from My Light; look at Me, face Me, flourish!

I'm weak. I feel sometimes it's hard to carry Your Cross.

---

[1] That was last night, in our new flat the concierge closes by lock the main entrance to the flats by 10.00 at night. We had forgotten our key in the flat. On seeing the door closed we knew we were locked out. I went to the door pleading, "O God, don't tell me it's locked let it be open! please!" It was locked, but at the same minute one of the neighbours was just arriving too and opened it.

My remnant, unite with Me and be One; together, together we will restore My Church;

July 12, 1987

Vassula, I rejoice when you realise;

(Sometimes I fully realise that I'm really with God and that He communicates with me in this way so I have my heart leaping! It comes in waves, most of the time I realise but not really fully.)

Do You know this, Lord?

I do, I know very well; Vassula, have you remembered Juan?
  we will unite him to Me,

My God!

I am;

You think a lot about Juan!

he is My beloved soul, I love him, I want him near Me, I wish to guide him and make a great servant out of him, O Vassula! what great things he can do for Me!

But Lord, it's impossible!! To start with he is not believing in You, then he's got other occupations in his life!

child, do you realise who is leading you?

Yes My God ...

I am the Alpha and the Omega, Creator of all, do you realise he has been looking for Me for years!

Has he? I thought he didn't believe.

he has always believed, only he has been misled; I love him and will guide him to find Me; I am Love and to Love he will come, I will fill him with My Love, all My blessings will restore him;
  beloved, now you must rest;

Lord, do You still always want me kneeling while writing?

I do, honour My Presence;

Yes, Lord.

July 13, 1987

Vassula to be My bearer you are to love Me as I taught you; alive, finally alive! I raised you from the dead!

What about the others?

creature, the others are yet to be risen; My dew of Love will fall upon them, My Light will cover them and they will revive; creation I will revive you! reviving you was not for your glory, I revived you for My glory,

Yes, Lord.

little one call Me Abba; yes, be close to Me; I will never abandon you;

July 18, 1987

(I do not feel fit to write. Since my arrival to Switzerland I'm not well. First the flu followed by an infection in the mouth – I could barely eat – then followed by a <u>piercing pain</u> in my side, which stopped me from sleeping for five nights and which I still have, the flu all over, plus a lip infection.)

come; let Me tell you, all are coming from Me; these are My purifications;
  daughter, I love you, learn how I work; I will sustain you even if you will have to suffer; I am caring for you and will not allow any stain on your soul; understand how I work, but <u>feel Me</u>, let

Me hear you talk to Me, remember Me; never will I let anything come before Me; I am First; polishing your soul will make it shine like gold and now I will remind you why I chose you; I chose you because of your ineffable wretchedness and weakness; I am a God of Mercy;

now you may work, but have Me in mind always; I never leave you from My sight; watch My lips when I am talking to you; I love you, come; get up, face Me and let Me hear you now;

(True, I had neglected God for some time, our moving countries occupied me with other things.)

allow Me to use you still for just some more time;

Yes, Lord.

have My blessings;

I bless You, Lord.

July 21, 1987

(Stockholm)

(Today I had two ladies from Jehovah's Witness as they call themselves. I let them in. We had language problems. They seemed very determined and somehow attacked the Catholic religion! They said they would come back with books in English. I will listen to see what they want. They had arrived while God was writing to me. My son came later on. Briefly we showed these revelations and they both giggled and I understood the word 'demon'. I let them; hasn't God told me that soon I will be mocked upon and He gave me His thorned crown to feel the mockery? (Predicted May 7, 1987.) I fear that this is only the beginning ...)

Vassula, I am near you, do not fear;

July 22, 1987

Vassula can you see all these souls? all are waiting in line;

(I saw Jesus with a group of souls behind Him.)

Jesus?

I am; yes, they were souls!

(Immediately after I saw those souls another image appeared to me: an image of many years back. I must have been 17-18 yrs old. I used to see often in e.g. the sitting room where I would be, on the floor, sitting, many souls who were hushing each other to keep still, and just be there around me. Like as if they would come to listen to a speech. At the time I was wondering why I saw these dead people as I used to call them, but paid no more attention to them since they never bothered me and sooner or later I was quickly distracted by other things around me. It was very often and rather common, but I paid not much attention to all this.)

yes, Vassula, they were waiting!

Waiting for what, Lord?

they were waiting for you to grow;

Did they know?

yes, they knew; I have waited for you to love Me and amend, loving Me fervently repairs and so those souls in Purgatory are healed,[1] snatched from the purifying fires and can finally come to Me;

Vassula, do you know how much they suffer while in Purgatory? their desire to see Me but being unable to? how much they depend on you! ah Vassula, will you help them?

Yes Lord, I would love to see them with You finally!

---

[1] That is: purified.

have my Peace, I the Lord will show you how you will help them; seek Me always; sacrifice and never complain; I will help you to indulge My desires; beloved, love Me for your love cures them,

Jesus will You let me know if they are back with You?

I will;

Jesus, what about the 'Jehovah's Witnesses'?

let them give you all they want, receive them with Me; you will understand why I have sent them to you; lean on Me, beloved;

Jesus will I not meet any of Your <u>own</u> World?

let Me tell you at once; I will take and place you among My own; daughter, had you merited any of My graces, I would have shown you how Love leads, without having had to face difficulties and having all "doors"[1] open;

Meaning?

meaning that you had not merited at all these graces I have given you, and it is out of My Infinite Goodness that I have looked upon your misery; <u>from now on desire Me more than ever</u>; you will earn every single grace, by giving Me acts of love; every act of Love will restore all what you have destroyed;

What had I destroyed, my God?

all good things given by Me and having them turned into evil; honour Me, I love you;

Lord, will You help me do these good acts?

I will; remember, all I gave will have to be given freely too; I want My altar pure;

(Later on:)

(God showed me that I never merited any of His graces. So now I come back to Him rather timidly, begging.)

Lord?

I am;

Allow me to be in Your Light?

be in My Light and stay;

Allow[2] me to lean on You?

I allow you always;

Allow me to hold Your Hand and be near You?

come in your Father's arms;

Allow me to talk to You!

be One with Me, face Me, be My reflection and let Me speak for you;

Allow me to be consoled by You?

little one, I will be your Consoler; come, feel Me, synchronise with Me; be One, annihilate in Me; let Me possess you entirely and reign over you; let Me thrust you in My Heart, approach; be in Me and I in you, how I love you, daughter!

(I felt God pleased.)

---

[1] "Doors": meaning Satan and his adepts are allowed to infiltrate and write his insults or give me the wrong word. God has taught me though because of this how to recognise the demons: Satan can never leave a soul in tranquillity by his presence – it's a give-away.

[2] The word "allow", to ask was taught to me by Him, because He as God and Sovereign always asks me His creature, in this way: "allow Me to so and so …"

I love You, Lord.

(I felt His love covering me entirely.)

be with Me now; stay,[1] refuse Me nothing, Vassula; I cry out loudly, My cry resounds and shakes the entire heavens; My cry should have been heard by My souls who love Me; they must have heard Me, tell them that they have not imagined it; it is I, Jesus, Beloved Son of God; I want them to unite and to propound unity, peace and love; I want them to be like an army of salvation, repairing all what has been destroyed and distorted; My cry is coming from the very depths of My Wounded Soul; bless Me, daughter;

I bless You, My God. May Your wishes come true.

stay faithful to Me, integrate into My Body, hold on to Me;

July 24, 1987

(There I come and kneel at my table and Jesus is opposite me, sitting on the sofa. I look at Him expectantly for His words to come.)

beloved, augment your love to Me thus healing souls; love Me and free them; now you have guided five souls back to Me, satisfy Me by giving Me souls; I want to redeem all those wretched souls who are near Satan's doors, I love you all so much!

(Later on:)

agapa Mé,[2]

Jesus?

I am, tell Sirka Lisa to love Me more; why does she not come to Me, I am her Counsellor; I am He who watches over you, I am your Consoler; does she know what an abyss of Love My Heart is? I love her, Vassula; I shall wait for her, I shall keep calling her, "respond soul! respond to My cry, invoke Me in your prayers, talk to this Heart which loves you; I will be waiting;"

(Jesus gave a message above for a friend of mine.)

July 25, 1987

I am your Heavenly Father who loves you; call no one else Father but Me who am your Creator; learn from Me; Vassula have I not said that I am still among you; I am Love, bring forth to Love My flock that I may redeem it; reduce paganism,[3] induce Love; help My children by giving them the same food I have given you;

I will do Your wishes with Your help. Be the Light to guide me.

(Later on:)

(The thought of Jehovah's Witnesses who are going to come puts me in discomfort. What to tell them?)

write;

(Jesus made a sign with His hand indicating this copy book.)

love them,

(?)

do what I ask you to do, love them, all are My children;

But I'm afraid that they'll advise me wrongly. They seem to want to say that they are the only ones in the whole world that carry the right religion and that all the

---

[1] I was preparing to get up and go.
[2] Greek: Love Me.

[3] Atheism.

rest, like Catholics, Protestants, Moslems, Hebrews etc are 100% wrong! and that by their beliefs one can reach Heaven.

(Jesus seemed inflexible.)

beloved, love them,

All right. But what if they start misguiding me?

would I stand still if I hear them misguide you?

No.

daughter do not fear, I will guide you;

I am happy to be with You, my God ...

why?[1]

Because I love You. Because You are my happiness, my joy and smile. You are my happy life; that's why.

fill Me with joy, Vassula; love Me, Vassula; trench into deeper depths of my Heart and let all My Love utterly consume you in nothing else but a Living Flame of Love's Love! beloved, rest in Me and let Me rest in you; be My heaven;

ΙΧθΥΣ ><>

July 26, 1987

My God?

I am; little one, who else would lead you by this special path unless I, God, had chosen it for you?

In the beginning, I was very much hesitating, afraid that it's from evil.

---

[1] Jesus seemed eager to hear the reasons. He enjoys it!

the devil would have fled when you worshipped Me; he would be unmasked, revealing his insidious designs in mind; he would not bear humility, love, and devotion; <u>have this always in mind</u>; grip My hand and climb[2] do not weary, repent often;

how will you now proceed?

You are asking me, Lord?

I am;

I can't, unless <u>You</u> do by helping me.

good; he who fights against My wishes will be kicking against a goad;

July 27, 1987

(I come with a feeling of desolation, I feel God is not so near as before.)

grieve not, My Vassula; I will clarify to you all this; I am near you;

July 28, 1987

(Still with this feeling of desolation.)

Jesus, I am so afraid to be misleading people when I tell them that I feel sometimes your hand caressing my head. Maybe I'm wrong? It would be terrible if I'm wrong!

grieve not, believe in my Redemptive Love; I have caressed you so many times in the past as well as now; no, Vassula, you have not imagined it; it is I, Jesus;

July 29, 1987

(Still with this desolate feeling.)

Jesus?

---

[2] 'Climb' means to progress spiritually, in here.

I am; I have told you that My bonds are eternal bonds; what have you to fear? erroneously you believe that because you are not used[1] as before I am less with you, or that I have forsaken you, or that I am angry with you; no; no, Vassula, it is none of these reasons; My Love has not changed, I have not deserted you, I will continue inspiring you;

July 30, 1987

(I'm still worried. Why can't I feel God as before?)

Jesus?

I am; come, look at Me; look, yes;

(I looked into God's eyes and melted.)

regardless of what you are have I not raised you and placed you in My Heart? Vassula, My Vassula will I ever forsake you?[2] reflect, I am Love and until I come to deliver you I will pour My Love into you; ela thipla mou, imé o Christos;[3]

July 31, 1987

Vassula, come; I will clarify your groundless fears of desolation; it is insight I am teaching you, do not take this as abandonment from Me; write;

I am giving you My grace to reach a higher degree of meditation while, at the same time, I am purifying your soul for this higher attainment; be assured, My beloved, that I am with you and never far; I am stimulating your love to Me and strengthening you; a deeper devotion and a fuller love for Me will be the results of all this;

Vassula, I desire you to achieve this higher degree of meditation; you must grow; beloved remove all shadows of doubt from your mind – shadows that distress you; I want you to progress, I want your soul to attain perfection and purity; I want to advance your soul into this higher and more delicate light; your soul thus cleansed will be able to offer Me virtues shelled in perfection and purity;

from meditation, you will reach in a higher level of contemplation; this aridity and feeling of desolation which leaves you to think 'all is gone', it is because I withdraw from you part of My Light; do not fear, though; be glad you feel the difference; by withdrawing part of My Light I reinforce your desire of seeking Me and thus I infuse you with more delicate Light in your intellect; yet, all Light is never totally withdrawn, for I always leave you with some Light for you to be able to see and follow it and to sustain you from stumbling;

I give you this vigour to continue seeking Me more fervently than ever; seek in Me My desires; Vassula, I will never ever leave you; why, I am your Heavenly Father who wants you to grow and flourish and these are My Ways; have no fear but be alert, never fall asleep; be seeking from Me; you will learn, I am your Teacher; love Me, Vassula; smile at Me when you see Me and take My Hand when I give to you; have My Peace and trust Me; come I love you;

O Father, thank You for relieving me and explaining to me all this. Thank you for Your teachings. I love You!

August 4, 1987

(Back in Switzerland)

(I'm almost fearing what I think is happening, is this the insight God talked about last week?)

My God?

---

[1] In the sense of being an instrument of God.
[2] He said this in so much sweetness that God only can talk in this way.
[3] Greek: 'come near Me, I am Christ'. (Jesus was trying to reassure me and I somewhat felt better.)

I am, beloved;

Am I understanding You correctly, Lord?

you are! Love will make out of you, a mirror of reflections and agonies attuned to all those who suffer; you will feel their agonies and sufferings as though they were your own;

when you will hear or see any sufferings, or if someone is in great pain, I, the Lord, will offer you this grace of feeling these pains as much as the one who is suffering; thus you will be able to penetrate fully in their wounds and have a clear conception of their feelings;

Vassula, beloved, with this insight I am giving you, you will be of tremendous help to them; suffer when they suffer; and if you deny them, I will remind you all the time, you will share their sufferings;

O My God, will my system take all this? Not that my spirit fears, but my flesh is weak ...

remember, I will give you enough strength for both your soul and flesh till the end; believe Me, this is a grace, little one; love My children as much as I love them; be My reflection, synchronise with Me and them; I love you and out of Sublime Love I am giving you this grace; tire not, come, I will infuse you with My Love by giving you My Nails; feel all sufferings; daughter will you do all this for Me?

Yes My God, if this is Your wish.

come, Love will guide you;

(I have suspected this, and here is why:-
Three days ago on the TV news, they showed two kids who died trapped underground. I felt sorry for the kids and the parents. I prayed for the parents. The following day they showed a tornado in Canada and terrified people talking about it, still afraid. The same night I prayed for them too. I felt sorry but not as if I'm in their skin. Suddenly, God threw His piercing Ray on me, I felt It piercing my chest and going out through my back. It burnt me and gave me such agony that I wanted to run and drink water, it was as if I was ablaze! Then, later on, as I slept, He gave me a vivid image of how I should have felt. In my dream my own son died. I woke up from agony and God told me while I'm in this terrible agony I should immediately pray for the parents that lost their kids. I prayed fervently like they were my own. I slept, and immediately God again gave me an image of myself being caught in the tornado. I went through desperate fears of death. He woke me up again and told me to pray for those who experienced this. I prayed fervently as I was still under a vivid image of the disaster.)

August 5, 1987

Jesus?

egho imei;[1]

Thank you for this grace. Although I know it's meant for feeding others too, it's with me.

for timeless hours you and I will be together; Vassula, have I not said that the wise will not understand what comes from the Spirit? philosophy cannot be compared to spirituality, never; that is one of the main reasons why all those in power and who call themselves wise will mock you, will scorn you, will deject you, will scrutinise you; so be prepared, beloved, for the wolves to hound you; do not fear, I will be near you;

(I sighed.)

all, Vassula, is but a passing shadow; do not get discouraged; I will be near you;

(Then I remembered how I feel unfit to be out in exile, and how I dislike it. What I thought was amusing in my past life is a

---

[1] That is: 'I am', in Greek.

pain now, and I can't like these things any more, I can't stand them ... I'm a misfit.)

I know, lean on Me;

(I felt desperate.)

Vassula, Vassula, no, you cannot enjoy these earthly solicitudes as before for this is My will; I do not want you to bear those things;

Jesus?

I am; look into My Hands; look, Vassula they are bleeding; Vassula, revive My Church; hear Me, have you seen all this blood streaking down My arms? I suffer;

Lord, why do You give so much pain showing me all this?

(The vision was so vivid, I thought His Blood will drop on this note-book.)

to let you understand how I suffer, beloved, seeing so many souls under Satan's power; let Me use you till the end;

I love You.

be with Me; "us," I will always remind you; we;[1] love Me;

August 7, 1987

Jesus?

I am;

(Jesus was again giving me images of His scourging, His right side of His face swollen. Again I felt in pieces.)

Vassula, I love you all so much!

Quickly, quickly[2] ...

---

[1] In saying "we", He indicated it with His index as a Teacher talking.

with My power I will raise even the dead; Vassula, I want to clarify My message of last week; do you know that I withdraw just a little bit of My Light? do you feel this?

I do.

good; by withdrawing My Light but just very little I nourish your intellect in the sense that I make you seek Me more, raising you to contemplation and enlivening it, flourishing it and thus becoming fruitful;

How did You nourish me before bringing me into this?

I had given you recourses which lie out of your intellect; now I wish to have you penetrate into a higher degree of meditation; Vassula, you have to progress; I am only enriching your food with this slight change; I want this to be clear to you; I have told you that I will detach you in every sense, have I not?

Yes, You did, Lord.

by being now detached I will enliven your faculties;

The insight You talked about?

yes, your insight, giving you this spiritual grace will help others;

How others, Lord?

you will be able to understand My children and thus you will be able to help them; do not relate this slight withdrawal of my Light as abandonment; no, Vassula, I am only advancing your soul into holiness;

---

[2] Here I meant, "hurry up and complete Your will so that You don't suffer more"; I couldn't bear Him suffering.

Lord, I was fearing to become like a boat without oars and be drifted backwards, losing all what I was taught by You! I panicked!

Vassula, I have to purify you; learn that by purifying a soul, the soul will go through terrible fears and anguishes; but I am telling you this, that languishing for Me inclines you to be raised into this blessing;

Which is?

which is contemplation; I want your love to reach perfection, giving yourself entirely to Me;

Jesus, my soul longs for You.

little one, do I not long for you too?
[1]we, us; come, let us go;

(Now I understand Jesus is teaching me two things at the same time: contemplation and to have insight.

On July 26, it was as if God was preparing me for this change; for already the following day I felt as if His Light was withdrawn slightly, I panicked. Immediately my soul started to search the reason, as I'm guilty and full of sin. I searched which were those sins that might have angered Him so much as to withdraw slightly His light, had I offended Him? Or could it be Satan doing this to me? I thought that if it's either, I because of exactly this should all the more cling tighter on my Saviour, pray more than usual, meditate more, fully use all other graces given to me, feel His Presence, talk to Him more than ever, never forget His Presence, work like I never worked so hard. If it's Satan, he'll flee fuming, so I'll let him fume and he'll leave me alone. On the other hand, if it comes from God, a test, I would like to pass it like a good student; I want Him smiling.

Several days passed, no change, my strength was giving in, I was beginning to panic now, I tried to serve Him with more fervour and devotion, but I could not understand yet why all this was not helping, at least that's what I believed. Then my Saviour and Teacher explained to me what was happening. When I thought He had abandoned me, He was but purifying me, lifting me into a higher level of meditation, developing my intellect, and infusing it with a subtle[2] light, nourishing me with insight.)

August 10, 1987

(Last night I was wakened up by the Lord and He asked me to surrender, all over again. My words were:

"Thank You, Father,
for having looked upon me,
who is but the personification
of the sins of this world.
Thank You for Your Mercy
when I denied You.
Thank You for the Love You have for me.
In spite of my guilt,
You have lifted me into Your Heart.
Allow me to be near You, near Your feet.
Already by allowing me this
it is more than I deserve.
Allowing me to talk to You
is more than I merit, I merit nothing.
Father, I surrender completely.
I know I'm nothing
but this nothing belongs to You.
You want to throw me in a corner, do it.
You want to trample me, do it.
You want me to suffer only, do it.
You want me in Your Heart
then it is more then I ever deserved.
Whatever You wish, Lord,
I will but thank You, and Love You.
Use me if You wish

---

[1] We, us = He reminds me to talk to Him, using those two words.

[2] It's obvious that even when I explain my own feelings, God is dictating them to me. The word 'subtle' was loudly said to me as I was hesitating how to describe this light. I looked it up in the dictionary to find out what it meant, I didn't know ...

*to my last strength to help others.
Make me worthy so that You are able
to use me completely,
I am Yours and Yours only,
wretched, but I love You."*

August 10, 1987

Jesus?

I am; Vassula, August is when I started to teach you; Vassula, it is a sort of anniversary between us; rejoice! beloved, it is our feast; let me place a wreath of Love on you; come, celebrate with Me; I will let you go now,[1] but come to Me to celebrate My August;

(By telling me this I ran and searched in my old copy-books for the date of August; I jumped with happiness to read in my notebooks what my angel Dan (the guardian angel) was saying to me: "I, Dan, bless you in the name of God our Father, His Beloved Son Jesus Christ and the Holy Spirit. Blessed are the pure in heart, for they shall see God." Then my angel handed me over to God and from there on Yahweh started to teach me. Dan ended by saying: "Glory be to God, I have done all that God wanted me to do."

I ran quickly and told my cousin, I was flying with happiness! I was celebrating with God! She was happy too but warned me that others who don't understand might believe I'm in love with God. Loving Him wrongly. What she said saddened me a lot, and scared me. Could she be right?)

Jesus?

daughter;

I'm scared for this.

I know; Vassula, have My Mother; I would like you to understand how wrong your thoughts are;

---

[1] I had to rush for an appointment.

I have taught you to love Me, your God, as I want everyone to love Me; I am celebrating the end of a year; beloved, will you be My daughter of Peace and Love? I have seen many lives taken by hatred; I filled My Kingdom with Eternal peace, would I not see My creation toil for peace?

little one, I have approached you in spite of your wretchedness, denials, and failures; I am a God of Love; I look upon My children with loving eyes, let everyone learn to recognise Me until I come to deliver them; let every soul approach Me without fear; let them know that I will receive them with open arms for I am a loving Father; let them know how I can turn the stones into devout followers of Mine; let them know how I liberate their soul and give them real freedom;

Vassula, I will not abandon you, but because of your fear, have My Mother teach you how wrong you are, I will be always near you; us, we?

Yes, Lord.

(I understood. St. Mary is for some time going to teach me and prove to me that my fears are wrong.

Between the 10th and 14th, I felt St. Mary close to me, talking to me and I started to realise that my emotional feelings were as strong as Jesus'; they were the same.)

August 14, 1987

My God?

I am; have My words of today; "whoever seeks Me will find Me;"

beloved, always love Me with fervour and glorify Me; narrate Me, saying to Orjän, "believe ... believe ... believe; come, beloved, I have indeed called you brother! how I love you! I, your Saviour, offer you My Love, I am Peace; come; come to Me and penetrate deep into My Wounds, feel

My Heart, feel Me ... live in My wounds brother;"

flower, beloved, remain;[1] here is My Mother;

ah Vassula, let Me tell you what will come; you will glorify My Son; daughter, eat from Him;

Oh St. Mary, You have always encouraged me! Since the beginning, You were my support.

(I felt a love for Her as much as I have for God. She is so very motherly!)

wear My medallion always for I blessed it on you; have our peace;

(I then fell prostrate and venerated Her in prayer.)

August 16, 1987

My God, I love You!

Vassula, you are becoming to My eyes; listen and write; today's Abel shall live; just depend on your God, Abel will live! Abel will live this time; beloved, the world in its weakness is filled with Cains; would I bear forever to watch My Abels condemned and killed by Cains? how many more should perish before My eyes? no, Vassula, I have wounds that are re-opened; this is a breed of Cains; beloved, every time an Abel rose, a Cain repeated his crime without the slightest hesitation; you see, little one?

(God seemed sad telling me this and I became sad too.)

What is the reason for this?

it is because the Abels are My seed, they come from Me;

And the Cains?

the Cains? they belong to the world; they come from men; this time I will step between Cain and My Abel; I will extirpate everything coming from Cain; I will cast away from Cain's hand his weapon, leaving him naked; he shall have to face Abel unarmed; Vassula, I will clarify to you all this, face Me and when you do watch My lips and you will understand; would you still work for me?

Yes, My God, if You allow me? Jesus?

I am Jesus Christ, beloved Son of God and Saviour;

$$ΙΧΘΥΣ \rightarrowtail$$

we, us?

Yes, Lord.

(I'm happy and He is smiling!)

come then, we will work together;

August 20, 1987

My God?

I am;

I think I understand Your previous message.

you have understood only part of it, child;

A part of what I understood is also Cain technology coming from men, unspiritual items?

yes, Cain represents all the things belonging to the world, write; Cain represents all what My eyes dislike; he represents in this era, iniquity, materialism, revolutions, hatred,

---

[1] I was getting ready to leave.

paganism, [1] oppressors upon those I blessed, immorality; Cain never understood Abel whom I fashioned to my likeness; Abel comes from Me, he is My seed;

Meaning that he is spiritual and loves You?

precisely, and because of this difference he was disliked by Cain; I have said that the wise will not understand what comes from the Spirit;

Lord, I'm worried about something.

(I don't wish to write it.)

I know, all I want to do is stir up his wisdom; which is more important to you, to leave him under heavy millstones or have you worried? even to have you suffer, what would you choose?

Without hesitation I'd choose to suffer for him.

I stirred you up from your sleep; would I not do the same to others?

Yes, My God.

well then, let Me free to act through you, hallowed by My hand; My Spirit is upon you, betrothed, beloved of My Soul; I have given you freely, so freely give too; come, annihilate in Me and be one with Me! I love you, My Vassula;

Jesus, I will do all what You wish.

(I find no words, because whatever I say it's not enough.)

come then, I will restore My creation; us? we?

Yes!

August 23, 1987

(Yesterday something very special happened! It was one of those busy days. It was washing day. So I had the machine working and the dryer, drying. As it was a beautiful hot day, my husband took our son to the pool. He left at 11.00 and said they'd be back at 3.00; so I should have lunch ready at 3.00. So I was left alone at home, working. It was ten to two, when I thought I'd better start lunch. So I lit the plate of the stove to melt butter and suddenly all the lights went off. The 'main' fuse blew out. All machines stopped. I checked in all parts of the house if any electricity worked, none worked. I looked to find a fuse to change the fuse, but my husband had moved them. The shops were closed, for it was Sunday, our car was out of order, and so I felt frustrated ... I went, out of frustration, and laid in bed. After five minutes I heard some noise in the kitchen. I got up to see what was this noise and to my great surprise I saw the lights of the oven lit and the plate warming the butter. But the machines were not working and the rest of the house was without electricity still. I couldn't understand, if the main fuse is out and everything was out, then...? I prepared the food and placed it in the oven to roast. At 3.00 my husband returned and I told him what had happened. So he re-checked all the electricity, which was still out except for the stove, which was working. He checked the main fuse and he saw that it had blown out. By then the food was ready. While checking the main fuse we saw that the meter was rolling. The minute I said: "The food is ready," the meter stopped rolling, although the oven was still lit. I went in and switched off the stove. My husband changed the fuse with a new one and again all the electricity worked as normal. He too could not explain this.)

August is our feast! We do not want our celebration spoiled;

Do You mean that...[2]

---

[1] Atheism.

[2] Jesus did not let me finish.

I mean that I will not see you grieve during our feast; Vassula, you are My flower, do you know what flower stands for? flower symbolises frailty; that is why I take good care of you lest your frailty harms you;

Thank You, My God. I know You are very near me and I love You.

(I'm feeling embarrassed, for I deserve nothing. Yesterday in the evening while in my son's room I was covered with incense. The odour was just at one particular spot. I felt happy!)

My God?

I am; I love you, do not doubt! alone you are not; I, Jesus, I, Jesus, am with you, flower; I have always loved you to distraction; propound your fragrance like you were taught to; embellish My garden, delight Me, come; you see, Vassula, you start to understand Me; now I have justly withdrawn you from everybody, beloved, you were not quite aware of what I was doing to you; have you not felt My arm over your shoulders pulling you away from everyone, while whispering in your ear My Heart's desires? now that you have lifted your head, you suddenly realise that you have no one around you but Me; how I love you! I feel so happy! adapt yourself to be alone with just Me; yes, just us two, Me and you, you and Me;

ah Vassula! face Me now; face <u>Me</u> your God, Vassula; from now on it will be <u>I</u> and <u>I</u> alone; I am your God, I am your Holy Companion, I am your Saviour, I am your Bridegroom; I will provide you with all you need; beloved, you need help? I will rush to you; courage? and I will give you My Strength; consolation? fall in My Arms, abide in My Heart; praise Me Vassula! praise Me daughter! come and glorify Me! glorify Me, fall prostrate in front of My feet! worship Me! be Mine, ah Vassula, love Me as I love you! bless Me like I bless you, cover Me with your fragrance like I cover you with Mine; I stand before you, I, your Saviour! worship Me, feel My Heart this time and this hour; night is soon to come, will you not replenish your lamp from Me? never wait till the day is over; let Me fill up your lamp;

come and draw from Me; let Me be alone with you; live for Me, I delight in our solitude! I love you to jealousy! My Love is such that I withdrew you from everyone; would you try and understand Me? I longed to be alone with you; Love is enflamed and when Love is ablaze, I allow Myself to do what pleases Me; now you are Mine and I desire you to imbue Me with wreaths of Love, infatuate Me with your childish words; leave Me free to Love you as I please now; have you not yourself given Me the liberty of using you as I wish?

Yes Lord, I have.

I will then use that liberty; My finger will just touch your heart and when it does, you will reserve nothing from Me; it is our August after all, I will always remind you that we are celebrating;

August 24, 1987

Vassula, repent!![1]
I forgive your sins; now I want you to praise Me![2] Vassula say: "Glory be to God Almighty"; do you know who I am?

You are the Alpha and Omega, Creator of all.

you said well, My child; now I tell you this: blessed are those who will read My Message and believe <u>I</u> wrote it, without having <u>seen</u> Me writing it; blessed are those who hear My Message and follow it; blessed are those that unite and propound peace and love; diffuse My

---
[1] I repented.
[2] I hesitated finding the right words.

Message, diffuse My Peace and let it reign in all Hearts, never doubt of My Love;

How do you want me to diffuse, how could I do anything? I am helpless.

wait Vassula and you shall see; I will help you; come, us, we?

Yes My God. Us, we.

August 25, 1987

remember, My child, the love I have for you; Vassula, little one, I have blessed the red cross you are wearing around your neck; believe! believe in My heavenly Works, Vassula;

My God! Thank You. The more You give me the more I feel I deserve less and less.

I love you; come, keep close to Me, I like to hear you say the things I told you, about My Presence and about other things too; teaching Ismini, live for Me, glorify Me;

Sometimes, Lord, I feel less Your presence, thinking, "Now God is not so near me." Why is this, Lord?

erroneously you believe I am not near enough, whereas these moments I am as close to you as one can be; alone you are not, NEVER!

(Suddenly I discerned Him so clearly. He proved to me with certain gestures of His, His so alive Presence! It went on for a few minutes. It was wonderful!)

all is spiritual;

(By this I understood all is supernatural, impossible to comprehend if you place these actions in the physical state. It is not physical, thus not possible to explain it physically. These are placed in the supernatural sphere and not in our realism sphere.)

many of you tend to forget that I am Spirit[1] and that you too are spirit;

August 26, 1987

Vassula, are you still willing to be My bearer?

Yes, Lord, if You still want me in all my incapacity and failures.

child, I will help you accomplish your task, then I will deliver you; Wisdom will instruct you; are you willing to forgo your leisures and sacrifice more for Me?

Yes, I'm willing.

have My arm, I will support you; Vassula, your era has lost all spiritual values, nevertheless I will be always near you to help you; I am Jesus Christ beloved Son of God; I am preparing you, allow Me to guide you blindly, believe in Me blindly till the end;[2]

August 28, 1987

Vassula, come, have My Works translated in French; I will help you; let My Bread be given freely;

I will, Lord. I know You'll help me.

August 29, 1987

Vassula, I have showered upon you discernments and learnings; you have been taught by Me; I have given you My Bread from My storages; I have given you fruit from My garden; I have poured into

---

[1] 2 Co. 3:17 and 1 P. 1:11.
[2] Meaning: 'have no proof of this, and just believe'. Believing blindly glorifies Him.

you My Works to enlighten this world revealing My Face; come, do not forget why I chose you; content yourself with what I give you daughter; I have given you abundantly from the tree of Life to feed others too; lean on Me, depend on Me, would you give Me all you have?

All what I have is Yours, I want to keep nothing for me alone.

everything you have is indeed Mine, but I have given you liberty to choose;

To choose what, Lord?

to choose between evil and good; I have given everyone this freedom of choice;

Then if this is the only thing I have, I choose to stay with You.

let Me bind you closer to Me then let Me guide you where I am sought most;

I love You, Father. May Your will be done.

love Me, child; hear Me, not until I complete My Works will I unchain you to come to Me; I will allow Myself to use you writing down My desires; Love loves you; draw My Sign,

ΙΧθΥΣ ><▷ Jesus Christ beloved Son of God and Saviour;

August 30, 1987

(Evening.)

Jesus?

I am;
 will you let Me rest in you?

Yes, Lord.

My flower seek Me, desire Me fervently, bless Me,

I bless You, Lord.

have My blessings too; <u>alone you are not!</u>

(I felt Him as though I could touch Him.)

August 31, 1987

Vassula, in the stillness of the night, I shall come; the hour is near, alone you are not; the world seems to forget My Presence; I am God, but how many think of Me? very few;

(I saw a night filled with stars, still, and beyond those stars God's Eyes upon us.)

stay awake, for in this stillness of the night I shall descend, I have laid My plans before I created you little one; I will lift you to Me and show you something;
 rest, beloved, now;

September 1, 1987

fidelity is what I love; Vassula, I will give you a vision lifting you to Me; I will show you how heaven will appear;

(The sky was shown to me. It looked as any night, with its stars, then it changed. It resembled spots of paint. Like a painter's palate, but one colour was dominating surpassing all others, in command, it was red, thick, <u>and it grew</u> in its thickness, like yeast, pouring from above on us.)

Vassula, I will open the heavens, letting you see what eye has never seen; you have well discerned, keep awake; I will watch over you, hear Me; write; I have, since the beginning of times, loved My creation, but I created My creation to love Me too and recognise Me as their God; I have, since the beginning of times, sanctified all that My Hands created; I am a God of Love, I am the Spirit of Sublime Love; creature, since the beginning of times, I have shown My

Love to mankind, but I have also shown My Justice too; each time My creation rebelled against Me and My Law, I hardened at Heart, My Heart grieved by their iniquities; I came to remind them that I am the Spirit of Love and that they too are spirit; I came to remind them that they are but a passing shadow on earth, made out of dust, and that My first drops of rain upon them, will wash them away leaving nothing behind; I have breathed into them, My Breath, giving them life;

the world has incessantly been offending Me and I, for My part, have incessantly been reminding them of My existence and of how I love them, My Chalice of Justice is full, creation! My Justice lies heavily upon you! unite and return to Me, honour Me creation! when you will, then I too will lift My Justice; My cries resound and shake the entire heavens leaving all My angels trembling for what has to come, I am a God of Justice and My Eyes have grown weary watching hypocrisy, atheism, immorality; My creation has become, in its decadence, a replica of what Sodom was; I will thunder you with My Justice as I have thundered the Sodomites; repent, creation, before I come;

I have indeed forewarned you many a time but you have not followed My instructions; I have raised up saints to warn you, but daughter, they have closed their hearts; My creation would rather live in lust and ignore Me; I have given them signs to awaken them;

My God, Your children are only sleeping. Please come and wake them up, they are only sleeping.

they are sleeping hour after hour, year after year;

But Lord, who is to blame if they have not been taught, they are almost innocent if they know nothing about You.

I have raised servants and teachers on earth to teach them;

But Lord, Your teachers and servants do work, but what can they do more when multitudes are <u>negative</u>, they are helpless!

helpless? they should repent, they should come to Me and repent; I have through times given them signs, but they have rejected them as not from Me; I have given them warnings through weak and wretched souls but they doubted My word; they have rejected all My blessings, grieving Me; O men with hearts out of rock! men of little faith! have they had more heart and have they had, <u>now</u> even, more heart, I would have helped them; I stirred them up from their sleep, but how many times have they closed their eyes, falling back into sleep;

But why don't they make it known to the world when You give Your signs?

some do, but the majority of My sacerdotal souls have closed their hearts, doubting, fearing; many of them fear; Vassula, do you remember the Pharisees?

Yes, Lord.

let Me tell you that many of them are replicas of the Pharisees; doubting, fearing, blinded by vanity and with hypocrisy, do you remember how many times I have given them signs? I have given them signs hundreds of times and what have they done? times have not changed, many of My sacerdotal souls are just the same, replicas of the Pharisees! I have given them signs but they want signs which could be explained by proofs; they want proofs;

Will You give them of Your past signs <u>a proof</u>, and of this revelation <u>any proof</u>?

all that I will give them is you yourself, child;

But Lord, it's not convincing, I'm not convincing, I'm nothing to convince! They'll laugh outright in my face.

I have blessed you;

But Lord, I know that it's You, and a few others too, but <u>many</u> will disagree, since there is no solid proof it's from You. I am nothing and You know it.

daughter, let Me be everything, remain nothing and let Me be everything; the least you are the more I am; I have now laid My Justice on mankind, upon them is what they have reaped;

Isn't there a solution, I mean that somehow everything becomes like You want and so Your Justice is lifted?

Vassula, when I will be received and not denied by My sacerdotal souls now, I will lift My Justice; I have warned them, but they keep My warnings hidden;

Please tell me the reason why they do this?

they seem to forget My Omnipotency and My Wealth, they tend to amass everything into one thing; [1] they will believe only if <u>they see</u>; grieving Me, counting not My blessings;
   [2] creature! creature! revive My Church, Vassula honour Me; the hour is near, beloved, the hour is at hand; <u>Love will come again as Love;</u>

Thank You, Lord. I bless You.

(These last three days I felt in my soul an inexplicable agony; between the 1st and the 4th.)

September 4, 1987

(In my private pad Jesus gave me a message which startled me. I got up leaving alone that message. Later on, when I went to write, Jesus repeated that message. I started to fear. My thoughts as once before raced to confusion, asking myself and God, "Why me?" Why has really all this writing started, why do I feel like this, bonded with God? How was I before a year and a half ago, and how I am now. I'm living in the Truth and I feel responsible for all that's happening. I feel I should please God. Then again doubts, doubts which made me test Jesus. I came to him doubting. He knew it. I had in mind to write my own thing controlling my hand <u>myself</u>.)

Jesus?

I am; well? you can try again;[3]
   write ... write! Love Love Love Love;

(The 3 dots show how I was struggling to write but couldn't, then he wrote "write" and He forced my hand down writing Love four times; while I was struggling to stop my hand.)

I am Love; I will remind you that on your shoulders I have placed My Cross of Peace and Love; up! up! lift! lift! daughter, do you realise why I have brought you up? I have brought you up to unite My Church, altar, have I not said that from the babe's mouth you will hear the truth and not from the wise? I have said that the wise will listen and listen and not understand, see and see again but not perceive, for their hearts have grown coarse; they have closed their ears and shut their eyes;
   Vassula, I have raised you from the dead, instructing you with Wisdom; fear not and advance,

(Jesus gave me a vision of myself, facing Him. I felt uncertain. He held my hands and while He was walking backward He was pulling me to walk, advancing.)

O daughter, how I love you! flower, everything you feel comes from Me, advance;

---

[1] Solid proof, concrete, touchable...
[2] Then He turned to me, laying His command on me.

[3] Trying to control my hand.

(I felt as if I was doing my first steps and thrilled!)

Vassula, by being timid you infatuate Me; daughter, write down the word:

Garabandal

Vassula when I stirred you from your sleep it was not just to wake you up, it was also to be able to use you, beloved; purifying you was not just to cleanse you, it was so that you feel My Presence and <u>be in My Presence</u>; using you was not just to use you writing My Messages and desires, it was so that I write down My blessings for My little children of Garabandal; I come to have My Message glorified, altar keep this flame ablaze, by My Power I will restore My Church; love Me, do not falter, lean on Me and rest, I will help you advance; the hour is near, pray with Me,

> "Father,
> deliver me in Your arms,
> let me rest near you,
> sanctify me Father
> when You receive me,
> forgive my sins as I forgave others
> Glory be to God my Father,
> I bless You; amen"

September 5, 1987

Vassula do not fear, write the word, <u>Garabandal</u>;
Garabandal is the sequel of other signs; Garabandal's apparitions are <u>authentic</u>, believe all you who have not seen; believe, believe, daughter, I have used you to be able to manifest Myself through you; My Mother had appeared to My chosen souls; out of their mouths, the Truth was said, but many of My sacerdotal souls declared them as uncertain and some of them denied them altogether;
I have manifested Myself through you to lift this doubt of Garabandal's apparitions are authentic and My children have indeed seen My Mother and heard Her Messages; Vassula, a harder trial will come upon you making My Cross heavier on your shoulders and augmenting My Cup of Justice; I have forewarned the world;

My God, very few probably know of this happening.

true, many do not know, because of the doubts and fears My sacerdotal souls bear; by doubting they deny My Heavenly Works, they have forgotten that I am Omnipotent; hardened at heart they have lost their spirituality, blinded they seek without light and without Wisdom;
all My Works have always been given to mere children and never to the learned; My Works appear unorthodox in their eyes, but it is because they compare themselves to Me;
I have, since the beginning of times never abandoned you;[1] Vassula, do you remember the Pharisees?

Yes, Lord.

they at one time accused Me of preaching against Moses' Law; what difference is there today? I have been accused of promiscuity and going against their Law; today's accusations and uncertainty is not far from this; let Me tell you, those who defy revelations, apparitions and Messages, are those who wound Me; they are the thorns of My Body; I have told you some time ago[2] that I will lead you with Heavenly Force right into the very depths of My Bleeding Body; I said that I will point out to you with My finger, those who wound Me; I am Jesus Christ,

---
[1] He made me understand that the signs given are to remind us of His Presence among us, <u>encouraging</u> us.
[2] On the 11th June God told me this same message. He said He would not spare them. At that time I did not know to whom He was referring to.

Beloved Son of God; Vassula, fear not, for I am before you;

September 6, 1987

Jesus?

I am; will I ever abandon you? flower, surround Me with wreaths of love; assemble My children around Me, let Me bless them; I, who was waiting for them, I waited for this hour; I come to welcome them and bless them; assemble My beloved ones, My own, My lambs; hug them for Me, caress them for Me, remind them of My Promise; love them, unite them; come nearer to Me, let Me instruct you with Wisdom;

September 7, 1987

peace be with you;

With You too, Lord.

absorb Me flower, let My Light shine upon you and let your worries fall into diminishment; My Breath will blow them away and their structure will but fall, swaying them away, leaving you smiling; My dew of righteousness will embellish you, flower, have My message of today; fear not, for I have laid My plans long before you were born;

Does that mean that whatever happens to me, to Your Messages and everybody, it is by Your Will?

yes, beloved, everything that will come, will come from Me;

I'm worried of failing You, Lord.

how will you fail My plans, think, you are nothing; so how can a nothing be something and that that something, if at all, fail My plans? but you are nothing so do not worry; leave everything in My Hands; Vassula, I am your Teacher; fear not when you are with Me;

I want to say something please.

feel free;

Do You know that there are times I think I'm absolutely mad? Insane?

I know;

Then just imagine those to whom I will one day show this to them! They'll be shocked, they will say that they can find a natural explanation. They will simply not believe.

to believe is also a grace; to have faith is also a grace, to see, hear and understand My Heavenly Works is also a grace, all given by Me;

Yes, Lord.

Vassula, I have worked with you; honour Me, daughter,

With Your help I will not fail You.

listen then to these words that come from My Mother;

Vassula, pethi mou,[1] do not fear, I am with you; My Son Jesus expressly limited you with the proofs and signs you were asking Him to give you, but He has His reasons; He has though, given you the grace to believe, He has instructed you with Wisdom; Vassula, you have indeed believed blindly;

Have I?

you have, otherwise you would not have had this fervour in coming to Us and write, letting yourself be used at His Will; having done this, beloved, proves that you believe blindly and God delights in this; your faith is great; Jesus wants by

---
[1] Greek: "My child".

this to teach others too to have faith and believe blindly in His Heavenly Works, be innocent, be like children in whom God delights;

What if they don't, St. Mary?[1]

your sufferings will be great; you will be like a mirror reflecting Jesus' image; upon you child, His sufferings will reflect;

You mean Jesus will suffer if they show disbelief and contempt?

precisely; Jesus will suffer; upon you will show His sufferings;

But since He has laid His plan before, why couldn't He have made them so that there won't be any contradictions?

child, this is the way men tend to think; do not forget His teachings; Jesus wants that His works are acknowledged with grace;[2]

Jesus told me that He would not stand by if He sees someone wanting to hurt me.

He has indeed said it, and I tell you this daughter; I will not stand by either! I love you and I will not see them hurt you;

(Here I felt very emotional.)

I am a coward; I fear, but I will cling onto You and Jesus.

daughter, I will tell you still something more; God has laid His Justice upon men, His cup is now full; listen to Me carefully, beyond these words lie many more; glorify God, Vassula; I am your Holy Mother; daughter, rely on Me; weary not of striving; remember, Jesus was abandoned by everyone on the way to be crucified; He bore His Cross alone;

Yes Mother. I will not ask anything more than what He gives me.

Vassula, let Me answer your question withheld in you; if they do not believe again, God's wrath will grow, augmenting His Cup of Justice; it will be like the vision God has given you;[3] pray and amend for the end of Times[4] is near;

Yes, Mother, may God bless You.

it is I, Jesus; little one, remain small; let us talk to each other; let us share this day; allow Me to be your Holy Companion;

Lord, allow me to talk to You. I will remember your Presence.

come, us, we;

September 7, 1987

peace be with you, daughter; remember those words I will tell you once again, remember them particularly more now;

"<u>I, the Lord, am standing at the door, knocking</u>; if one of you hears Me calling and opens the door, I will enter to share his meal side by side with him; those who prove victorious, I will allow to share My Throne, just as I was victorious Myself and took My place with the Father on His throne; if anyone has ears to hear, let him listen to what the Spirit is saying to the Churches;"

daughter, tell them, tell them; remind them of My words for they have forgotten them;

Jesus, help me.

I will always help you, Vassula;

---

[1] St. Mary's voice suddenly changed tone and became very grave.
[2] In other words, we are free and we have our own free will.
[3] September 1, 1987.
[4] End of one era.

(I sighed.)

Thank You, Lord.

September 8, 1987

Vassula, delight Me and receive Me; I want you to follow Me; I will take you to meet Me at My Tabernacle; receive Me and I will bless you;[1]
    I love you;

I love You, Lord. I'll come.

September 9, 1987

Vassula I want those words I will give you to be known, I wish that those words be diffused all over, "I, the Lord, bless My children of Garabandal;"
    Vassula bless them, unite them;

All with Your help I will, Lord ...

(Then, 'all hell broke loose'. Satan raged. His adepts as well. They have names even. I know those who are attacking me.)

Vassula, come; I will make you understand how they hate you; do not fear;

(Jesus dragged me underground. There we stood. I recognised hell, as my feet were in slimy and sticky black mud. A grotto cave. Jesus told me to listen. "Aha, it's her again, another hag! bo beware now wound her, cripple her forever, wound her, so that we win, ill-treat her she feels the hate I have upon her and the rest of his creation, sabi, go too and wound her, I hate you all!" Satan was again like a madman. Jesus pulled me back out.)

now that you have heard his hatred you must realise with what determination he is after you to have you stop writing; I, Jesus, love you and under My wings I am guarding you, never leaving you an instant from My sight;

(Later on:)

Vassula, do not read these books, they have neither Wisdom nor Truth; wisdom is found in the Holy Bible; I am glad you heard Me;

(I had not done much as I was mostly meditating the whole day. When I realised time was gone I went to prepare our meal, as soon as I started to work, Jesus who was watching me interrupted my work saying: "Vassula have you got a moment for Me?" I said: "Yes, I have millions of moments, not only one for You." I left my work and went to write. He told me to stop reading a book I was reading, advising me it's no good. It was talking about things, I never had heard of and about legends, religions and all written by non-theologians.)

(Later on in the evening:)

all these parts of My Face were harmed;

(I was looking at the Holy Shroud photo.)

All what I see, Lord?

yes, all, they tore off part of My beard, they harmed My right eye;

Jesus, I don't know what to say.

tell Me; I love you!

I LOVE YOU.

Vassula do not get discouraged, NEVER; I am with you; together we are bearing My Cross;

---

[1] Jesus again calls me to receive Holy Communion.

September 10, 1987

I love you; until I come and deliver you; <u>believe in Me blindly</u>, Vassula;

Jesus I know there are times You must be very displeased with me. Those times I fell into doubt, at these times I am the result of a multiplication – if You multiply Thomas by 10, the result is me.

flower, you are frail and it is out of your frailty that I am attracted, do I not know all this beloved? I am your Strength;

(Jesus whispered in my ear something; I'll keep it secret.)

Vassula, Garabandal is the Sequel of Miracles, in between these Miracles I have been giving other signs;

Can You write down which miracles?

write; Lourdes, then Fatima, I want you to write now Garabandal in San Sebastian; Glorify Me! remember I am the Light of this world;

(Suddenly Jesus reminded me of a dream I had last night, and I had forgotten. It was <u>the vision</u> I saw lately, but it appeared worse in my dream.)

listen, I have let you see the vision in your sleep, to make you feel it; no, there is no escape!

(I remember when I saw it coming like a giant wave I tried to run and hide, knowing it's impossible.)

But why do this if You love us? Why?

I am known as a God of Love, as well as a God of Justice;

What can we do to stop this?

tremendous amendments are required now from all of you, uniting and being one, loving one another, believing in Me, believing in my Heavenly Works, for I am among you always;

September 11, 1987

Vassula, let Me tell you, Wisdom has not just instructed you to find Peace; Wisdom has not just covered you with myrrh, fragrancing you with Her Sublime Love; Wisdom has not led you through winding ways bringing you fear and testing you to abandon you now; <u>no Vassula</u>, I have led you to be where I wished you to be; what I have commenced and blessed I will finish, come, rest on My shoulder;

(Later:)

little one, seldom do I find fidelity in men;
  I want to warn you against men's weakness which is infidelity; I love you and I will support you knowing how frail you are; allow Me flower to kiss you;

(I leaned towards God and He kissed my forehead, I, His child.)

I love you, I hallowed you, I freed you; come, I and you, you and Me, we, us, honour Me loving Me ardently;

(I love You. Holy Father, may I kiss Your hands?)

always do, daughter;

(I kissed His wrists.)

September 12, 1987

Fidelity always finds a way to be with Me; love Me and be faithful, child; unseen are My Works from the wise eyes; I have them hidden from them; My hidden Wisdom I give to the humble and to mere children;

daughter, I am Spirit[1] and I have approached you teaching you as Spirit to spirit; My teachings were given to you spiritually and not in the way philosophy is taught; Vassula, be aware of what has to come for an unspiritual person will not accept these works as from the Spirit of God; he will defy them, because they are beyond his understanding, as this can only be understood by means of the Spirit; I, the Lord know what the wise think and I tell you truly, they do not convince Me;

(That same evening my soul, for an unknown reason, suffered. I longed for God. I repented. I asked Him if He wanted to hear me and if He had a few moments to listen to my repentance, I was facing God with a load of sins again ...)

September 13, 1987

(Jesus, on the 8th, called me to Holy Communion. I went today and received Him.)

Father in Heaven:
"Do not let men
be the cause of my destruction,
Do not let them take away
what You already have given me.
My fear is their insensitivity,
and when they close their hearts
upon Your Heavenly Works
and when they shut their ears
I am very weak and vulnerable.
With one word,
they will be able to break me
as easily as one breaks a reed."

O Vassula, Vassula, take My Hand; if they persecute you, they will be persecuting Me; if they mock you, they will be mocking Me; Love is suffering;

Help me, Father, from these people.

Love will help you; adorn Me with purity, be My altar; bear with Me My Cross; altar, grieve not;

I bless You, Father. I long for You.

(Later on:)

(This Sunday, September 13, was the second time from the beginning of this revelation that my soul felt in complete anguish, a sadness of an unexplicable reason; a bitterness that I thought I would not survive. Physically it hurt too. My chest was heavy and the pain ran down my arms. Jesus called me:)

Vassula, synchronise with Me and feel My pain; they are recrucifying Me;

Why, why do they do this to You?

beloved, they know not what they are doing;

Who's doing this?

many souls; I love them and yet they despise Me; Vassula, share My pain, be one with Me;

We, us, Lord?

yes daughter; together we are suffering because of the infidelity of men; hold My Hand, together;

Together, Lord.

September 15, 1987

Jesus, I can't stand to have them wound You constantly. Hurry and let those thorns out!

O daughter, I will point them out to you, one after the other, I will tell you where they are placed and with My Strength you will pluck out one by one; and instead of those thorns that wounded Me, I will let

---
[1] 2 Co. 3:17 and 1 P. 1:11.

you offer Me only flowers from My garden of delights; for they have been growing under My Light, exhaling on earth their sweet fragrance, embellishing My garden; within My Heart and in Its most intimate depths, I still have the lance's blade; Vassula, this too will be removed; with My Power I will pull it out; I will not spare them this time!

unite My lambs and tell them that, "I, the Lord, bless them"

September 17, 1987

Vassula, I am sending you to him[1] so that he hears of My Message; will you ask him to receive you? will you ask him to guide you?[2]

(In an instant I suddenly saw in a vision given by the Lord, the demons who roam earth, overthrown! It was as if the dry soil they were standing upon, shook and cracked, lifted itself upward like a fist, overthrowing them and helplessly fell backward, powerless.)

I come to unite My children and bless them;

September 18, 1987

(This Friday I met the Greek priest inside the Greek Orthodox church. I told him everything. He listened, accepting all that I said. He wants to study now the revelation.)

September 20, 1987

daughter, by now you must have understood how I work; believe, My Vassula, for in you I will breathe many more revelations; abandon yourself entirely to Me and let My finger imprint

---

[1] The Greek Orthodox priest, Alexanthros.
[2] There God means, advise me.

on you My Word; come, little one, and caress Me;

Yes, Lord.

(By this Jesus means to caress Him on His big portrait I have from the Holy Shroud. It is in my habit while I meditate and talk to Him to often stretch my hand on His portrait caressing His Wounds and as if I want to wipe away the streaks of blood, soothing Him. This I do without thinking because of my meditation, which absorbs me entirely.)

September 20, 1987

Vassula, Garabandal's apparitions of Myself and My Mother should be authenticated; hear Me, Vassula, every time My Mother appeared to My chosen souls illuminating them with Her grace, I stood beside Her, but no eye could see Me; I sometimes appeared as an infant to bless those that glorified Me;

daughter, I wish that these places of apparitions are honoured more; I wish that the Holy See would honour Me by blessing those Sacred places; Vassula, I do not mean Lourdes and Fatima, I mean Garabandal as well; I come to glorify Garabandal's apparitions;

I wish to see My Holy See there and bless that place, rectifying all that has been distorted and wrongly proclaimed by My sacerdotal souls who wound Me, lift the doubts and efface the abuses given by those who defied the apparitions, would My Holy See do this for Me?

Lord My God, how will they know all this?

leave, Vassula, this work for Me; I will find a way of letting them know; daughter, I wish that each time I give them a sign of My Presence, no matter how small, I wish that My Holy See glorifies My sign by blessing it; I want the world to know of My Presence, of My Riches, of My Mercy and of My Heavenly

Works; I wish that My Holy See propound My given signs in larger scale, feeding the world; I want My land fertile; do not let them pluck the few flowers left; I want this wilderness irrigated, who will water My garden? why do they neglect My flowers?

Beloved Jesus, if I'm not mistaken, it took them seven years to confirm your miracle of Fatima. My God, I can see refusals, rebukes, difficulties of accepting.

flower, do not grieve; let Me help you; Vassula, I always reach My goals;

September 21, 1987

My God, how much I want everyone to love You and turn to You, recognising You.

O daughter, how much I want this too!

(God seemed longing for this to happen!)

How I wish that the world realises that You are among us ever so present. How much You love us, how I wish that they realise we are only passing by on earth, and that you are waiting for us, how I wish that they love one another, stop their hatred and egoism, live for one another, care for one another, worship You our Father, unite, how I wish them to believe in Your signs and not hide them away thinking they are making You a favour. How I wish they realised how wrong they are and see your Riches!

Vassula, your desires are given by Me to you; they are infiltrating in you I will keep My Flame ablaze in you, altar, forever; diffuse My words, "I, the Lord, bless My children of Garabandal"

Lord, I diffuse in the capacity I have. I need channels to diffuse it broader.

Vassula, I have given you witnesses;

You mean my friends?

others too;

You mean from the Church, the priests?

yes, Vassula, they are your witnesses;

Yes, Lord.

let Me engrave My words on you;

Jesus, I just remembered, there is this man who doesn't believe at all it's from You, the revelation. It's the first one.

I know;

But why?

for the simple reason that he is wise;

Oh My God, I have so many desires!

just ask Me;

Just ask?

yes, beloved, ask;

Anything?

anything;

I desire a change, My God, for the better. I desire that their hearts get enflamed with love for You and that billions worship You adoring You, all on their knees. I wish them to feel like I feel, how much You love us, and how near You are to us and how close we can be with You; a Father, a Friend, a God everything in one. Couldn't You shine Your Light on them and wake them up as You did with me? I want them to share the same happiness and closeness I have with You. Please, Father, they are also Your children.

Vassula, all will be done; I will guide many back to Me, despite their wickedness, I will help them; weary not of striving with your God; we, us?

Yes, Lord.

September 22, 1987

little awareness pleases Me! daughter, I am pleased;

(Jesus told me this because I concentrated on His actual Presence, trying to see how He looked. His hair today was all pulled backwards.)

when I see you trying to be aware of My Presence, it glorifies Me; let us pray; daughter, start in this way,

"O Beloved Creator,
Holy Spirit,
I bless You for the Works
You have showered upon me,
I bless You for the Light
You shed upon Me,
Glory be to God Almighty,
amen"

(Jesus knew I had difficulties in finding the right words of praise for Him; this prayer is just for me.)

September 23, 1987

betrothed, do not listen to those who are in deep sleep, for they know nothing, feel nothing, see nothing, hear nothing; how could they, since they are sleeping and thus totally unaware!

(Jesus made me understand of the two worlds. One which is material, physical, then the other one, invisible and spiritual.
Later, much later, when my apostolate started, I was invited to meet one of Garabandal's seers. It was as if God carried me on His Wings so that I bless her as God wanted me to do and give a blessing too to the others through the phone. I started to realise how God works. He asks something almost impossible for us to do, but He helps you do it with the Power of the Spirit.)

come, it is I, Jesus Christ, Beloved Son of God; I can, if I wanted, give you more proofs, but I am limiting you for the reasons I have; guiding you blindly pleases Me, it glorifies Me;

then, I want that this become a lesson for those whose wisdom blinds them; I want you innocent, simple; guiding you in this special way was so that My religious souls understand that I, the Lord, give abundantly; daughter, tell them that it is not difficult to believe in My Supernatural Works; why, am I not God and Spirit?

be like children and believe; who of the children would doubt that it is I, writing, guiding in this way, if you showed them My Works? be innocent!

September 24, 1987

(I felt St. Mary near me.)

Vassula, yes, it is I, your Mother; I have appeared to My children of Garabandal; I let them see Me and hear Me; I have appeared to them and they know it; I want you to bless them;

St. Mary, help me accomplish Your wishes.

I will guide you, Vassula;

Thank You.

(I felt amazed. Later on I smelled incense odour around me.)

it is I, Jesus, I blessed you and fragranced you with My incense;

ecclesia will revive! we are one; when I will unite My Church I will not wait further, can you feel how My Soul longs for you? I will fetch you beloved, I love you;

(I was pleased hearing this.)

I feel I do not belong here anymore and Earth is indeed an exile.

beloved, having you in this exile makes Me suffer too, but all will not be in vain; I love My creation and you are to bring My creation back to Me; I suffer seeing you down on earth; live for Me, daughter, you must remember how I sacrificed Myself; would you do the same for Me, your Father?

Make me worthy for You and for any sacrifice, Lord.

beloved, I the Lord, bless you; come, all will not be in vain;

September 25, 1987

(This morning I smelled incense smell again. I knew that He was standing at that particular spot.)

My remnant, all I ask of you is love; love Me; diffuse My words which are:

"I, the Lord, bless My children of Garabandal, I love them"

beloved, assemble them, unite them; accept all that has to come, whether it may be joy or suffering; I am before you;

Yes, Lord. May Your Will be done, and your wishes realised.

come, feel Me; let us share everything;

September 26, 1987

Vassula, let us deliver a soul, very dear to Me, who is very near Satan's flame; she does not realise his insidious game he has laid for her;

Who is this soul, Lord?

she is one of My brides;

A nun?

yes, a nun, she has neglected Me, taken by her vanity; beloved, bring her back to Me with your love; I love her; love Me and she will be delivered; Vassula, these Works are mysterious to you and to many, but believe Me, I am Jesus and Wisdom; now you will bless Me; feel Me, it glorifies Me; all will be done according to My plan;

Jesus! It's SO wonderful to be with You in this way!!

Vassula,

It's wonderful, marvellous!!

Vassula, will I ever abandon you?[1] love Me, amend for others whose hearts became icy-cold towards Me; altar, live for Me, replenish your flame from Mine altar! never forget how much I love you; stay ablaze, enkindle hearts, quench My thirst,

Beloved Jesus, keep me near You for without You, I'm lost.

near Me you will stay, have you forgotten our links? you are bonded to Me with eternal bonds;

Thank You, Lord, for taking care of me, the zero of zeros, the one who denied You.

I have been denied even by Peter, but on him I laid My first foundations of My Church, have you forgotten? I am the Lord, who loves you ineffably, and upon

---

[1] When He says this I almost die each time. God can have this tone only.

you, soul, I have engraved My Words; I am your Strength; keep Me in your heart now and forever;

I shall, Lord. I'll keep faithful.

come, let us share this day; be my companion;

September 27, 1987

(It was again as though all hell broke loose. The devil raged. He tormented my soul, to the point that I found myself asking the Lord to go on without me; that I would always love Him but I simply have no strength left to continue. Immediately I regretted my words. I then asked the Lord to leave me for my unworthiness. During my rest I saw myself on a rough road, fallen. Near me I saw Jesus' feet, bare. He bent and lifted me again. Then in front of me I saw a large staircase of around 100 steps, and at the top the Saints were standing, calling me to climb up there. I turned around and saw a familiar figure. A priest, he had humour and was talking to me in Italian. I recognised Padre Pio! Near him I saw St. Francis of Assisi. St. Francis approached me. All were encouraging me to continue.)

Jesus?

I am; Vassula, do not fear;

Jesus, forgive me for being weak.

your weakness will be annihilated in My Strength;

io, sono con te, Padre Pio;

My God, is this happening?

yes, he is with Me, Vassula, and beatified by Me; I am with you, My Mother and all the Saints;

(Later on, after the Charismatic group, I couldn't follow what was going on, because of mere ignorance; also that I craved for silence. I felt guilty, very guilty with ignorance.)

Vassula, do not worry, every man has got his own way of glorifying Me and praising Me; I have given you this way;[1] I and you, you and I; you are to worship Me in Silence; remember, I have already instructed you a few months back;

(True: May 31, 1987.)

at your side I stand;

(I felt Him so near I could touch Him solidly. My soul was happy again and in peace.)

little one am I not your Spouse? well then, will I not console you when you need to be consoled?
come to Me and I will lift your burdens, come to Me and I <u>will</u> console you! Confide in Me daughter, I am your Spiritual Director, I am your Spouse, I am He who loves you most, I am your Creator and God; come and fall in My arms and feel My warmth;

(Jesus left my soul in total harmony and peace.)

September 28, 1987

(Jesus was calling me. I was as eager to meet Him as He was. I don't know but it seemed ages since we were together.)

O come, beloved! how impatiently I have waited for this moment to meet you in this way!
together Vassula, together you and I will sanctify Garabandal; for Holy it is,[2] since My Mother and I appeared;

---

[1] In writing.
[2] Even that was done, without my planning to go there. It came about in a natural way.

May Your will be done, Lord.

Vassula, to be timid[1] is not a sin; I am telling you this;

(I was happy hearing this. Suddenly my soul longed for Him.)

look at Me, little one; to languish for Me glorifies Me; languish for Me, I paid for you with the price of My Blood;
 Vassula, why look around for a Spiritual Director?

I don't know.

with Me you will learn, for I am Wisdom and Truth; come to Me and I will instruct you; Vassula, I love you;
 tell him[2] this, that I am going to restore My Church, I will revive My Church; I have selected you to work with Me; Vassula, meet him, talk to him, caress Me by saying how I taught you to caress Me glorifying Me;[3] love Me, Vassula for love wards off divine justice when it is about to strike sinners;

(Later on:)

Vassula, are you happy that I have liberated you?

Yes, My God. I'm very happy to be with You. I feel attached to You and happy.

do you believe Me now that I have bonds of Love on you?

I do now, Lord.

little one, bless Me;

I bless You, Jesus, and I love You and thank You.

Vassula, do you know that signs I have been giving and will continue to give, to make My Name be known to you, so that the Love I have for you all, may be in you and so that I may be in you; but many of My sacerdotal souls have disowned Me in the presence of men;

How, Lord?

by disowning My signs, they have disowned Me their God; have I not said that the man who disowns Me in the presence of men will be disowned in the presence of My angels?
 have I not said that I will continue to make My Name known to you? why, then, do they doubt that I am among you and that it is by My Mercy I give you signs and miracles which are barely honoured; for let Me tell you, daughter, they have taken the key of knowledge! neither have they gone in themselves nor have they let others in who wanted to;

My God! You seem so angry, Lord!

Vassula, the time has come to Glorify Me; be alert and stay near Me; I love you little one, be one with Me;

Yes, Lord.

us, we?

Yes, us.

come;

September 29, 1987

My God, You seem to be unhappy with some of your sacerdotal souls.

Vassula, they are responsible for so many souls; not only do they fall, but with them they drag so many other souls,

---

[1] I was wondering if to be timid is a sin.
[2] Him: is the Charismatic priest. He is new here; just transferred.
[3] On the Holy Shroud picture.

But Lord, there must be many who are good, loving You, working as You want them to. I know some.

ah Vassula, there are many following My instructions, immolating, living humbly, loving one another, feeding My lambs; they are the salt of the earth, the beloved of My Soul; they are My Abels, they are the balm for My Wounds, assuaging My pain; to My sorrow, among them are the Cains too, the arrows of My Body, treacherous, blinded with vanity, wicked and with despicable inclinations; they are the thorns of My Head, numerous are their sins, hypocrisy is their master and it is to those My divine justice flares up;

take My Hand daughter, keep close to Me and I will point out to you those thorns; I will lead you with divine force into the very depths of My Body, I will let you recognise the lance's blade; I will not spare the Cains, Vassula, for what have they to offer Me? their hands are empty and have nothing to offer My lambs; they love to show themselves in public, they love to be greeted obsequiously, they are like salt having lost its taste; I tell you truly daughter, they are today's Pharisees!

Oh God, this is terrible.

Vassula, for this reason, everything that has been hidden will come to light and everything covered will be uncovered, for this is My will;

come now, do not forget My Presence;

No Lord, I look upon You as My Holy Father, Holy Friend, Holy Brother, and I look upon St. Mary as My Holy Mother, You are my Holy Family. How can I forget You?

beloved, I am your Spouse too, this is the way I wish you to love, love Us intimately, nevertheless never forgetting that we are Holy, honouring Us; We are your Holy Family, I am your God; be alert;

Yes, Lord.

let us go;

Let us.

October 1, 1987

(Morning. I had been occupied all morning with a visitor here who was trying to sell me cosmetic products. It was all unnecessary as it was all a waste of time. But she was sent by a friend of mine.)

little one, I love you to distraction; I am your well-Beloved; why Vassula? do not withdraw from Me! you are guessing correctly;[1] My love is again inflamed and when It is, I allow Myself to demand love; I desire you to live for Me only; I want you to fix your eyes on Me; look at Me, love Me, fragrance Me, adorn Me, bless Me, desire Me, breathe for Me, smile only for Me, tell Me how much you love Me your God, seek to bring others to Me, satisfy My insatiable thirst; <u>I am thirsty</u> Vassula! I thirst for love, I thirst for souls; Vassula, why bring Me rivals, do not bring any more rivals, do not! eulogise Me, I have given you abundantly, will you not gratify Me for all I am giving you?

I have walked with you in My garden of delights, we shared its beauty; I have shared My joys and sufferings with you; I have laid My Cross on you, we are sharing It together, sharing Its anguishes, sorrows and pain, we share Its Love; have I not lifted you to My breast feeding you, healing you? I have taken you as My bride sharing My Cross as our matrimonial bed; will you look at Me?

(I looked at Jesus' face.)

could I ever abandon you flower? I am He who loves you most; remain near Me;

---

[1] I could feel Jesus' Heart inflamed again, overflowing with love.

here,[1] listen, I will tighten our bonds even more now; I want you closer, I want you one with Me; who was first to hold you?

How, Lord?

I was first to consecrate you and lay eyes on you; Vassula I have created you for Myself; let Me remind you who you are, you are nothing else but dust and ashes and it is out of My immense pity I lifted you to life from among the dead; remember always this;

(The pastor came and I showed him the revelation. To start with he did not believe.[2] Then he denied St. Mary as our Holy Mother and never heard of apparitions. He did not believe in any Spiritual Works. He is against Holy pictures. He probably thought I was not normal.)

Vassula, I am Wealthy, but very few know of My Riches! when I was in flesh, have I not been despised, have I not been looked upon with contempt, have I not been called a blasphemer? have I not been rejected as the stone rejected by the builders that became the keystone?

honour Me by accepting contempt, mortification, humble yourself, be like Me, remember? have I not said that you are to serve Me among wretchedness, have I not said that you will have no rest? accept what I offer you, fear not of mortifying yourself;

I will leave two drops of Blood from My Bleeding Heart [3] on your heart covering it entirely; hallowed by My Hand, live under My Light, learn to be rebuffed;

---

[1] It was as if He had a sudden idea, stopped, pointing at our ankles which I saw tied to each other.
[2] Later in the years, I found out he was an evangelist. At that time I still did not know the differences.
[3] Jesus saying to me this seemed to be very sad. My pain was nothing compared to His. I wanted to console His pain forgetting my pain.

(I felt St. Mary near me.)

St. Mary?

light a candle for Me, Vassula, and repair his fault;[4] ask Jesus to forgive him; would you do this for Me?

I will, St. Mary.

amend, beloved; do not doubt of Jesus' Works; honour us;

I will, St. Mary.

October 2, 1987

it is I, Jesus; let it be known that any image of Mine or of My Mother's is to be honoured, for it represents Us as My Cross is representing Me; let it be known that My Holy Shroud is indeed authentic, It is the same that covered Me; blessed by Me, Vassula, enter in My Heart, let Me Hide you in there; rest; come, come to your Father;

(I felt like God was enveloping me, I was enwrapped by Him and happy.)

October 5, 1987

(I would go and repair for the pastor, as St. Mary asked me to do. Later on my cousin Ismini rang me up telling me they will go visit Turin in Italy, and asking if we'd like to go with them. Finally, I thought, it was my dream always to go there and visit the Cathedral that has the Holy Shroud. Jesus has arranged it again for me. I would go.

My cousins drove us to the hotel where they usually go. Turin is an enormous town, but our hotel was 500 meters from what I went for! Jesus made it easy for me. We arrived Saturday lunchtime, and after a while I went to the Cathedral. I was very impressed. Upstairs was the Holy Shroud

---

[4] For rejecting Her.

in the dome of the Cathedral. I thought I saw the Holiest of places. Peace and Holiness reigned in that dome. I felt it in me, it was wonderful.

Later on I left for the hotel. It was evening when my cousin returned from shopping. I rushed to her to tell her where I was, but she seemed to be flying towards me, she didn't want to hear me, she wanted me to hear her, for what she saw and discovered was so wonderful.

She said, "Vassula, that road we passed by 10 times and I, for so many years, I never saw St. Mary's statue there. But it's enormous! Almost three meters high. It's so beautiful, Her dress with so many pleats, and her blue cape. She looked so beautiful, and She has Her arms opened like She'd like to embrace the world, you must come and see Her. You passed by Her, haven't you seen Her? At each side of Her were satin curtains, red-scarlet, shiny and beautiful." I said I passed it but I only saw the curtains which were worn-out, half red and half yellow. She told me that she too for years did not notice it. I had seen no statue.

The following day, Sunday, she wanted me to go and see the enormous statue so I said, "After I take you to the Cathedral where the Holy Shroud is." So she followed me. It was Sunday Mass. We stayed half an hour, then after lighting a candle we left for the big statue of St. Mary. We arrived there and my cousin almost fainted. For there was no big statue, or even small. There were no shiny red-scarlet curtains. There were the ordinary worn-out, yellow-red curtains I had seen, but no statue.

She did not understand it. But I did. Below the curtains was an interior door. She pushed it and it was a church. I said to her, "This is why we came to Turin, to go to this church, called Madonna di Rosario, to repair. The Church of St. Mary. The huge beautiful statue you saw was to pull and bring us here. Our Mother called us. She gave you the apparition of Herself in statue, big so that it impresses you, to pull us here. And She wants Her candle lit in Her Church, to amend for the priest's words." We entered and it was such a beautiful Church. Mass was on. We stayed till it was over. We went forward to a golden statue of St. Mary and Jesus as a Child, and it was there we lit her candle praying for Jesus to forgive us and him.)

Jesus, is this correct?

Vassula, yes, it is exactly as you recounted it;

I will lift you to Me as soon as you accomplish your mission; My Soul longs for you; Vassula hear My Mother;

Vassula, tell Ismini how much I love her; child, I gave her this image of Myself to attract her attention and lead you into My Church; beloved ones how I love you; honour Us, beloved, honour Us; amend for your brethren;

remember how close We are to you all; Vassula never get discouraged for I am beside you; lean on Jesus always; daughter, think of Jesus' Passion; live for Him, glorify Him;

Only with Your help and the help of Jesus am I able to do all this. I want to honour You.

I love you all; I bless Ismini; I have blessed her and her husband in My Church;

I bless You, St. Mary.

I bless you too;

(Later on:)

Forgive me, Lord, for My total unworthiness and failures and lack of every good, making me offend You by this in Your presence.

I forgive you fully;

I love You, dear Lord.

every time you tell Me I love you, I overlook all your wretchedness, letting it pass by and stop My divine Justice from striking you, Vassula, for indeed you are wretched beyond words; you soothe My anger by telling Me you love Me;

(Jesus seemed severe, I feared Him.)

I fear You.

I am Love, so do not fear Me;

Oh Jesus, I wish I wouldn't be so wicked and ungrateful and spiteful.

I pity you and it is out of pity I seldom flare up against you;

I know I don't deserve a drop of grace on me, You have been too good to me, patient, You never got angry with me. You only loved me with my mistakes. You spoilt me.

Vassula, for such is My Mercy!

Jesus.

I am;

My God.

I am;

I ask You to teach me to love You more and as You wish so that You can spare me and so that I may honour You.

little one, I am your divine Teacher who will teach you; never doubt, never doubt of My Forgiveness;

No Lord, I will not doubt. Make me worthy of You because of your Grace and approach to me, allow me to glorify you. Forbid me to sin and from constantly offending You with my sins, Beloved.

bless Me;

Jesus, I bless You. Father, I love You.

at My Stations I desire to see you;

Oh Jesus, how? I want to but how, with who, who will guide me?

(From desperation my eyes filled.)

reserve your tears for the time you will hear offences being said on account of My Mother;

Oh Jesus, help me.

daughter lean on Me, let Me instruct you, please Me by being pliant as you are, come, be near Me, I love you;

I love You, Jesus. Have mercy on my ignorance.

I have; delight Me and say:

"Lord, let Me be your victim,
the victim of your burning Love;
I desire to worship You and You only,
stretched on Your Cross with You,
never looking left or right;
I desire to quench Your
thirst by earning souls for You;
victim of Your Love I will be,
I love You;"

say it!

(I said it.)

from now on you will never leave My Heart, Vassula; select, Vassula; either your life or a victim's life, select;

Jesus I don't want You to leave me. I want to be with You, at Your side.

then you have chosen well, you will resemble Me, be a victim of Love; flower, you will flourish under My Light;

I thank You, bless You, for all that You give me and for the compassion You have upon me.

have My Peace, daughter; never forget My Presence; allow Me to rest in you, for this is My home;

Jesus You make me happy and I learn from You.

flower, I am your Master and God; come, us, we?

Yes, Lord.

October 6, 1987

(I felt poor. And I am. I am not pleasing God because of my ignorance and slowness to understand. I'm not happy with myself. He was so right about me as being "by far" the most wretched of His creatures. I hate now talking about how this has started, because I find I am talking about myself. It's ugly, very ugly. But friends and people want to hear about how it started so I was obliged to explain and the more I went on I could not avoid despising every time I said something about myself, to the point that it made me decide that from now on I shall not explain how it started, thus I will avoid talking about myself. I thought they could find out from others. If they are curious, they will not be appeased by me. If they want to read because they believe, God will enlighten them. I shall not be my own witness. I shall leave everything in God's hands. He makes the impossible possible, so I shall be from now on just His pencil and paper, His secretary, a secretary taught by Him to love Him, and, taking down His words, I shall be His tablet.)

yes, be My tablet, letting Me engrave on you My Word; be soft though so that My Word can be deeply engraved on you;

(I forgot myself and was sitting on the floor. He looked at me, reminding me. I knelt.)

I love you, Vassula together you and Me, we are sharing My Cross;

hear Me Vassula, you are the beloved of My Soul have you not yet understood? feel, feel how I, your God, love you, My child, My well-beloved bride;

(I felt Jesus enveloping me in Him.)

listen Vassula, all the heavens resound with My cries, My desire is unshaken, it must have reached your ears; I desire flexibility, how will you unite if you are inflexible? I wish to unite My Church, will you feel Me and listen to My Voice?

My God, why don't You let the heads of the Church know about Your message?

I will, daughter; embellish My Church; love Me; ecclesia will revive!

(I saw a wonderful image of Jesus, Majestic, Glorified, a beautiful image of Jesus, triumphant as a King, showing me a sign with His Hand raised and making a sign with His Fingers lifted. It was as though He was signalling me VICTORY.)

October 8, 1987

Jesus?

I am;

Jesus, I wish to repair for every offence said about our Blessed Mother. I cannot bear to hear offences said from Your creature about Her, especially from ministers. I would see my head roll and defend Her.

Vassula, I will let you understand how Love suffers hearing those offences;
Vassula, let it be known that I the Lord honour My Mother; let it be known to those who offend Her that She is the Queen of Heaven and that on Her Head I the Lord placed a crown, a crown of twelve stars; She reigns beloved and this is written in My Word; I honour My

Mother and as I honour Her you should honour Her;

I love you, both My Mother and I, bless you;

Lord, the pastor denied Her as our Holy Mother, that we should venerate Her, and when I told him that You said it from the Cross, he said that You meant it only for John, and that nowhere in the Bible is written that She is our Mother too, and that we are Her children.

but again I tell you daughter, that My Mother is your Mother too, you are Her children, it is written in My Word and I am telling it again for those who do not know, Scripture says,

Where, Lord?

in the book of Revelation, that when Satan failed in his pursuit of My Mother, he was enraged with Her and went away to make war on the rest of Her children, that is, all who obey the Commandments and bear witness for Me;

Thank You, Lord Jesus, for helping me.

Vassula, I have told you, before you I always am; stay small so that I may accomplish My Works; I love you;

I love You, Lord, and bless You.

us, we?

Yes, Lord.

October 10, 1987

Jesus?

I am;

Oh Jesus, I never knew that Christians do not believe, I mean venerate St. Mary, I never knew how they felt about Her. I never knew there was such a tremendous difference between Christians. I didn't know it is so bad.

oh Vassula, it is worse than you think!

Oh Jesus, why is it so bad?

because, Vassula, My Body has been torn apart; I want My Body united!

Would they then venerate our Blessed Mother if they are united?

child, they will;

Do I understand that "they will" means they will, it will be?

I will bend them, I will bend their knees and they will venerate and honour My Mother;

Yes, Jesus.

little one, I will revive My Church;
  come, us, we?

Yes, Lord.

October 12, 1987

(While visiting somebody, I found a magazine of science which promote the scientific resolutions of thought and discouraging any spiritual work. Nowadays every supernatural thing has its 'natural' explanation. Words like, double personality, ESP, subconscious, suggestion of thought, hypnosis, or mass hypnosis, or auto-suggestion. e.g. for the stigmatics it can be explained by auto-suggestion, thus self-imposed, schizophrenia, or sex-complexes. People seem to want to find always a logical explanation. There would have been no big prophets like Isaiah these days because their case would go into scientific files. There would be soon no saints with stigmatas without classifying them as schizos and self induced by auto-suggestion and hysteria. For me it appears that they are trying to compete with God

and prove that they can prove to Him He is not Omnipotent.)

Oh God, why?

Vassula, numerous are those that do not believe in Me;

But I ask You one thing, I really mean it. I ask You to destroy all these theories and teachings that try to wipe You out. They are Your enemies. Why let it multiply? Destroy it, otherwise it will destroy our faith. Please do it.[1]

I will; hear Me, grieve not, never doubt, have faith; never weary of writing, beloved; this is why I come; it is because I cannot see you lost; do you now understand, Vassula; little one I will never see you fall;

What about the others, I don't want to see the others fall either. I desire You to support them as much as You support me.

Vassula, I will help all of you;

(God seemed pleased.)

Oh God, forgive me for demanding things, I'm impulsive but I can't bear injustice. Forgive me for being so direct.

I forgive you, child; say it;

(I had other things in mind.)

I must tell You that as it is right now, these people will not be convinced to their dying last breath, at the most they will file it under the word UNEXPLAINED; but would not say, "Well then this or that comes from God."

I will convince them; My power is beyond theirs, I will show to you all that I am Omnipotent; My Omnipotency will be seen wherever you may be; no eye will be able to deny it, no man will deny that this sign comes from Me;[2] beloved, how will their theories appear then?[3] how will their men of science feel? what will happen to all their wisdom? I will show to them how their wisdom appears in the face of My Wisdom;

I will efface from this world what they believe is wisdom; this is one of the reasons I use you engraving My words on you, to be able and foretell My Plan; I the Lord Am, I was and will always be and it is not up to you to look at Me as not; I Am;

O beloved God whom I adore, I wish that this plan is for now, today, or next week!

I will fulfil My Plan Vassula, as I have always fulfilled everything I started;
little one let us pray,

"beloved Father
I love You, I bless You,
I thank You for Your Mercy,
make me worthy of You
so that You are able to use me fully,
use me as You wish,
I love You, amen;"

beloved, I bless you; look at Me;

(I looked.)

You are smiling.[4]

write it;

And You are showing me Your dimples when You smile.

I love you;

I love You, Lord.

---

[1] I had found myself telling God what to do, it was beyond my strength.
[2] Will this be a sign in heaven one day?
[3] God did not reply.
[4] I hesitated writing the rest.

October 13, 1987

(I saw Jesus at the door of the bedroom. I knew He was indicating to me to write, like somehow He was waiting.)

I was at the door, come you will work with Me;

(Sometimes Jesus wants to prove to me that my discernment was right.)

I will foretell you what has to come so that from now on those that call themselves wise will believe in My Works and follow Me;

daughter, I will heal many; <u>Love will return to you as Love</u>, fulfilling My Word; in a short time I will prove to you that this comes from Me Vassula; I am the Lord, beloved, to Me you will come; hear Me, I want to remind you what I have asked you a few days ago; let it be known all over, diffuse My words: "I, the Lord, bless My children of Garabandal;" I want them to hear Me; oh Vassula, how I long for this;

Lord Jesus, I will try within my capacity, with the sources You have given me. I am impotent and You are Omnipotent; would You help me, Jesus?

I will help you, remember how I work;

Vassula, let it be known that in a short time I will send you all a sign coming from above, you will understand that it comes from Me, I will shine on you, I love you all;

how I love you all! I love you beyond your understanding; I am your Creator; have I not said that your image I have it carved in the palm of My Hand? how can I ever abandon you?

I'm thinking of the vision You gave me. The punishment that I feared.

I will make you see it again so that it bears a mark on you; *Again Lord, help us to avoid it. I know You don't like doing this to us and get no pleasure out of it. Tell me what to do.*

Vassula, true; I get no pleasure in punishing you, I wish that My creation returns to Love; tremendous reparations have to be done; amend, those that can amend for others; My creation has to change; daughter, My creation has to learn and believe in My Spiritual Works; My creation will have to accept Me as Omnipotent; My sacerdotal souls must understand how wrong they are denying My Works of today;

Yet there are many who do accept.

there are those who do not and it is to those I speak; I also speak of those who have split My Body; believe Me, daughter, My cup of Justice is full for having torn My Body apart; I will not spare them any longer;

Vassula, allow Me to till you for just some more time, soon I will be collecting My crops; come, beloved;

Lord, may all Your Will be done.

October 15, 1987

I will mortify you like I was mortified, I will humble you; Vassula, I love you and it is out of love I watch over you; since I am directing you I know what is best for your soul; I will give you this penitence so that it washes away your tendencies of vanity; I, the Lord, will see that your soul lacks nothing; I will always watch over you;

Thank you, my God, for helping me.

I am using you now but in a short time you will be delivered and in My arms you will be;

daughter, remember when I was in flesh among you, My life was nothing else but sufferings, sacrifices, anguishes, sorrows, the lot; I had no rest;

Vassula, I have brought you up for this Message; My flower, you are to bear My Cross together with Me to the very end; I love you infinitely;

I love You, Lord, and if You want me mortified, I will do Your Will.

be pliant so that I may do whatever I please with you; little one speak of Me;

(Jesus means to the Greeks on Rhodes island. The Greeks are very eager to hear and easily open their ear.)

October 16, 1987

Vassula, I always reach My goals;
come, I will tell you; one day My Kingdom[1] on earth will be as it is in Heaven; My Church will be united and blessed for all My devout ones will understand one another; exalted by My Hand, purified by My Blood, My Church will be One;

May Your desires come true, Lord. Many of us desire this; – enlighten those who need to be helped to understand Your desires.

October 18, 1987

daughter, will you take My hand and continue My Works?

Yes Lord, I never want to leave Your Hand.

I want it to be clear to you, what I have said previously; I said that I will foretell events that will take place so that there would be no doubt that this comes from Me;

Jesus, have You not said that the only sign You will give is me?

yes, I have said that you will be the sign of My Works, I have designed My plan long before you were born;

flower, stay open so that My dew of righteousness drips in you; sip from Me My Virtues; I want you perfect; I want My flower embellished, saturated with My Perfection; I want My flower to fragrance My divine Myrrh; look at Me, Vassula;

(I looked at Jesus.)

all My wishes will be accomplished; would you devote more of your time for Me, Vassula?

My time is Your time. I live for You.

replenish then your lamp, take from Me;

Jesus, what can I say? You give me so much when I deserve nothing. You keep giving me and I can't even offer You anything that's close enough to what You are giving me. You give me Light. You woke me from the dead. You healed me and poured on me Your works.

glorify Me; who freed you, Vassula?

You did, Lord. Can I say something?

beloved, tell me;[2]

My God with Your Mercy, Love and Power, do unto my brethren as You have done unto me ... free them ... lift them to You, unite them to You, let them feel Your love as I feel it. I want to rejoice seeing souls approach You. Then unite all Christians and those who deny our Blessed Mother.

Vassula are you willing to perform sacrifices?

Yes Lord, if I can be used that way.

I will show you what I desire from you, beloved, derive from Me always; I love

---

[1] The Church.

[2] God sounded like a tolerant father.

you flower;[1] remember, reserve your tears for later on when your ears will hear how My own treat My Mother!

Do not let them anymore.

Vassula, the day will come, and that day is very near, when My Church will speak one language, but before this glorious day there will be tremendous upheavals, partly because of man's vanity, sin and lack of love, and partly because My Body is torn apart; let Me tell you once more, that My Body I will glorify and unite; flower, Love will unite you all; write down this too, stay small so that all authority will come from Me;[2] let it be known that My wishes are inflexible, they stand firmer than ever;

Which of Your wishes, Jesus?[3]

Vassula, I desire to diffuse those words to My children which are:

   "I, the Lord bless you, come to Me;"

Lord, lead me to them and help me diffuse Your words.

Vassula, lean on Me; live in My Light and rest;

October 19, 1987

(I want to add here, that while in Greece, I was reading St Thérèse of Lisieux; her biography. She was in my mind constantly, and while I was on the local bus and in deep contemplation on her, thinking of her with love, the bus stopped and there in my deepest contemplation I saw the Greek words for "I love you" and two hearts, each letter a foot tall; they were written on a bus station roof, four metres away from me. My senses being in another plane I knew she was telling me this. It was her message.)

daughter, do you realise that My plans have been laid out long before you were born?
   wait and you shall see; rest now, replenish always from Me; I love you;

Jesus, I love You, Beloved.

have My peace, daughter; I will see that you will lack nothing; seek your rest nowhere else but in My Heart;

Lord, I am asking You if there is anything one can do to help Mrs X's son.

hear Me, works of love are able to deliver him;

By who, Lord?

Vassula, by all of you;

Jesus, Beloved, I ask You with Your Divine Hand to bless the community in Bangladesh. I ask You to bless them all. Support them.

Vassula, tell them to cradle My love for it is within them; I am in the midst of My beloved ones; daughter, with My Hand I bless them;

(I prayed for Mrs X's son.)

believe in what you ask; little one, have faith in Me;

Jesus, can You see what's wrong with him?

I can;

Wouldn't You want him near You, Lord?

ardently I want him; beloved, Satan has a hold on him;

(I heard Satan yelling, "I refuse to let go!" He was furious.)

---

[1] My eyes had filled.
[2] I think Jesus means it for everybody.
[3] I think Jesus went on without answering.

Lord, Jesus, if You want me to suffer for him but bring him near You, let me do it. What can I do? Maybe I'll go without water for two days?

(Switzerland's climate is extremely dry and one drinks a lot.)

Vassula, suffer for him; do not drink any liquids while you bear My Cross;

I'll do this as a sacrifice.

beloved one, later on you will understand; care for your brother, sacrifice for him; I love him;

Jesus, I will.

October 21, 1987

(Today I had discouraging news. The Catholic theologian from Lyon whom I had put my hopes on, when he learned that I do not belong to the Catholic community, his enthusiasm became cold. He said I am experiencing God, but he does not understand that it's far beyond this, for God is giving a message to all of us, as far as the ecclesiastical authorities and the Holy See. But of course, why should he believe? I come from nowhere, so to speak; as I once said, if I was one of them I would have been accepted and they would have tried to glance at the message. And this is exactly what God is trying to teach us, not to differentiate from one another. We are all under one authority, God's authority. Why make a distinction? A distinction even upon the character of the person. I'm not wearing the habit, but does it matter, can I ask God why? He has chosen me as I am and wants me that way.)

Vassula, you are experiencing the same things as when I was in flesh on earth; remember Vassula, when the Pharisees questioned Me about who had given Me the authority to preach?

Yes, Lord.

beloved, My Message comes from Me; all authority will come from Me; you belong to Me; have I in any instant written that your authority will be given by mankind? little one, towards Wisdom lean your head;

(I became distressed and sad. Tears flowed out and I had to stop for a while to recover.)

My victim, I have chosen you to be the victim of My Heart, the sweet torture of your soul, victim of My Body and of My Soul; by the denials, anguishes and sorrows, Vassula, you will experience My life on earth; I will give it all to you in small doses with the capacity your soul can bear; you will, and you have already been, disbelieved, accused, mocked upon, rejected; Vassula, there will be more to come, yet, on the other hand, I have given you those who believe in My Message of Peace and Love; they are your witnesses;

let me remind you, that you too will be betrayed;[1]

Vassula, I love you; I, the Lord, am your support; to Me come and get consoled; let My Peace enwrap you, come, all authority comes from Me and not from men; you belong under <u>My Authority</u>, which is One; <u>One Authority</u>;

My God, thank you for giving me Your support. Thank you for giving me witnesses too. I will not raise my voice anymore, I should keep my words which were, "Do what you please with me, if you give me delights or sorrows, I will thank You all the same. You want me thrown I'll be thrown, You want me cuddled, I do not merit it. Do what Your Heart desires most. I am Yours."

yes, be soft so that I may engrave deep in you My Words; remember My Presence and My Love;

---

[1] By one?

October 22, 1987

(At 2.30 in the morning I woke up with my mouth and lips as dry as parchment from thirst. Jesus told me: "get up and drink now, two days are over;" I went and sipped some water, not much as I could not stand it.
This morning my soul, sad beyond imagination, longed for Him. Why has He awakened me, to refuse me the privilege of being among those who live in His house? If they knew their privilege! and I, to infuse in me the desire, but prevent me from entering and be surrounded by His Peace, instead, I have to be in exile and so much temptation ...)

O daughter! blessed of My Soul, blessed of My Heart, from within Me exhales My pain too; but, Vassula, I have created you to stay among mankind and integrate among them; I love you ineffably to the extent that fondness becomes folly; Vassula, wretched beyond words, sacrifice, beloved, yourself and be among wretchedness and Godless people, for you are to be My Net; let your Holy Father rejoice at your catch; let My Heart fill up this time with joy; draw souls to Me;

reserve your tears, for there will be none left when your ears shall hear the infamies said about My Mother!

Jesus do not let their tongue articulate when it comes to infamies.

Vassula, I, the Lord, will grant them My pardon for they know not what they are saying;

Will they ever learn, Lord?

all will learn, every creature will learn, provided that they listen; let Me answer the question in your mind;

But Lord You say 'provided', that means that there will be some who will not listen.

to My great sorrow there will be those who will shut their ears! those that will refuse to hear will not be spared this time; come now, get up and follow Me;[1]

October 23, 1987

(This morning I was wondering how Jesus must have felt when the Pharisees never believed Him and how difficult it must have been for Him to convince them that He was actually the Son of God. How misunderstood He was by them. It was beyond men's capacity to comprehend that it was possible at their time; they simply would not understand or accept such a miracle.)

and how many now understand or believe fully in My Message?

Quite a few do, more than those who do not.

tell Me, which number is greater of those who listen, believe and understand fully My Message, My sheep or My lambs?

(Here sheep represents the sacerdotals, and lambs represents the laity.)

who are more willing to hear?

I find that Your lambs are more willing, by experience now.

today is like yesterday; daughter, times have not changed; today is like yesterday; when I was on earth in flesh, some believed in Me as another prophet, only a few believed in Me as the Messiah; when the Pharisees heard Me they rushed to stone Me for blasphemy, and now Vassula, why are you surprised at what people believe? you come from Me and today I am sending you as My bearer with My Message of Peace and Love, I come to

---

[1] Jesus standing near me was urging me to get up.

unite My Church, but today is being like yesterday;

let Me tell you; the authorities will be perplexed and many will refuse to believe fully that this Message descends directly from Me, some will mock you; they will scrutinise you, others would not bother to spare you even a minute of hearing, some will misunderstand My Message, for this is beyond their wisdom again;

here I come, with My Heart in My Hand, offering It, All Merciful; using you who is weak and wretched, to be My instrument and manifest Myself through you to descend on earth and unite you; but I tell you truly, had they but looked into My beloved Johannes' inspirations,[1] all coming from Me, they would understand that the hour is at hand; seek his words, for every prophecy told by him comes truly from Me; little one, let them all see how I work;

My God and Beloved Father, I sometimes fear to face all the denials, mockeries, deafness, rejection for I truly believe that this is truly You. What happiness they would receive if they had really believed that out of Your boundless Mercy and Love You have descended to us and help us again, to unite us!! To redeem us!! To revive Your Church!

My remnant, fear not; if they mock you, they will be mocking Me; if they deny you, they will be denying Me; all that they do to you, they will be doing to Me;[2]

happy is your soul to discern what you discern, for I tell you that many souls of great esteem in My Eyes would have wanted to discern what you have discerned, but never could; to hear what you hear, feel what you feel, but never heard it or felt it; Vassula, upon you lies My grace;

> *I bless You, Father,*
> *for having looked upon*
> *Your most wretched creature*
> *and having poured on me*
> *all those graces.*
> *Glory be to God Almighty*
> *for shining on me.*

keep close to Me, for you will still face many more trials;

us, we?

Yes, Lord. We, us.

October 26, 1987

(In the night of the 24th God enlightened me to understand further the meaning of the Apparition of St. Mary as an immense statue to my cousin. It was to confirm that God is willing and allows statues in His Church which represent His Image and this of St Mary. Then in the night of the 25th God enlightened me again and made me understand that He agrees and allows us to decorate the Churches in images representing Him; photos, paintings etc.)

I allow My Church to bear My Image; do not strip My Body,[3] adorn Me, embellish Me, leave It as It is;[4] listen Vassula, I am the Church, trust Me;

(Later:)

beloved, I am Yahweh; write, daughter:

O creation, have I not raised saints and prophets to warn you of the end of times? have I not foretold that I will send you from My Celestial Hall an angel proclaiming My secret intention so that it may be fulfilled? the constancy of My Words will be reaffirmed;

---

[1] Pope John XXIII was praying for a Second Pentecost in which a renewal could take place; the renewal of God's creation, of God's Church, and a revival, so that the Church brings forth UNITY.
[2] God reminds me that He is sharing all my sorrows and anguishes, which consoles me.

[3] The Church.
[4] As the Orthodox and the Catholics decorate the Church.

have I not foretold you that My messenger's mission will be to communicate My Revelation? My testimony is the spirit of prophecy; rejoice and exult all you who are faithful to Me! woe for the unfaithful, for My Word will come upon them like a Sword striking them, destroying all their false wisdom, wisdom which inspired My creation to fall into Satan's nets, transforming My lambs into Godless, fearless, immoral people;

I have, Vassula, given you a vision of warning, an allusion of what I have done to Sodom and Gomorrah, let them take heed of My warning, for I the Lord, have foretold My creation that unless they repent and accept Me as their Creator, My Sword will strike them;

it is out of My boundless Mercy that I descend on earth[1] to warn you; I am the Spirit of Truth who speaks; listen to what I have to tell to My Churches, creation; do not stand still; forward My warning; I am standing at the door knocking, if anyone hears My voice and opens the door, I the Lord will enter to share his meal side by side with him; do not fear, I am fulfilling My Word; before you I stand;

Lord, are You maybe hinting to me personally to forward Your warning? If yes, how Lord, more than by photocopies?

all I ask from you, is love; let Me engrave on you; I have already selected those who are to forward My Message;

come, I am with you; feel Me, feel My Presence, yes;[2] love Me;

I love You, Jesus. Teach me to love You more, just like You want us to love You.

I am;

October 27, 1987

(The latest Catholic theologian lost interest immediately in me because I did not belong to his community.)

but, Vassula, of course you do not belong to them; you belong to Me; I am your Creator and Holy Father;[3] you belong under My Authority;

Lord, yes we are under Your Authority[4] but it is organised and there is a system of belonging in one of the Christian Communities, so I was told.

all are the same in My Eyes; I have never wanted My Body parted; it is you who have dismembered Me! you have decided upon My Body! you lamed Me;[5]

Oh God...

daughter have I not told you to reserve your tears for My Mother?

(Although He sounded strict, I could not help noticing that He was as sad as I was.)

Yes Lord, but You seemed so hurt. I am only human.

Vassula, this is because we are sharing My Cup; My Cup tastes bitter; tell the Holy See that it is I who sends you to them; hear Me, if they ask in which community you belong, tell them that you belong to Me and that you are under My Authority;

Lord, I do not like to argue but can't I tell that I am an Orthodox? I am an Orthodox.

orthodox! catholics! protestants! you all belong to Me! you are all One in My Eyes! I do not make any distinction, so then

---

[1] Figurative way.
[2] I discerned Jesus.

[3] Is. 9:5-6.
[4] Christ being the Head of the Church.
[5] There was one moment of silence and Jesus sounded so disappointed and sad. I felt guilty for having brought up the subject.

why fear? ask for My beloved Pope John Paul, he will not make any distinction; Vassula, tell him this: "beloved, I, the Lord, am standing at your door, knocking, will you hear Me calling? will you open the door? if you do, I will enter your house and share your meal side by side with you; prove victorious and I will allow you to share My Throne; hear Me, listen to what the Spirit is saying to the Churches;"

I am your Shepherd,
with Me you will lack nothing,
in meadows of green grass
I let you lie, beloved soul,
to the waters of repose I lead you,
where I revive your soul
by paths of virtue I guide you
for the glory of My Body
although you pass through
a gloomy valley, do not fear,
beside you I am to hearten you
I will feed you
under the eyes of your persecutors,
I have anointed you
and will always fill you;
for I am an abyss of Love
with boundless Mercy,
come and live
in the middle of My Heart;[1]

O Lord,
You are my Light and my salvation.
I need not fear.
I know You will shelter me.
I thank You with all my heart,
Lord my God,
I glorify Your name forever.
Your Love for me is so great,
pity me in my incompetence.

remain small, flower; grow in spirit, sip from My Virtues; come let Me always engrave on you My words;

Yes, Lord. I am happy to be with You.

Love will never abandon you; come, us, we?

Yes, Lord.

October 30, 1987

I have given My creation innumerable signs warning them; I raised up saints declaring My desires but have they [2] listened? has anything changed?

Lord, suppose they do this time, suppose they are willing, suppose they read and believe and unite and seek to glorify You rather than seek their own interests this time, had they believed in this message.

Vassula, ah Vassula, many would fear, even those who would believe in My Message and admit that it is I, through fear of being mocked upon and fear of their superiors; many would put honour from men before the honour that comes from Me; honour Me and diffuse My message;

Suppose, Lord, they do bend.

I would uplift My Justice then that lies heavily upon them; but they still hurl venomous arrows at one another, afflicting My Body; there will always be disharmony reigning among them because love is missing;

Vassula, had they followed My command to love one another as much as I love them and humble themselves, My Body today would reign in harmony; have they ever humbled themselves washing each others feet,[3] have I not given you this as an example so that you may copy what I have done? bend! bend to be able to unite!

---

[1] Ps. 23.

[2] The creatures.
[3] I had the impression here that Jesus meant that this gesture should be done from one church to the other.

soul, the time has come where My beloved servant John Paul should hear Me; I have indeed heard his cries, his cries have reached Heaven, his cries resound in the entire universe, his cries have reached My Ears!

let Me tell you: in a short time there will be one flock and one shepherd; I will lead all My sheep, even those that are not of this fold; Love will unite you, but before this, there will be tremendous tribulations, the entire Heavens will shake! be vigilant, daughter; hand over My instructions, they are all within My sacred writings; by forwarding [1] My Message you will understand;

Jesus, oh St. Mary, what will they say? Understand me St Mary, it is not in my position to face all those superior people.

Vassula, do not fear; your incapacity infatuates Jesus; stay small;

St. Mary, suppose they didn't listen?

little one, this divine revelation will be His last warning; if they do not want to listen or understand I will allow His Hand to fall on them and strike them; Vassula, all you have to do is love Him; be vigilant because Satan is furious and will try all sorts of traps; do not fear, I am guarding you;

Thank you St. Mary for encouraging me. Thank You for guarding me. I bless You.

Vassula, I bless you, child;

November 3, 1987

come, Love will instruct you; let it be known that I delight hearing the words, "allow me Father," and "if it is Your will"; these words, said in your prayers, infatuate Me; ask and it shall be given,

---
[1] Making it known.

but always remembering those words; come, Vassula, have My Peace;

I love You, Jesus. Allow me to bless You.

beloved, I bless you;

November 5, 1987

trust Me, let Me guide you where I wish; keep your hand in My Hand; have no fear, I will lead you into the very depths of My Wounded Body; Vassula, fulfil My Words;

daughter, <u>fear not</u>; I wish you to embellish My garden;

*Father, Righteous One,
I cannot deny my fear. Help me.
Allow me to receive Your Strength.
Allow me to grow in Your Light, in You.
Do not forsake me.
If it is within Your Will, make me worthy
so that You may use me and may share
in accomplishing <u>Your</u> desires.
I ask You to forgive my weaknesses
and incompetences in Your Mercy.
Do as <u>Your</u> Heart desires.
Let <u>Your</u> will be done, not mine.
Amen.*

Love will help you; remember though that as soon as My Word will be established, <u>to Me</u> you will come! I bear no more having you out in exile; My Soul longs for you!

Father! What joy you give me! What happiness and consolation your words give my soul! I'm so happy!

beloved, yes, love Me, desire Me; please this Heart that sought for you; I will soon be coming to you, but, while still in the world, be near Me by drinking Me and eating Me, by praising Me, by honouring Me; let Me rejoice <u>fully</u>;

do not be discouraged if the world denies you, because you do not belong to the world, no more than I belonged to the world while in flesh; you come from Me; I am your Father and in you I live as you live in Me; honour My Name, glorify My Body, remain in My Love; I will not fail you or desert you; so fear no one, beloved; sow My seeds which will bear fruit in holiness; be holy, for I am Holy;

"I am listening.
    What is Yahweh saying?
What God is saying
    means Peace and Love
for his children, for the earth, for His Body,
    if only they renounce their folly;
for those who fear Him,
    His redemption is near,
and the Glory will then live on earth.
    Love and Mercy now descended,
Righteousness and Peace
    now will embrace us;
Righteousness always preceding Him
    and Peace following His footsteps."

(God guided me to write this passage taken from Ps. 85:8-13, changing a few words.)

beloved, I said: <u>I am</u> going to water My orchard, I intend to irrigate My flower beds; hear Me: My rivulet will grow into a river and My river will grow into an ocean; and I will make discipline shine out; I shall send My Light far and wide glorifying My Body; so come, take My Hand and let Me lead you;

daughter, do no more today; rest in My Heart;

November 8, 1987

Jesus?

I am;
    if I had not delivered you, you would have been still today in deep sleep;

I feel very ashamed. I am indeed the last to talk. Whatever I do to try to repair and thank You, Lord, will not come near enough to what You've done again for me. Even when I want to pray for others, I feel guilty and hesitant because, Lord, how would I dare pray for others who are so far better than myself? How could 'the most wretched' pray for someone better than herself? It reminds me of Your words about the plank in the eye and the splinter in the other one's eye. I feel I've got a plank, a whole forest, so how could I with all this wood in my eye dare utter a sound? Unless, Lord, you deliver me. I ask You to allow me to ask You to clean me. Have mercy on my soul. If You want, make me worthy to enable me to pray with dignity for my brethren.

Vassula, I am pleased to hear your words, for not until you realise your unworthiness will you begin your way to perfection;

*If it is within Your will,
    allow me, Father,
to ask for Your help.*

daughter, replenish your lamp from Me, do not wait; grow in My light, little one; whoever will believe in this Message will believe not in you but in Me; I, the Light, descend into the world through you, so that whoever believes in My Message need not stay in the dark anymore; your witnesses know the truth, they know that these words are not your words, no, My Vassula, all what is written comes from Me, the Lord; I tell you truly that whoever welcomes you, welcomes Me;

No, My God, I'm not worthy!

why, Vassula, have I not purified you, have I not anointed you Myself to be Mine? indeed I will be manifesting Myself through you, so honour Me daughter;
    come, I will teach you My ways; I and you; let Me breathe in you, let Me rest in you, daughter; rest Me from those who wound My Soul; oh Vassula, if you only knew ... My Blood is gushing out again today;

Oh God and it's Sunday! Why?

little one, they are piercing My Heart through and through;

My God, let them pierce me instead!

hear Me, you will be; they will pierce you; come now, allow Me to rest in you, share My Cup daughter;

(Why, why is it like this, what is going on, why are they doing this to our God? A God of Love, of Peace, a Father, a Friend? How could they? I feel sick. Jesus is again today bleeding, suffering from our wickedness. The world, one could say, has been kidnapped by Satan, and Jesus is trying again to save us.)

My God, you give me so much pain to feel you so hurt. You, only Infinite Goodness and an Abyss of Love, why are they tormenting you? I cannot bear Your sufferings anymore, but I care for Your sufferings, Your pains. Lord, I care and love You.

Vassula, My Vassula, victim of My Soul, victim of My Heart, bear My sufferings and share them with Me, drink from My Cup, feel My scourgers; beloved of My Soul, what will I not do for you out of Love? I will allow you to share My sufferings; I have chosen you to be the victim of My Bleeding Heart, by all the sorrows of which yours is capable of bearing; victim of My Soul by all the anguishes, denials and mockeries your soul can bear; come, you will share My Cross;

I am your only Love; I have reached My goal; allow Me to be the sweet torture of your mind and soul; you please Me, for now I have extirpated all My rivals, they are all gone; none are left! it is I, your Jesus, only left with you! how I delight! and now let Me love you without restraint; let Me reign over you; I have found a place for My greatness and bounty; I do not love you for what you are, but for what you are not;

come, your nothingness infatuates Me, your incapacity leaves Me speechless;

Lord, I feel embarrassed.

Vassula never seek to be something; stay nothing for every divine work I will accomplish will be purely Mine and not yours;

My Church will be one, under one Authority; have I Myself not asked Peter to feed My lambs? have I not chosen him to feed My sheep, have I Myself not uttered these words:

"you are Peter and on this rock
I will build My Church;"

why this arrogance among the nations, these futile plots among the people? I had selected Peter, a man after My own Heart, the rock, on whom I would build My Church; why then distort My Command?

Whom are You referring to, Lord?

I am speaking to those who scheme and plot against My foundation, do you not realise that your plots will lay futile?

Lord, I do not know whom are you referring to.

I know, Vassula, all this is obscure to you, but it is as clear as day for those deceivers! My Eyes are fixed upon them; My sword lifted and ready to strike; they know themselves and believe Me, their days are numbered; yes, cast your eyes around you, deceivers! why are you surprised? you will perish for I am doing something in these days that it will be hard to believe had you been told of it!

beloved, let Me answer your question in your mind: My Message will be read by those deceivers too; beloved, feel Me; I am in pain as you; My Cross is on you, bear It with love; My Cross is the door to true life; embrace It willingly; Vassula, abnegation and suffering lead into a divine path, this one of holiness and virtues;[1]

O come, beloved, I am with you,[2]

Lord, I feel so terribly sad, I know I should shed no more tears and reserve them for later, to compensate. I am ready to shed my blood instead, replacing my tears, if none will be left.

My Vassula, remember you are not of this world, you belong to Me; can you see My Sacred Heart?[3] enter in My Sacred Heart; in its depths, you will find your rest; I will take you and thrust you in its depths; My pain is unbearable;[4] do you remember when you were but a mere child, what I had done to you?

(Jesus gave me the same vision of then, when I was 10 years old. That was the first call.)

you were unable to move; I am divine Power, beloved, therein you belong;[5] come now, I need to be consoled; let us rest in each other;

(Jesus was very much in pain and sad.)

How could I console such distress?

by loving Me ardently; love Me and console Me, Vassula; love Me with all your soul;

I do love You and You know it, Lord.

love Me without measure!

Teach me to love you without measure.

I am; come now, I have a secret I wish to tell you; fear not, I will whisper it in your ear;

(Jesus told me the secret that gave me so much joy!)

Oh God! Will you really do this?

I will, beloved, I will; never doubt, all will be done accordingly, My Vassula;

Jesus, My God, thank You. Allow me to bless You.

I bless you too, beloved; come, it is late; we will rest in each other;

Yes, Lord.

come then;

November 10, 1987

*My God,
may You use me to engrave on me
everything that Your Heart desires.
May Your Will be done
and Your Name Glorified.*

the time has come to scatter My grains among mankind; forward My Message, I will help you in all your undertakings, let My Words be known, let My creation know of My Great Love, of My boundless Mercy; My reign will be one of Peace, Love and Unity; I have chosen Vassula as an incapable and wretched being, useless and without speech; write this, too;[6] yes, without any basic knowledge of My Church, an empty canvas, where I the Lord was free to cover it with My Works only, so that it is clear that all what is written comes from My Mouth; all acts will be done by Me, through her; I will speak through her, act through her; I have formed her, pouring all My Works on her to enable her to be My bearer for this Message, which will be known;

will you forward My Message? will you do this for Me? remember, it is I,

---

[1] I felt hopelessly sad.
[2] Jesus was caressing my head.
[3] Jesus pointed at a lit Chest and Heart.
[4] For having me in exile.
[5] Jesus pointed with His index finger to His Heart.

[6] I heard Him say what follows and I looked at Him embarrassed and hesitant.

Jesus, Beloved Son of God, Saviour to all mankind, the Word, who blesses you; I bless your undertakings; whether you will encounter joys or sorrows, be confident; I will give you My countenance; I am before you always guiding you; uniting My Church will Glorify Me! I will lead you into the very depths of My Bleeding Body; I will point out to you My thorns, you will recognise them;

have no other interest but My glory, never doubt of My Works, Love shines on you, My well-beloved; endeavour and please Me; come, at your side I Am; have My Peace,[1] let us pray to the Father,

"Righteous One,
Beloved Father,
blessed be Your Name,
assemble all Your faithful ones,
let the heavens proclaim
Your Righteousness,
let every lip praise
Your Holy Name continually,
malice must be banished
from the deceivers,
help those whose spirit is crushed,
revive them as Your Word
has guaranteed,
the vow I have made
I will keep and fulfil,
I pray for Your Churches,
may they all be one, Father,
may they be one in You;
Amen;"

(Jesus helped me to pray. These were His words.)

November 12, 1987

beloved it is I, Jesus;
clutch at My Cross, just as I have taught you to do while resting;

(Jesus taught me to hold a crucifix while resting at night. In this way, when I happen to wake up I feel the crucifix in my hand and immediately my mind is on Him.)

never ever leave Me, not even for a second; I am All and Everything; by holding My Cross you both glorify Me and honour Me; I, your God, purify you and console you, My child; so honour your Father who so much sought you when you wandered away from My side, erring from My divine ways; you see, child, you always belonged to Me, now that I have found you, beneath My cape I shelter you and keep you; look!

(I saw Jesus Christ in a scarlet-red long cape. He opened it with both hands showing me a bright glow coming from His Breast. Suddenly like a flash, a tongue of fire came directly on me, piercing me. It was not painful, it only lit my love for Him, desiring Him more than ever.)

My Flame will enkindle your heart; My Flame should stay ablaze forever in you, altar, I have renewed My Flame in you; so that you proceed with My divine Message, since you are incapable of drawing from Me, I then will see to it that My Flame will remain in you ablaze; come, I love your incapacity, because I have given you the grace to realise it; I feel glorified when you need Me for everything; your weakness attracts My Strength, your misery entices My Clemency; love Me, Vassula, share My thorns and nails, share My Cross, crown Me with your love, honour Me with your faith, allow Me to lead you blindly all the way; I will never desert you! believe in every word spoken in the Scriptures;

November 13, 1987

My Vassula, all I ask from you is love; every virtue blossoms from Love, Love is the root for every virtue; Love is like a fruit-tree, that blossoms first, then later on gives its fruit; every fruit is a virtue;

---

[1] Turning to me, Jesus said this.

come, let us have a silent prayer together first, you and Me to the Father, let us pray in total silence; I will dictate:

"Father, Righteous One,
My Shelter,
send out Your Light and Your Truth,
let these be my guide,
to lead me to Your Holy Place
where You live,
I, for my part, love You fully,
I will keep my vow
to fulfil Your word,
Holy Father I am aware
of my faults, of my sins,
have mercy on me in Your Goodness
and Your great Tenderness
forgive my sins, purify me, Lord,
be my Saviour, renew me,
keep my spirit faithful to You
and willing,
I offer you my will, surrendering,
I am willing to be Your tablet,
I praise Your Holy Name
and thank You for all the blessings
and peace you have given me;
amen"

now repeat it with Me;

(We repeated it together.)

Thank you Jesus for leading me step by step. You are my Holy Teacher, teaching me with Love and patience, guiding me and guiding others too to know You better, to know what an Infinite Love You are, never deserting us, but always ready to search for us who were lost and bring us back to You. Never did I feel harshness from You, or impatience, I only felt loved. You gave Love and Peace to my soul. This is what You are. I will never leave You, Lord.

daughter, desire Me always; love Me and honour Me; remain faithful to Me;
let us be together; do not forget My Presence;

November 14, 1987

Jesus, are You happy when I also come to You in this way You have given me?

I am, how can I not be?
you come to Me, My Vassula, yet you are not telling Me what is in your heart; I feel your heart, Vassula it is laden with sorrow and pain; do you want to know why? I will tell you why, it is because Love suffers; when I suffer, you suffer too; I have given you the grace of synchronising with Me at all times; you are My reflection, what I feel, you feel; I am letting you feel Me, souls are piercing Me anew;

(My agony now reached its peak. I'm supposed to reserve my tears but I couldn't.)

daughter, do you think that My eyes are dry?[1] they fill up as much as yours, I suffer .... My eyes are wet too;
O Vassula! My flower, how you understand Me now, daughter; together we shed tears, together we suffer, together we bear My Cross;[2] My Heart is wounded by so many souls who embitter Me O Vassula, your tears are My tears; here, bear My Cross, take My nails too, will you let Me rest?

Yes Jesus.

(My soul has never reached such sorrow and agony as now.)

Vassula, O Vassula, how I dread in telling you this, still I must tell you the truth; wear My Crown of Thorns and you will understand Me;

I think I know, Lord. I will be ridiculed, denied?

---

[1] I looked up, because Jesus' voice shook with agony, and saw His Eyes full, and wet with tears all around His eyes.
[2] Jesus dictated very fast.

souls will not hear Me, they will sin, proved by their refusal to believe in My Merciful Message, proved by their reluctance and by their fear of admitting their fault;[1] here, wear My Crown;

(He placed it on my head.)

you will glorify Me; listen, the time will come, in fact the time has come, where I will give you My instructions to scatter My grains in great abundance; Love will instruct you to fulfil My intentions; prove victorious, Vassula;

daughter, delight Me and face Me like now; I have allowed you to feel My Bleeding Heart, leaving My Blood drip on your heart; I let you share My Cup; around your head I have adorned you with My Crown, I have laid My Cross on you, My Nails I give to you, what more can a Spouse offer? all what I have given you are My most precious Jewels; My beloved one, now that you understand Me; are you willing to proceed into the depths of My Bleeding Body?

Yes, Lord, take me there.

daughter, we will then proceed, hold on to Me, bless Me;

(I blessed Jesus.)

come, I will bless you too; lower your eyes too;

(Jesus blessed me.)

call Me Abba, now you know what it means;

Abba?

yes, how I love you! I have also created you so that I have someone with whom I can share My sufferings; you will get to know Me, Vassula; you will learn who your Father is; flower, dearest daughter, let it be known how much I love My creation;[2]

Vassula, do you know why I am giving you this powerful grace to call Me any time you wish?

For the reasons You've told me already, Lord.

there is still one more reason;

Please do not write it, I have heard You.

yes, you have heard Me;

But Lord, 'this' comes from You, it's not from me.

flower, remember I have given you all your freedom to choose;

Yes, Beloved, but You have also given us the grace of our intellect to enable us to understand and choose. You have taught me this.

yes,[3] I love you; come, us, we?

Yes, Lord.

(I suddenly felt the need of God, St Mary, and all the Saints. Then, with great power, St. Mary appeared.)

the hours are fleeing, Jesus is guiding you; fear not, My beloved daughter, have My Peace; Jesus is with you, Jesus is your Guide; love Him as you do, My Vassula; you repair enormously; be Jesus' balm, delight Him; I, your Holy Mother will help you, fear not and <u>proceed</u>; you are on the right Path; I love you;

---

[1] Jesus enlightened me to understand this passage. I know who this is referred to. It goes very deep into the Church.

[2] Here God is letting me know that He does not love me more than the rest of His creation, but shows how much love He has on me just as an example. I am like a sample.
[3] There was a slight pause.

I love You, St. Mary. If I have to hurry I cannot do it unless God will open the Path for me, I shall then proceed with Him, holding His hand. I trust Him. I rely on Him. I ask You, Beloved Mother, to be my support, encouraging me and helping me.

you will get support from Me and I will help you;

Thank You, I bless You.

November 16, 1987

beloved, I will be doing something that will be hard to believe in these days, what I will do will be to confirm My Message; fear not;

My God, already it is hard to believe for many that You are communicating with me, just as simple as that, at any time, anywhere.

believe in My miracles, believe in Me;

November 18, 1987

My God, since the day You revealed Your secret intention to me, I fear. I am afraid to proceed. I fear, sensing that trouble lies ahead. It's like You, before entering in Jerusalem. You knew what trouble lay ahead.

My Message fulfils My Word; you are to proceed, whether you will be rejected or not, you will accomplish your work; I am before you;
 little one, stay meaningless so that I may appear fully; the less you will be, the more I Am; let Me proceed, let Me be the one who acts and speaks;
 yes, little one, they[1] will all have to bend to unite, I will be coming humbly, bare-foot; I am not coming loaded with weapons; I will bring back to Peter My sheep; I will unite them and Peter will feed My lambs; I, the Lord, have spoken; trust Me, beloved ones; I love you all with all My Heart;

November 21, 1987

Vassula, I will bring back to Peter My scattered sheep; I, the Lord, guarantee this to you all!

(Suddenly the Lord gave me a vision of sheep still apart, another flock, then later on these too were united.)

flower, this will come after My Great Sign!

Father, forgive my impatience, I have to learn to be patient like You!

little one, exalted by My Hand, draw from My resources and fill up your heart; imbue it to be able to impregnate other hearts too; I, the Lord, bless you; visions I will give to you, I am enriching your sight to discern men's hearts and be able to read them; My well-beloved, I offer you this grace, but remember, you will only use it for My interests and My glory, retaining nothing for yourself;

Jesus, well-Beloved, My God, who never stops pouring Your gifts on me to be near You. Jesus, I am the zero and yet You pour on me so many gifts; what then would You not do and give to those who are really pleasing in Your eyes, honouring You?

yes, you see, Vassula, you seem now to understand Me better; if I give to you, who is indeed the most wretched of My creatures, what would I then not give to those who truly merit My graces, those who honour Me and those who sacrifice for Me!
 ask, beloved ones, and I will give you, believe in what you ask, have confidence and trust Me, do not be like Peter who lost his confidence while walking on the

---

[1] The different churches.

water; have faith in Me! be confident! believe!

November 22, 1987

Vassula, the wind is blowing, becoming stronger every day; it blows on this wilderness that My creation has become, sweeping the desert-sands, bringing it closer and closer to the little fertile land that is left; already it has covered part of it, outspread like a veil over it, if we do not hurry little one, soon there will be nothing left but wilderness;

Lord, please be patient for I'm slow to learn.

flower, remember how long I was outside your door? have I not been patient <u>all</u> these years?

Jesus, why didn't I hear you all these years?

because you were deceived by the world, you belonged to Me from the beginning, but the world deceived you, convincing you to believe you belonged to them; that is how treacherous and deceitful Satan is; today his work is to convince My creation that he is non-existent; in this way he works without being feared and like lambs, My creation is trapped and devoured by the wolf; this is his plan of today;

November 23, 1987

(Having been to Lyon I've talked to the Catholic theologian. He together with his wife did not quite understand my detachment from this world. He said I had responsibilities. I said yes, but I put God first. Then he could not understand either that God even detached my soul. He wasn't agreeing. (Was not Abraham ready to sacrifice his own son?))

little one, I love you to folly; Love has no limits and I wish you to love Me too to folly; My intention is to stretch your love; I intend to make you love Me by showing Me no limits; I delight to check[1] on your loyalty towards Me; I delight to hear you honour Me; now you sacrifice for Me, but your sacrifice will not be in vain either; give yourself unreservedly to Me; please Me by being pliant, allowing Me, child, to treat you as I please; soul, never fear Me, I am Love;[2]

Many, Lord, do not seem to understand me either when I desire to be with You, and that death is but a delivery.

beloved, be holy, stay holy and Divine Love will carry you still higher; fear not, My well-beloved; lean on Me, be loyal to Me, loving Me your God with all your soul and heart, with all your mind and strength; remember how I lean towards you, to reach for your soul;

November 24, 1987

Vassula, I will make you read the words that I said to Margaret Mary; I said: "I will reign in spite of My enemies and all those who try to oppose Me" so be confident, beloved ones;

Vassula, I would like you to design once more how the Holy Trinity is,

Yes, Lord. (This is after a vision once the Lord gave to me when I had problems of understanding.)

○→○→○

(A vision of Light, one coming out of the other. Then one light coming out then another one, making three. When the Son is in the Father, then they are one. The Holy

---

[1] Like He checked on Abraham.
[2] That means that God will never ask something that will hurt our soul.

Trinity is one and the same. They can be three, but all three can be one. Result, one God. God is in three Persons, and one in the unity of essence.)

November 25, 1987

(I saw Jesus seated near me.)

Are you, Jesus, there?

I am; you have discerned Me; you see, Vassula, for that little faith you are giving Me, a faith much smaller than a mustard seed, I can make you see Me, feel Me, write with Me; come, I will be your Holy Companion;

(Later on.)

beloved, you need not fear for I have laid out my plans long before you were born; from all eternity I knew you would serve Me, beloved; do not trouble your heart to what you will say or do, for I, the Lord, will place My Words on your lips;
 I am guiding you, you are in Me, in My Love; I have consecrated you, you are blessed, I am leading you into the very depths of My Bleeding Body, accomplish My desires in doing My Will;
 I will favour you by giving you the grace in achieving discernment; remain in Me; give Me all your weaknesses, beloved soul; give them all to Me and let My Strength annihilate them;
 you will accomplish all the work I have designated you for, glorifying Me; trust Me and I will uphold you; blessed by My Hand, keep Me in your heart as I keep you in Mine; imbue your heart from Mine to be able to impregnate others; I, the Lord, will nourish you; trust Me, feel confident; come, come, beloved soul, and rest in Me; I, the Lord, bless you and all your undertakings;
 Vassula, take My Hand, take My Hand and follow Me, see?

(Jesus led my spirit. I dragging behind Him. He took me to St. Peter's Basilica. He pointed with His Arm stretched out and with His index at a lonely figure. It was the Pope, John Paul II. There he was, seated, alone, in thought. He appeared in deep thought.)

see Vassula? he is waiting; he is waiting;

Father, may Your designs be accomplished. Amen.

My Messages must be handed to him, accomplishing all what is written;
 come, beloved, the time is near; do not fear, remember I am before you; what I have commenced and blessed, I will finish; come, Love loves you and guides you; keep your hand in Mine; us, we?

Yes, Lord. Together. O how I love You, Jesus!

(Jesus, who comes with His Heart in His Hand, offering It to us. Love, with His so Tender Heart, comes again to help us untangle from Satan's nets.)

I Love You, Lord!

beloved, how, how could I see all this and leave you; I love you with all My Heart; with all My Heart, I love you all;

(I felt His Heart and it's inexplicable how much Love Jesus has for us!)

November 28, 1987

little one, embellish My Garden; as It is now, I see nothing in It but aridity; aridity is reigning over It; the dry winds are blowing on It, drying out what little is left; My flowers need watering, otherwise every single one will perish; My buds will not make it for the blooming season, they will perish one after the other; O if they only listen!

My God, why is it so complicated to reach a decision? Why is it so difficult to come to this decision? Why does it have to take months, years? Is it really so complicated, to love one another and unite as a family? Aren't these very same ones that teach us to love each other and to learn to sacrifice and give? Does it have to take years to unite? Do they really have to have special councils and meetings? Why can't they make one gathering a decisive one, joining hands and giving Peter the authority you once gave him, and please You, leaving You smiling?

how I love your simplicity, My child; it is childish the way you think; children are My weakness!

you see, when children quarrel, their quarrels never last more than a few minutes because malice is missing; but, daughter, these are not children, they have lost all the innocence they once had; they lost their simplicity, their holiness; building up instead malice for innocence, vanity for simplicity, unholiness for holiness, bigotry for humility;

you see, child, this is the reason I descend again to remind them how I, Jesus, am, I will come barefooted and humble, I will enter My Own House and kneel at My servant's feet and wash them;[1] weep not, My Vassula, all is for unity; let Me use you; this time they cannot deny that it is I, Jesus, since I have foretold this event[2] well before time; I have let you read part of what I have inspired My servant John XXIII with, but the rest...

Rest, Lord?

I have, later on, whispered in his ear about the great tribulations My Church will undergo;
I, Jesus love you all; remain in Me, in My Love;

November 29, 1987

Vassula, are you ready to sacrifice more now for Me?

Lord, You can use me as You please. I have surrendered. I am surrendering every day.

remain in Me, remain in My Love; daughter, numerous will be your trials;[3] would you still sacrifice more for Me, your God?[4]

My God, take my life into Your Hands and do as Your Heart pleases.

My well-beloved bride, then, have a look at My Cross;

(I looked, and with Jesus was a gigantic dark-wooden Cross.)

I have been nailed on It, glorifying My Father; do you see what awaits you? I, the Lord, will share It with you; you will then bear all the sufferings your soul is capable of, I will stretch your endurance, little one;

Father, do as Your Beloved Heart pleases with me, anything that will give You more Glory. All that comes from You satisfies me.

be obedient to Me and please Me, obedience turns the devil helpless and makes him flee;

November 30, 1987

Jesus?

I am;
I, Jesus, <u>guarantee</u> to you all that My Church will be one, united; beloved, be faithful to Me; trust Me, and be confident;

---

[1] Jesus spoke in metaphors.
[2] The so longed-for UNITY.
[3] God was warning me.
[4] After the warning, God, accepting my freedom, asks me again.

December 1, 1987

I have chosen you to show the world how Merciful I am; finding you where most of My children still are, if I had not come to fetch you, you would be today still where the rest are; I come out of My boundless Mercy to warn you, likewise to draw you to Me and remind you of your foundations;

(I start to understand that this Message for Peace and Love among God's creation and the uniting of the Church, will be one of God's last attempts before enflaming His Justice upon us.)

how well you understand Me now, daughter; do you fear Me?

(God must have felt in me a fear of what He might do if we do not change.)

I do, My God, after the vision You showed me.

I have showed you only part of it;[1] Vassula, My creation has to be warned; do not let the same mistakes be repeated;

Like when, Lord?

when I gave them My big Miracle at Fatima, I warned then My creation, but they paid little heed to My warning; they spent their time instead doubting, arguing, never diffusing My Mother's words properly, so that very few knew of the urgency of the Message; they have blood-stained their hands from their crime, dragging with them so many souls; I shall remind them of their sins of the past,[2] <u>I will remind them the urgency of Garabandal's Message</u>;

why doubt of My Works? pass on to My creation My warning; tremendous reparations are to be made; My creation has to be warned and to believe in Me; remind them of My Love,[3] propound My Word, promote Me ... promote Me, do not remote Me! now you are remoting Me, you are <u>not</u> protecting Me! declare openly My Works of the past and of the present, I am Omnipotent;

the thorns in My Head are all those sacerdotal souls who hold the key of knowledge, neither do they go in themselves nor do they let others in who want to! these are My thorns! those thorns now should <u>find Me</u> and repent; their hands are still, with fresh blood from the past, responsible for all the crimes and atrocities; I want them to repent, they defied My Mother's Message of Garabandal, never diffusing It like It should have been, ignoring its urgency; O[4] what have I got, Vassula! stones, their hearts are petrified; accept the Truth! open your hearts! <u>Garabandal is the sequel of Fatima</u>! do not repeat your errors!... – Peter![5]

Peter be My Echo! feed My lambs Peter, do not deny Me again, beloved;

(When the Lord said: "Peter, be My Echo! feed My lambs Peter, do not deny Me again beloved;" I could have died there and then, the way I heard Him say it.)

come, let Me help you; rest in Me;

(I felt so moved, I wasn't myself anymore. Jesus was trying to sustain me. When I recollected myself, I said:)

Jesus, I will describe now: God was <u>begging</u>. He said it in a <u>begging voice</u>.

yes, yes, Vassula, out of Love;

---

[1] Meaning all the worst is hidden.
[2] Apparently God reminds us of our sins only if we have not asked to be forgiven and repented. Once this is done, forgiveness is granted and God never reminds us of our old sins again.
[3] Including God's actual Messages of Peace and Love.
[4] God saddened beyond description moaned...
[5] God cried out in a loud Voice as to someone who is far away and would not hear... then God seemed to beg...

I love You, My God. How could I see You and hear You as sad as this, without wanting to die a million deaths? If I had 1000 lives I'd give each one, one after the other for Your Glory, healing Your Wounds.

My Wounds will only heal when My creation will return to Love, accept Me as Omnipotent and unite; come, let us share My sorrow;

Jesus, I wish I could do much more to make reparations and glorify You.

stay near Me and I will share all I have, with you; come;

December 2, 1987

Garabandal's Message is authentic and should be diffused and honoured; sanctify Garabandal; can you not see or understand that your errors are being repeated? you are repeating your errors of Fatima; O creation, when will you believe in Me? "ie emphanises itan";[1]

My God, to hear and feel You in such sadness is terrible.

Vassula, comfort Me;

Oh come Lord, I want to comfort You. I wish every soul knew so that they comfort You Lord and so You will be comforted by many.

if they love Me they do;
come, I will remind you that I, Jesus, will stand in the midst, between Cain and My Abel; Cain will face Me this time, instead of his brother; if he raises his hand to strike, he will have to strike Me; he will be stripped and will find himself naked facing Me, his God;

My Abel, My well-beloved Abel,[2] thou shalt live this time; your blood will not be shed; and My fragrance will embellish My garden, this very garden that My Abel's blood was shed in; come, flower, I will remind you of My Presence, stay alert;

December 4, 1987

Jesus?

I am; daughter, I want My Words to be clear; I do not blame those who persecuted the apparitions; I only want them to realise and admit their errors and to come forward to Me for repentance; I will forgive them, pardoning their sin; daughter, many will persecute My Message again denying that it is I, Jesus, for fear of admitting their fault, for this is beyond their wisdom again, child;[3]

Maybe they do not mean to deny it is You, maybe in their subconscious. They believe they probably do not mean to, not on purpose, for I'm sure if they realised, they would praise You! Only they do not understand.

how I love your reasoning – why cover them?

Because they do not know and if they do not know and understand...

I am listening;

Then, if I dare ask You: I ask for their forgiveness and Your Mercy on them.

but child, they will be your persecutors, inflicting on your soul suffering – they will be your scourgers;

---

[1] In Greek: "the apparitions were" (were there).

[2] God said it in such a tender way that only He can speak in that way; no one else.
[3] It was beyond their wisdom then to really understand and believe Jesus was the Son of God among them, as it is beyond some to believe that this divine Work descends from God.

Even so, if they do not understand, then they don't mean it; they do not know what they are doing, because they are weak. You can with Your Divine Love help them <u>understand</u> it is You. My God do not let Your Divine Hand strike them, for in striking them many innocent souls might be punished too.

Vassula, My creation has degenerated; tremendous reparations have to be done, I want My creation to realise where they are heading to; I want My sacerdotal souls to draw from Me and imbue My lambs with love <u>and knowledge</u>; right now, they[1] live in total darkness;

Yes, Jesus, but enlighten the ecclesiastical authorities, <u>even</u> if this 'unorthodox' way of being with You is beyond their understanding; open their eyes and ears, Lord!

I will only give wisdom to mere children, and not to the learned;

But then Lord, their chances are slim, they're gone!

gone they will be, unless they come to Me as children.... Vassula, I will stretch your endurance in suffering for you will be scourged;[2] let Me free and do not interfere with My Works,

Lord, will You forgive them, and overlook their weaknesses?

(I still dared to interfere.)

I will not bear to see them hurt you, child;

I do not know what to tell You, but can I ask You to overlook their weaknesses?

flower, I do not want to see you trampled by them; I would not bear to have them crush you;

Yet do not strike them, <u>teach</u> them, Lord.

they will have to open their ears then; Vassula, do you know what is awaiting you? you have seen My Cross; remember, that although your trials will be hard, I never leave your side; near Me I have your Holy Mother; listen to Her Words:

"daughter, beloved, sanctify Garabandal; I have appeared in Garabandal, giving My Message; My Message was not properly diffused; many sacerdotals have denied My Apparitions, thus refusing Us a place in their heart; but I have not forgotten My beloved children; there were times where they themselves doubted, and falling into confusion, denied My Apparitions; this was given as a similitude; it is to show My children [3] how and what a confusion reigns in the Church of today; I have promised that I will confirm My Apparitions of Garabandal; the hours are fleeing and My Messages were <u>not</u> diffused properly, neither has My Holiness been honoured;"

My God, it sounds so urgent like it should be diffused today at this hour. I depend on You to open our path, we are willing to diffuse Your messages but give me the strength and courage and possibilities to accomplish Your desires. Amen.

will I abandon you now, My Vassula?

No Lord, I need Your strength to continue.

you will receive sufficient strength to accomplish what you have been designated in accomplishing;

December 6, 1987

write, Vassula; I, the Lord, wish you to honour My Stations of the Cross: introduce the light, first honouring My Mother, offering Her

---

[1] God's creation.
[2] Symbolises the suffering of the soul.

[3] The world.

a candle, then I wish to see your knees bend in all of My Stations, honouring Me by holding at My Stations a light;

Lord, You have laid out Your plans already. I beg You to open the path for us to honour You Lord.

I will; lean on Me and I will carry you; Vassula, when this is accomplished you will be reminded by Me that soon the second event will be coming, I shall remind you not to seek anymore your comfort;

My God, are You talking for all of us?

no, I am talking to you, Vassula; look into My Face; I will remind you that this event will be the beginning where you will feel My Powerful Hand on you; My Divine instructions will flow in you; you are to be pliant, willing to serve Me, loyal, honouring Me; I will use you, you will be used fully, even to be My target; you are My tablet, little one; I intend to bring back to Peter My sheep;

Lord, My God, I have been with You as a 'tablet' now for over a year. You have used me every day, and I love You because I'm nearer to You in this way. You can use me. I will be loyal and Your slave too.

Vassula how I love you; will you kiss My Feet after doing the Stations of the Cross?

Yes Lord, I will.

come, do not forget My Presence; you seem to neglect Me these days;

My God, give me the strength to manage everything. I want to please You as You know, but my capacity is limited. Will You forgive me?

O Vassula, how I love you; I forgive you; write what you saw!

(Jesus, in telling me that I neglect Him, looked sad and grave. When I asked Him to forgive me, His Divine Face lit up and with a bright smile, showing me His dimples, He opened His Arms wide, so that I fall in His embrace.)

forgiveness will always be given without the slightest hesitation; and I made you discern Me fully so that you are able to tell My children the way I forgive;

come, we, us;

(Jesus in saying this made a movement with His index finger, like a Teacher, warning me.)

December 7, 1987

I lead you in an 'unorthodox way', but I am God and I will choose any way, the hours are fleeing, the time is near; I will lead you like I wish, Vassula;

December 8, 1987

(After reflecting what can await me I started to panic. These were moments of extreme weakness. I was very disturbed.)

My God, can't I love You like any other normal being in a normal way? Can't You, Beloved God, guide me in a normal way instead of this way? Oh God, I feel so much responsible with all this. It's a torture to know that in spite of all the graces You are bestowing on me, I remain wretched and so sinful, wicked. Why Lord, why do You keep me? I can't face You any more; I'm not worthy of You; let me go in my corner. Do not have me so near You.

why? why?

My God, no, I'll follow You and love You like the others in the normal way!

beloved, I love you![1]

---
[1] I saw Jesus hurt by my words. I felt awful.

Oh Jesus, I am only wounding You. Let me go. I'll rest in my misery, but I won't stop honouring You and loving You.[1]

wait!

Lord, all of this [2] *is beyond my understanding, it's beyond me!*

no, this is not beyond your understanding, not anymore; beloved,[3] five of My Wounds are wide open; I am bleeding profusely; I am suffering; your God is suffering; will you not glorify My Body? five of My Wounds are open for you to see what sorrow My creation is giving Me;
 I love you all in spite of your wickedness, in spite of your failures, in spite of your doubts, in spite of your iniquity, in spite of your denials, in spite of your scepticism and in spite of your insincerity towards My Body; do you not yet understand? why have you closed your hearts forever towards Me? why have most of you abandoned Me, why have My followers changed path, why have they neglected My garden, why have they not watered My flowers, why?
 where are My lambs Peter? would you help Me find them and unite them? come; I will help you find them, I will bring food for them and nourish them; no Peter, you will find nothing in this wasteland; there is nothing left; the little that was left is now dry and wasted; for as far as the eye can see, there is nothing but wastelands; but I, the Lord, will fetch from My stores My Bread and I shall fill your storages with My produce; I will feed My lambs; I will irrigate this wilderness; trust Me, beloved; trust Me and I will unite you all again; together, My Vassula; flower, I will not see you trampled by them; I mean to use you for the Glory of My Body; I, God, love you;

(When our Lord said in this message: "in spite of your insincerity towards My Body..." He was talking about those working for UNITY. Usually when the ecclesiastical authorities meet to be able to find a solution, what happens is the following: the one who comes to face the other one hopes that the one facing him will be the one will give in 'something'; in the end it ends up by no one giving much. This was given me to understand by the Lord, yesterday night.)

December 11, 1987

Jesus?

I am;

Jesus, why is it that the media believes easier than the priests, theologians etc. Remember when You asked me the question, Lord?

I remember;

When they read the first book they want to read the rest, then most of them, after reading the first book, they kneel and pray. Even some who never prayed before in their life, it's wonderful!

Vassula, My children are hungry; when they see My Bread, they seize It to appease their hunger; if they want more, they come to Me[4] for more and I offer them all I have;

But Lord, it happened once or twice that those that read it because of their joy wanted to share it with a priest, thinking they too will feel happy, but to their disappointment the priest showed no interest. In fact, they discouraged them.

---

[1] I wanted to go to bed and sleep out my awfulness.
[2] The supernatural approach and all events to come.
[3] Jesus 'exploded', showing me how He suffers.

[4] In prayer to Him.

Vassula these are the ones that wound Me and pierce Me through and through; I suffer intolerably to see My own reject Me; they have nothing to offer My lambs;

Still Lord, in spite of the negative attitude and lack of enthusiasm from the priests, they are not discouraged, because they do find peace in finding You again. But they feel bitter that it should be this way, especially when they find out that they knew nothing about the apparitions and wonder why the Church does not speak more of this. One of them commented that these things are kept low and only in their circles.

yes, Vassula, My sacerdotals are repressing My Works of today; daughter, I have said and say again that they hold the key of knowledge, and neither do they go in themselves nor do they let anyone in who wants to! they are blocking The Way with scepticism, doubts and bigotry, I have lost them as children, their wisdom has blinded them losing their way to Me;
 – beloved, sacrifice all[1] that you have now and pray with Me;

Yes, Jesus.

"Father,
let peace be what they will discuss,
forgive their insincerity,
Father do not stand aside
if they will persecute me
come, come to my defence,[2]
be at my side,
enlighten them and teach them,
let them see their errors,
you are Righteous,
shine on them instead,
to praise you and say,
'Great is our God Most High
who wants to see
His children at Peace,

praise the Lord
who descends to unite us,
praise the Lord who comes
to announce His Works of today';
Amen;"

come, beloved, meet Me later on; remember now My Presence; I love you, daughter;

Yes Lord, I will remember.

December 11, 1987

flower, never doubt that it is I, Jesus, your Saviour; behold and look back where I had found you; [3] I found you in wretchedness where so many of My children still are! come, Vassula, do you see this crucifix?

(Jesus meant the crucifix, a wooden of olive tree from Jerusalem, and which was now near me and on the notebook. It is the one that does not leave my hand during the night.)

yes, My Vassula; take it in your hand now; lift it to My lips; yes, lift it;

(Jesus so sweetly kissed it when I lifted it to His divine lips.)

will you kiss it too?

(I did.)

lift it now; I blessed it... I love you all, beloved ones;

December 12, 1987

My God! It must have reached Your Ears, Lord, of what I am now accused of. It is the third time that the Jehovah Witnesses accuse me. Twice before they said that this is the work of the devil (without reading

---

[1] To leave for this time my housework, which is very behind, my son's meal, my husband who is severely ill with perhaps hepatitis; I was getting ready to go.
[2] To defend His Word, not me.

[3] A quick image of the past was given me.

it); and this time that I am a descendant of the fallen angels of the past! Lord, why? Why are Christians so different from one another? What went wrong?

never has My Church been in such a confusion; remember the words of your Holy Mother:

"the confusion of Garabandal was given as a similitude, to show how My Church of today is confused; <u>it is reigning in confusion;</u>"

My God, I'm so sad, so sad, Lord.

you grieve because you feel Me, you are getting to know Me; how I rejoice when you recognise what I suffer from; Vassula, I love them too, but they have been so misled by Satan; he blinded them; leading them when blinded into another path and in their delusion they not only disregard My Mother as Queen of Heaven, but disregarded My Peter too and the authority I Myself have given him upon all My lambs; they persecute My flowers as well and condemn all My Heavenly Works of today; Satan has conditioned them to abuse anything; they do not understand; stopping them from perceiving the Truth, their doctrine has infiltrated among you, beloved ones, and they are the ones I have warned you about;[1] they like to call My graces given to My children, "Satan's handiwork", rejecting your Holy Mother;

Vassula, it should never be up to you to accuse them, learn to say instead: "let the Lord be Judge and correct them;"

beloved one, the End of Times is at hand; I have said that I will give you signs and warnings; I suffer to watch them[2] sneer at My foundation[3] and follow nothing but their own doctrine; they are those Cains and dangerous to My Abels; an obstacle to the ones who want to grow in My House; a misleading torch of misguidings to My people, a hardened rock; they have rebelled against My foundation; how will I offer them a kingdom on earth, when inside them they have accepted doctrines which come from Cain?

I will resurrect you and your soul will come to Me; into My Arms! you are but a passing shadow on earth, a mere speck of dust which will be washed away with the first drops of rain; have I Myself not said these words: that there are many rooms in My Father's House and that I will prepare you one, so that where I am, you may be too? it is to Me, in <u>My</u> House that souls will come! [4] Vassula, they are scheming against My foundation; they are trying to uproot My domain; I love you; do not weep, flower;

(When I feel Jesus sad, I become sad too.)

I will place on you My thorned crown... and the lance is among them; they are plotting against My House, reunion after reunion to put an end to Peter!

Oh God no! No, Lord!

gather together, beloved ones; reinforce My Church; unite, beloved ones, come together again, be one; flower, stay alert,
Love will redeem you, My beloved ones; come flower, open; open and let Me pour into you My sap which will raise you, strengthening you to enable you to tread on My foes; remember, I, the Lord Jesus Christ, am before you;

(This message alarmed me very much.)

I long for them to listen, it's urgent!

---

[1] The false religions.
[2] Jehovah's Witnesses.
[3] Church in Rome.

[4] The Jehovah Witnesses, confused, believe that one can live forever in paradise on earth; and that our soul dies once we die.

December 19, 1987

I am Love;
tell them, tell them, Vassula, that sincerity will conquer evil, humility will debilitate the devil, love will unmask Satan;

(Later:)

<u>Fatima's shrine cries out for amendments</u>! come back to Me, creation! come and recognise Me, creation; come and pray to Me; <u>sin no more</u>; believe in Me and do not doubt; <u>come and repent</u>, come and receive Me; be holy, Vassula; O Vassula, bring back My creation to Me! <u>Altar</u>! I will pour into you My Flame, enflaming you with Love; you are to seek My Interests glorifying Me; do not be like the others who seek their glory and grandeurs;

Lord, I said and say again, I will only seek Your interests, Lord, and that which brings more glory to <u>You</u>. Take my will. I have surrendered.

yes, Vassula, satisfy My thirst; treat Me as King; honour Me, your God; never rebel against Me; sanctify your body to honour My Presence in you; beloved, come, all that is hidden will soon come to light; My Divine Hand will lift the cover and I shall reveal to you all that has been hidden; Garabandal is the sequel of Fatima <u>and My reign will reign forever for I Am</u>; I am the Alpha and the Omega;
how I love you creation! My own, My children, beloved come, come in My open arms; come back to your Father!

(God's Voice was full of love. He was almost begging.)

I love you;
listen, Vassula, when you will be among My Abels I will be among you; I will whisper in your ear My instructions; I have Bread to offer; My Bread is Holy; I have used only a small amount of yeast from My storages, and it was enough to leaven all the dough; this dough that is My New Bread now, so get rid of your old yeast; it has lost its effect, beloved ones, come and use My new yeast, renew yourselves altogether into a new batch of bread, attractive to the palate which will draw My lambs feeding them; honour My Bread which I sanctified; My Bread of Sincerity, Truth and Love; let Me rejoice, beloved; let My lambs taste My New Bread; distribute It among them and let the hungered masses eat; allow them to be full; I will not be convinced by the arguments of the wise; they will not impress Me so do not let them impress you either, daughter; My intention is to bring back My scattered lambs; bring them back to Love;
sign My Name,

ΙΧθΥΣ ⳨

December 21, 1987

My God, Righteous One, even in my nothingness and in this great incapacity I have, my desires have been implanted in me by You. They are Your desires. I desire that Your Name be Glorified and that Your lambs assembled again recognising You, recognising our Heavenly Mother, that Her Reign will last forever, overcoming Evil. I seek only <u>Your</u> interests ...

yes Vassula, seek My interests only, be real, not just a façade of holiness like some are; I, the Lord, know them, no matter how hard they try to appear like Abel, they do not deceive Me; wearing a mask will not help conceal their identity, I tell you truly, I will point out to you this time those deceivers; I will come to them in an unexpected hour; why have in My House Cains? seeking only their interests and not Mine? I will, with Heavenly Strength, unmask them; I will unveil what is hidden; do not fear, beloved, My Church, <u>I</u> will clean; I will sweep away all those that obstruct The Way to Divine

Love and from entering into My Sacred Heart; you see, Vassula, My Cup tastes bitter, the world is offending Me beloved; those Cains are blocking the Way, obstructing It with enormous blocks, blocking the passage for My lambs to come to Me; their hands are empty, they have nothing to offer My lambs, not anymore; Vassula, blessed of My Soul, follow Me; I will guide you, do not despair, will I ever abandon you now?

No, Lord, I'm clinging on You, Beloved Father.

here take My Hand, never leave It, accept all that comes from Me;

December 22, 1987

Vassula, the time has come to unite My Church; come together again beloved, come and rebuild these ancient ruins, rebuild My old foundation a foundation established by My Own Hand; honour My Mother as I, who am The Word and above all, honour her; would I then not desire you who are dust and ashes recognise Her as Queen of Heaven, honouring Her? My grief of today is to see how little My creation knows of Her importance; those under the name of Luther and who have isolated themselves entirely, must return to Peter;

Lord! They will be shocked!

Vassula, I will bend their knee to venerate My Mother; it is I, the Lord, who am speaking; I will bend them! and when they do, I will let My Light shine on them and raise them; I will strengthen your stems, and you shall be like an irrigated garden, like a spring of water whose waters never run dry; I will rebuild My Foundation;

come, beloved, be pliant and soft like now so that I engrave on you My Words, come never forget My Holy Presence;

Yes, Lord.

December 23, 1987

My God, the Protestants will be shocked!

(I couldn't get over it.)

Vassula, I have been waiting years for them to change; now leave Me free to write down My desires;

But they will be shocked!

listen, can one hear Me only when it is convenient for him, then shut his ears when what I say does not suit him?

They'll reject outright then the <u>whole</u> thing! Since they will not be able to select parts. They'll claim it's not You speaking.

if they do they would be then disowning Me as their God;

Lord, may I dare say that this is hard on them? They will not feel they are disowning You, they are after all loving You and they <u>do</u> worship You, Lord.

Vassula, <u>I have come to unite you all</u>; would any disciple of Mine deny My appeal?

No, not if they are sincere, Lord

with this statement you gave Me, hangs all what there is to say: "<u>if they are sincere...</u>" then they will listen;
 I come to shine on you all and enlighten you to be able to unite you; but, Vassula, to My great sorrow there will be those who would prefer darkness to the Light because <u>their deeds are evil</u>, they would refuse to come under My Light for fear of exposing their deeds, but My

devoted ones and those that sincerely acknowledge My Works and follow Me will come under My Light, exposing without fear their deeds, because they will show that what they do is done in Me their God;

I have said that if you make My Word your home, you will indeed be My disciples; you will learn the Truth and the Truth will make you free; and now, I say to you this: if you give credit to My Word of today, you will indeed be My disciples; you will learn <u>Sincerity</u> in the Truth and the Truth will free you and enable you to unite in Love and Glorify Me;

I come to you all, with My Heart in My Hand, offering It to you, but in spite of My appeal many would reject Me, disowning Me as God because their hearts have hardened; if they loved Me they would listen to My appeal; if they refuse to listen, it is because I have lost them as children; their wisdom has blinded them; but I tell you truly, the sheep that belong to Me will recognise My Voice; those that would not recognise My Voice are no sheep of Mine because they do not believe in My Omnipotency;

do you know why My lambs are scattered and My Body maimed? do you know why disharmony reigns in My Church? it is because they have been walking at night without any light to guide them; <u>seek Me who am the Light</u> and I will guide you, cast away your bigotry and your obduracy; be meek and humble; open your hearts and let My Sap fill you up; I am your Good Shepherd who loves you;

Vassula, talk to me; treat Me as your Holy Companion;

I will My God, I love You Lord. I wish to glorify Your Name, Lord.

beloved, My Name I have glorified and I will glorify It again; My reign will be forever;

come, courage, daughter, I am with you;

December 26, 1987

(On the night between December 25-26 Jesus was emphasising the importance of Garabandal's message with those of Fatima's, and that they are similar. It was as though I did not rest that night. The message was ringing in my ears repeatedly, and Jesus was emphasising His Presence.)

<u>Fatima's Shrine cries out for the sanctification of Garabandal</u>; I have taught you to read the Signs of the Times, are you looking for those Signs? how can you not tell the Signs? have you no perception? why are your minds closed? why do you refuse to see? why do you refuse to hear? have you forgotten My Words? why repeat your mistakes? beloved, why all these venomous attacks on the Message of Garabandal given by your Holy Mother who is the Ark of Alliance of My Word to you; the opposition My sacerdotals have towards Garabandal's apparitions and message are all manoeuvres of Satan; <u>once again as in Fatima, he is trying to prevent My Message from becoming universal</u>;

have you not understood that Satan knowing the value of My Salvation Plan given through My Mother at Garabandal to mere children, is trying once again to erase My Plan? thus leaving you all in darkness to fall; Satan is redoubling his efforts more than ever now to triumph over your Holy Mother, manoeuvring My Church to deny these apparitions which are the sequel of Fatima's Message of Salvation; Satan, in his fury, is trying to prevent you from feeding upon Me;

My Salvation Plan is clear; I come to redeem My children; <u>recognise My Voice</u>! do not be surprised at the kind of instruments I use; I have chosen a nothing, knowing nothing, a blank canvas so that it is clear that the Works covering this sheet[1] will be from Me, and that you believe that it is I, Jesus, Beloved Son of

---

[1] Canvas.

God, who speaks this time; among you is My Kingdom;
 My Abels I know <u>you</u> will recognise Me again; O beloved how I love you! I will unveil to you My Plan soon;

Lord, if the sacerdotals do not recognise Your Voice, then Lord, what happens?

Vassula, it is not up to you to ask; dust and ashes;[1] let Me guide you as I wish, leave these things for Me;

Yes, Lord.

O come do not misunderstand Me, I am Love, learn to accept; come us, we? I will replenish your lamp;

Yes Lord, I thank You for taking care of me with Love.

let us go;

December 28, 1987

(If I forget myself and dare utter a judgement upon anybody, or think that I understand more than others, in no time God reminds me whom He has, to give His Message: just by a penetrating look of His Eyes upon me He puts me in my place, fixing me where I should be. Just by His words: "dust and ashes," He reminded me that I'm nothing, and the least of all His creatures. No, some will not understand this; they would think that because He has chosen me to take His Word, I am worthy, but don't you understand? By choosing me, who am the least of all, God shows what fathomless Mercy He has on us; that even to the least He gives. Wouldn't He then give a LOT more to those who are so much more worthy in His Eyes than I, if they ask with faith? Have you not noticed His patience with me? Instead of striking me, His Love flows with more abundance. How could His creatures reject Him? But I shouldn't talk since I belonged in these sort of people before. Now I'm saying: "Cherish your God as much as you cherish your breath, for without your breath you will die. God gave us life by breathing in us; His Breath is our life. God is our Breath, God is our Life.")

O Vassula! My Abel shall live this time; sincerity will abolish evil; [2] blessed are those who stimulate My Word; blessed are My sheep who recognise My Voice, blessed are those who will feed My lambs again,
 blessed are the simple in heart, blessed are those who will pray the Rosary on the day of Garabandal's sanctification[3] and whose knees are bent and hail My Mother; blessed are those who will carry My Cross of Peace and Love, uniting; blessed are My sheep who return to Peter; blessed are those who humble themselves and follow My example; blessed are those who follow My command and love one another as I love you; blessed are those who bear witness of Me and are not scandalised of Me;
 Vassula, beloved of My Soul, have faith and trust Me; I am your Heavenly Teacher; never doubt of My Word; come, you are weak, come lean on Me who am your Strength;

Yes, Lord, I need You. I cannot do without You ever.

love Me, desire Me; be My heaven; ah, Vassula, now you sacrificing for Me, but soon I will have you near Me;

I'm longing for that day.

stay near Me, I have got something to ask you;

Yes, Lord?

---

[1] With these two words God reminded me that I am the least of all His creatures.

[2] "Sincerity will abolish evil". This could be as well: "Abel will conquer Cain".
[3] God foretells this event.

for My sake, Vassula, for My sake, will you learn the Rosary? Hail My Mother at all times, will you do this for Me, Vassula?

Yes, Lord, I am willing to learn; Lord, help me learn.

this is what I desire to hear from all of you who do not know, the same words: "yes Lord, I am willing to learn; Lord, help Me learn;" I will teach you all, you who are willing to learn;
   come, daughter, rest in Me; I shall not forsake you ever;

(Jesus must have felt how I long for Him and suffer out here. It's the wave again of 'desiring God', wanting to be His sacrifice, detached totally. I seem to waver. Remaining here, I might 'feed' some of His lambs who never refuse His new Bread, pleasing Him for the return of new souls. Being with Him will be marvellous too for me. What is best?)

December 31, 1987

My God, I am praying that the churches will believe in Your Message!

Vassula, to believe in Me is a grace given by Me,[1]
   hear Me, Vassula: you will speak from My Mouth and will speak of the tribulations that My Church will undergo; this revelation is My Voice; recognise the Signs of the Times; accept My Message, taste My Message, <u>eat My Message</u>; woe for the unfaithful;

(Later on:)

little one, do you love Me?

I adore You endlessly, Lord.

yes, Vassula, love Me; make up for your past; make up for those who do not love Me; flower, every flower needs light knowing what effect it has on its petals; daughter, will you repent?

(I repented of my old sins and the present ones, as He was preparing me to receive Holy Communion.)

resent all these things from the depths of your soul; resent impurity[2] for this was the vice of Sodom;

---

[1] One has to pray and ask God for this grace.

[2] Impurity of the soul.

Prayers

Three Daily Prayers
Daily prayers recommend, by Jesus, to pray. [1]

Novena of Confidence to the Sacred Heart

O Lord, Jesus Christ
To Your Most Sacred Heart,
I confide this intention...

(Here mention your request)

Only look upon me
Then do what Your Heart inspires...
Let Your Sacred Heart decide...
I count on It... I trust in It...
I throw myself on Its Mercy...

Lord Jesus! You will not fail me,
Sacred Heart of Jesus,
I trust in Thee.
Sacred Heart of Jesus,
I believe in Thy love for me.
Sacred Heart of Jesus,
Thy Kingdom Come.

O Sacred Heart of Jesus,
I have asked for many favours,
but I earnestly implore this one.
Take it, place it in Thy Sacred Heart.
When the Eternal Father
sees it covered
with Thy Precious Blood,
He will not refuse it.
It will no longer be my prayer
but Thine, O Jesus.

O Sacred Heart of Jesus,
I place my trust in Thee,
Let me never be confounded. Amen.

Prayer to St. Michael the Archangel

St. Michael the Archangel,
defend us in the day of battle,
be our safeguard against the
wickedness and snares of the devil.
May God rebuke him,
we humbly pray, and do thou,
O Prince of the Heavenly Host,
by the Power of God,
cast into hell Satan
and all the other evil spirits,
who prowl through the world
seeking the ruin of souls. Amen.

The Memorare of St. Bernard

Remember,
O Most Gracious Virgin Mary
that never was it known
that anyone who fled
to Thy protection,
implored Thy help
and sought Thy intercession,
was left unaided.
Inspired with this confidence,
I fly unto Thee,
O Virgin of virgins, my Mother!
to Thee I come, before Thee I stand,
sinful and sorrowful.
O Mother of the Word Incarnate!
despise not my petitions,
But in Thy Mercy,
hear and answer me. Amen.

---

[1] See the message of May 4, 1988 for the three daily prayers that Jesus recommends we all say.

A Prayer of Repentance and Deliverance
This prayer will be very effective if prayed with the heart and sincerity.[1]

...let them repent before Me with these words:

Lord,
you have endured me
all these years with my sins,
but nonetheless You pitied me;
I was led astray in every way,
but now I will sin no more;
I have wronged You and I have been unjust;
I will be so, no more;
I renounce sin, I renounce the Devil,
I renounce iniquity that stains my soul;
free my soul from all that
is against Your holiness;
I entreat You, Lord,
to rescue me from all evil;
come Jesus now, come now
and abide in my heart;
Forgive me, Lord, and allow me to rest in You,
for You are my Shield,
my Redeemer and my Light
and in You do I trust;
From today
I will bless You, Lord, at all times;
I repudiate evil
and all other gods and idols,
for You are the Most High over the world,
far transcending all other gods;
By Your mighty arm,
rescue me from ill health,
rescue me from being a captive,
rescue me from trouble
and defeat my enemy, the Devil;
come quickly to my help, O Saviour!
Amen

Vassula writes: *Jesus Christ dictated to me this prayer which is a prayer of repentance, healing and deliverance. He said that this "exorcism prayer" is needed for our times so evil.*

People do not know how to totally repudiate Satan in their prayers, who is controlling them, blinding them and giving them a lot of suffering, either through illness or by making them captives. Jesus also says that a lot of people worship false gods (idols).

---

[1] See the message of November 13, 2006

TRUE LIFE IN GOD

CLARIFICATIONS

WITH THE CONGREGATION FOR THE DOCTRINE OF FAITH

Office of the Archbishop
Archdiocese of Lipa
San Lorenzo Drive
4217 Lipa City, Philippines
☎ (043) 756-2573 • Fax (043) 756-2964
E-mail: bparguelles@catholic.org

✠ Ramón C. Argüelles, DD, STL
Archbishop of Lipa

FOREWORD

God's favorites are not free from controversies. In the film *FIDDLER ON THE ROOF* the Jewish patriarch, the protagonist of the beautiful musical, in the face of persecution of the Russian Jews, addressed God in an amusing way: "Lord, I know we are your favorite people. But can't you favor other people once in a while?" St. Bernadette of Lourdes would have preferred another young girl to be the visionary rather than herself. Bernadette affirmed the opinion of the Mother Superior who never believed the illiterate Bernadette. If God and the Blessed Mother should favor anyone it should be one, like her, who had lived all her life in the cloister in the midst of selfless dedication and self-sacrifice.

The New Testament shows Jesus praising the pagan and non-Jewish centurion who asked his help for his ailing servant. His words: "Lord, I am not worthy that You should enter under my roof..." became a timeless statement worthy of being repeated in the Eucharistic Liturgy. Certainly among God's most favored ones is Mary Magdalene who became the apostle to the Apostles. Can it be that even in our days God uses a non-Catholic (although deeply faithful to the Pope and a great believer in all that Catholics must believe in, especially regarding the Eucharist and even more profoundly attached than most Catholics to the Blessed Virgin Mother) and one whose marital past is under question, not of course like that of the Samaritan Woman, another favorite of Jesus whom He had to see by all means at noontime near Jacob's well?

Cardinal Joseph Ratzinger showed such Christlike open-mindedness when he spearheaded the review of Mrs. Vassula Ryden's case. Through Fr. Prospero Grech, Consultant of the Congregation of the Doctrine of the Faith, the good Cardinal asked Vassula to respond to five questions (see letter dated April 4th, 2002) to clarify some difficulties suggested in the Notification of 1995, regarding the writings of True Life in God, and about her activities related thereto. The responses will immensely help some doubting Thomases, who are entitled nevertheless to peace of mind.

It will help many to know that the Congregation sent a letter dated April 7th, 2003 to the Presidents of the Episcopal Conferences, wherein Cardinal Ratzinger asks them to provide him with information about Mrs. Ryden, and the influence she might have had on their faithful in their respective countries. Of all responses received, five countries, unfortunately including my own country the Philippines, replied negatively. Cardinal Ratzinger deemed it convenient to inform the bishops of the said countries, that the Congregation had reviewed Mrs. Ryden's case and that the suggestions made in the Notification towards the writings of True Life in God and her marital situation were clarified. This latest communication, dated July 10th, 2004, mentioned the said countries at the bottom of the said letter.

Cardinal Ratzinger asked P. Joseph Augustine Di Noia, O.P., Undersecretary of the Congregation of the Doctrine of the Faith, to provide Mrs. Ryden with a copy of that same letter to enable her to inform everyone about the exchange of clarification letters.

I am extremely happy that Cardinal Ratzinger perfectly mirrors the attitude of the Holy Father whose great obsession and probably the reason for the life and energy he manifests is the **UNITY OF CHRISTIANITY**. One very touching event is the Holy Father's coming back from a visit to Armenia. He brought with him to the Synod Hall a gift of the Orthodox Patriarch of Armenia, a precious lamp with a plea for the unity of all Christians.

No matter what Mrs. Ryden's past life may be, she can and already is an insrument of God in our days to bring to reality God's dream, the Holy Father's dream, the Church's dream which may be the greatest event of the early years of the Third Millennium: THE UNITY OF ALL DISCIPLES OF CHRIST! People like Vassula who suffer for Christian unity with the Holy Father need encouragement, understanding and prayer. I am willing to give her that if only to join the Holy Father, Cardinal Ratzinger and many unknown souls who sincerely desire a renewal of Christianity, a renewed thrust of Evangelization, unity of all Christian brethren. May Mary help us grow in the TRUE LIFE IN GOD.

Archbishop Ramon C. Arguelles
September 30, 2004
107th Year of the Entry into Life of the
Patroness of the Universal Mission

CONGREGATIO
PRO DOCTRINA FIDEI

00120 Città del Vaticano,
Palazzo del S. Uffizio

10 luglio 2004

Prot. N. 54/92-19631
(In responsione fiat mentio huius numeri)

Gentile Sig.ra Vassula Rydén,

a riguardo delle preoccupazioni da Lei espresse a questa Congregazione con lettera del 4 giugno 2004, ritengo opportuno informarLa che questo Dicastero ha scritto ad alcuni Presidenti di Conferenze Episcopali la lettera di cui Le accludo copia (cfr. Allegato).

Nel comunicarLe quanto sopra ed in unione di preghiera, profitto della circostanza per porgerLe distinti ossequi e confermarmi

dev.mo

P. Joseph Augustine Di Noia, O.P.
Sotto-Segretario

(con Allegato)

Gent.le Sig.ra
Vassula Rydén
Via Fosso della Castelluccia, 45/B
00134 Roma

TRANSLATION

CONGREGATIO
PRO DOCTRINA FIDEI

00120 Città del Vaticano
Palazzo del S. Uffizio

10 July 2004

Prot.N. 54/92-19631

Dear Mrs. Vassula Rydén,

With reference to the preoccupations expressed to this Congregation in your letter of the 4 June 2004, I take the opportunity to inform you that this Congregation has addressed to some Presidents of the Episcopal Conferences the letter of which I enclose a copy (see attached).

In informing you of the above and in union of prayer, I take the opportunity to send you my most respectful greetings.

Yours faithfully

(signed)
P. Joseph Augustine DI NOIA, O.P.
Under-Secretary

(With attachment)

Mrs.
Vassula Rydén
Via Fosso della Castelluccia, 45/B
00134 Roma

CONGREGATIO
PRO DOCTRINA FIDEI

00120 Città del Vaticano,
Palazzo del S. Uffizio

10 luglio 2004

Prot. N. 54/92-19631
(In responsione fiat mentio huius numeri)

Eminenza/Eccellenza,

come Ella sa, nel 1995 questa Congregazione ha pubblicato una Notificazione sugli scritti della Sig.ra Vassula Rydén. Successivamente, a seguito di una richiesta della medesima, vi è stato un dialogo approfondito, a conclusione del quale la suddetta Vassula Rydén, con lettera del 4 aprile 2002, poi pubblicata sull'ultimo volume di «True Life in God», ha fornito utili chiarificazioni circa la sua situazione matrimoniale, nonché circa alcune difficoltà che, nella citata Notificazione, erano state avanzate nei confronti dei suoi scritti e della sua partecipazione ai sacramenti (cfr. Allegato).

Dal momento che in codesto Paese vi è stata una certa diffusione degli scritti in oggetto, questo Dicastero ha ritenuto utile informarLa di quanto sopra. Allo stesso tempo occorrerà richiamare i fedeli cattolici, per quanto riguarda la partecipazione ai gruppi di preghiera di carattere ecumenico organizzati dalla medesima Sig.ra Rydén, ad attenersi alle disposizioni dei Vescovi diocesani.

Nel comunicarLe quanto sopra profitto della circostanza per confermarmi con sentimenti di profonda stima

dell'Eminenza/Eccellenza Vostra Rev.ma
dev.mo

✠ Joseph Card. RATZINGER
Prefetto

(con Allegato)

Ai Presidenti delle Conferenze Episcopali di
Francia, Svizzera, Uruguay, Filippine, Canada

TRANSLATION

CONGREGATIO 　　　　　　　00120 Città del Vaticano
PRO DOCTRINA FIDEI 　　　　Palazzo del S. Uffizio　　　　10 July 2004

Prot.N. 54/92-19631

Eminence/Excellence,

As you know, this Congregation published a Notification in 1995 on the writings of Mrs Vassula Rydén. Afterwards, and at her request, a thorough dialogue followed. At conclusion of this dialogue, a letter of Mrs. Rydén dated April 4th 2002 was subsequently published in the latest volume of "True Life in God", in which Mrs. Rydén supplies useful clarifications regarding her marital situation, as well as some difficulties which in the aforesaid Notification were suggested towards her writings and her participation in the sacraments (Cf. annex).

Since the aforementioned writings have enjoyed a certain diffusion in your country, this Congregation has deemed it useful to inform you of the above. Concerning the participation in the ecumenical prayer groups organised by Mrs. Ryden, the Catholic faithful should be called to follow the dispositions of the Diocesan Bishops.

In communicating to you the above, I use the occasion to assure you of my lasting and profound esteem.

　　　　　　　　　　　　　　Your Eminence/Excellency's
　　　　　　　　　　　　　　　　　Most Devout

　　　　　　　　　　　　　　　　　(Signed)
　　　　　　　　　　　　　　Joseph Card. Ratzinger
　　　　　　　　　　　　　　　　　Prefect

(With attachment)
_____

To the Presidents of the Episcopal Conferences of
France, Switzerland, Uruguay, Philippines, Canada

Rome 30.03.03

Dear Readers of TLIG,

Since the year 2000 I have had the honour of being in communication with H.E. Cardinal Joseph Ratzinger, Prefect for the Congregation for the Doctrine of Faith. On the 6th July 2000 I presented to him my humble request of my writings being submitted to further study by the same Congregation and that I be granted the opportunity of answering to the reservations expressed in the *Notification* of 6th October 1995. His Eminence benignly has granted me this occasion and at the hand of Fr. Prospero Grech submitted a letter to me of 4th April 2002 containing five questions for me to answer. My answers to these questions were then submitted to The Congregation for the Doctrine of Faith on 26th June 2002. Cardinal Ratzinger has now requested me to publish the questions with my replies to them and I am happy to share them with you as an expression of my official standpoint.

I pray that the publication of this document may serve the dialogue of truth and of love, so important not only to ecumenism, but also to rendering God's graces fruitful in the church.

May God bless you,

Vassula

Vassula

Collegio Sta Monica,
Via Paolo VI 25,
00193 Rome
4th April 2002

Dear Mrs Rydén,

On the 6th of July 2000 you addressed a letter to His Eminence Cardinal Ratzinger regarding the "Notificazione" of the Congregation for the Doctrine of the Faith concerning your writings. His Eminence has taken note of your letter and, together with his collaborators, has decided to give you the opportunity to clarify the meaning of some assertions contained in your publications. For this purpose I have been delegated to contact you personally both in conversation and in writing so that the Congregation may have a clearer idea of the exact interpretation of these assertions. I wish to make clear from the very outset that not being a Roman Catholic you do not fall under the jurisdiction of the Congregation and that yours is not a personal censure. However, as many Catholics follow the "True Life in God" they too have a right to know where they stand regarding points of doctrine and practice prompted by your writings. We are also aware of your works of charity, your efforts to lead all Christians towards unity with the Bishop of Rome, of your great devotion to the Blessed Virgin Mary, of your presentation of God as the God of Love even to non-Christians and of your antagonism to rationalism and corruption among Christians. Your latest books, too, seem to have laid aside some ambiguous expressions contained in your earlier ones. This notwithstanding I would be grateful if you can reply, as clearly as possible, to some questions to help the Congregation to obtain a clearer idea of what you are doing.

1. You know very well that, for both Catholics and Orthodox, there is only one Revelation, that of God in Jesus Christ, which is contained in the Holy Scriptures and in Tradition. Within the Catholic Church even accepted "private" revelations as in Lourdes or Fatima, although taken seriously, are not matters of faith. In which sense, therefore, do you consider your writings as revelations and how should they be accepted by your hearers and readers?

2. You belong to the Orthodox Church and often exhort priests and bishops of that faith to acknowledge the Pope and to make peace with the Roman Church. For this, unfortunately, you are not welcome in some countries of your own persuasion. Why do you take up this mission? What is your idea of the Bishop of Rome and how do you foresee the future of Christian unity? One sometimes gets the impression in reading your works, however, that you stand above both Churches without being committed to either. For example, it seems that you receive communion in both Catholic and Orthodox churches but in your marital status you follow the custom of oikonomia. As I have said already, these observations are not meant as a personal censure as we have absolutely no right to adjudicate your conscience, but you understand our concern about your Catholic followers who may interpret these attitudes in a relativistic manner and are tempted to disregard the discipline of their own Church.

3. In your earlier writings, as observed in the "Notificazione", there was some confusion of terminology regarding the Persons of the Holy Trinity. We are sure that you subscribe to the teaching of your Church. Do you think you could help us to clarify these expressions? When

dealing with matters of faith would it not be useful to follow the official terminology of standard catechisms to avoid confusion in the minds of the readers of "True Life in God"?

4. There are also some difficulties regarding protology and eschatology. In what sense does the soul have a "vision of God" before being infused into the body? And how do you envision the place of the New Pentecost within the history of salvation in relation to the parousia and the resurrection of the dead?

5. What is the real identity of the "True Life in God" movement and what does it require of its followers? How is it structured?

Dear Mrs Ryden, we are sorry to disturb you with these questions and you may rest assured that we appreciate your good works and intentions. However, in answer to your letter to Cardinal Ratzinger, we felt it was our duty to clarify some ambiguities in your writings which might have escaped you. We owe this to your Catholic readers who might experience a conflict of conscience in following your writings. Please take your time to answer; it would be better if you and I could meet and have a few informal chats before you put anything in writing. Pray that the Holy Spirit may illuminate you, and consult any spiritual director or theologian you can trust. We are certain that our queries will also help you to understand the deeper implications of your writings to render them more acceptable to both Catholics and Orthodox. I shall personally be at your disposal to clarify their meaning.

His Eminence sends you his regards and trusts that you will provide a satisfactory answer to ease his task of complying with the requests in your letter.

Yours sincerely in Christ,

Fr Prospero Grech, OSA

Consultor of the Congregation

Rome, 26.06.02

Most reverend Fr. Prospero Grech
Collegio Sta Monica
Via Paolo VI, 25,
I-00193 Rome

Re: Answer of Vassula Rydén to the letter of Father Prospero Grech, written on behalf of H.E. Cardinal Joseph Ratzinger of the Congregation for the Doctrine of Faith and dated 4th April 2002.

Dear Fr. Prospero Grech,

First of all, I wish to thank you for granting me the opportunity of responding to the questions you have to my writings and my activity, expressed most respectfully in your letter of 4th April 2002, and that reiterate the points of critique contained in the "Notification" of 1995.

I am aware of the task and responsibility assigned to your most holy congregation of "trying the spirits" (1. Jn 4:1). I have somewhat realized, during these years, the complexity of this task of discernment and how delicate it is, as I myself have met along my way many people who approached me claiming they had divine experiences as well, which they wanted to mingle with mine. For prudence and for reasons of responsibility I have made it a principle not to notice any of them. Therefore, I do appreciate the importance of your work of protecting the faithful from any harm and keeping the faith pure from unauthentic experiences, but equally to safeguard the true charisms that could benefit the church.

I am also grateful to you that you are giving me the opportunity to clarify and shed light on certain expressions that might appear unclear as they are written in imagery and poetic or symbolic style. I am equally aware that my speaking to Catholic Christians though being Greek Orthodox is unusual, but rather than seeing it as disorder, I humbly desire this to be my small contribution to the healing of the dissentions between Christian brethren. And so, I will respond the best I can to the questions you have designed to present to me in complete honesty and lucidity, assured equally of your generosity, good will and comprehension towards my limitations in expressing the full panorama contained in the 12 volumes of the books entitled True Life in God (TLIG).

Question 1: Relationship between TLIG and Revelation.

> *You know very well that, for both Catholics and Orthodox there is only one Revelation that of God in Jesus Christ, which is contained in the Holy Scriptures and in Tradition. Within the Catholic Church even accepted "private revelations" as in Lourdes or Fatima, although taken seriously, are not matters of faith. In which sense, therefore, do you define your writings as revelations and how should they be accepted by your hearers and readers?*

I never had any lessons of catechism let alone theology, nor did I know of any theological nuances as the ones mentioned above at the beginning of my call and my conversion. I was taught these differences gradually as the gentle guidance of the Holy Spirit proceeded. In the very beginning of this call, I was very confused and early, during the manifestation of my angel, this is what I said: "But I can't understand. We have already the Bible, so why do we need messages?" My angel replied: *"So you do feel that all has been given in the Bible?"* I responded: "Yes. That is why I do not see the reason of all this. I mean nothing is new." Then the angel said: *"God wants these messages to be given."* I said: "Is there a special reason why me?" The angel responded: *"No. God loves you all. These messages are just a reminder to remind you how your foundations began"* (07.08.1986).

A Protestant minister once said to me that there is no reason why God would want to speak to us now that we have the Holy Bible. Confused, I said to Christ: "Lord, there are some ministers who refuse to hear or believe that You can manifest Yourself like this, through me; they say that You, Jesus, have brought us all the truth and they need nothing else but the Holy Bible, in other words all these works are false." The response of Christ was the following:

> *I have said to you all that the Advocate, the Holy Spirit, whom the Father will send in My Name, will teach you everything and remind you of all I have said to you. I am not giving you any new doctrine, I am only reminding you of the truth and leading those who wandered astray back to the complete truth. I, the Lord, will keep stirring you up with Reminders and My Holy Spirit, the Advocate, will always be among you as the Reminder of My Word. So do not be astonished when My Holy Spirit speaks to you – these reminders are given by My Grace to convert you and to remind you of My Ways. (20.12.1988)*

Another passage 11 years later our Lord asked me to write the following:

> *All of these messages come from on high and are inspired by Me. They can profitably be used for teaching and for refuting error. They can be used for guiding the Church into unity and for guiding people's lives and teaching them to be holy. They are given to you for a better explanation[1] to the Revelation[2] given to you. They are an inexhaustible source of amazing grace for you all to renew you. (30.07.1999)*

I believe that there is but one Revelation and I never said the contrary, nor do you find this in the writings. I do not expect the readers of TLIG to take the messages for more than Holy Scripture and I am sure that nothing in the TLIG books can induce all those who hear and read me to think in another way. In fact in my witnessing I quote all the time many passages from the Scriptures, sometimes even more than the messages themselves. Within the messages there is a clear and continuous insistence of focusing on the Holy Bible and of living by its truth. The writings are an actualisation and a reminder of the one and only Revelation in Christ, held in Scripture and Tradition, transmitted through the church; they are but an appeal to this Revelation. In fact, these writings never affected readers to take them above the Scriptures, but testimonies shed that they helped them to understand much better the Word of God. Yet, we know that God can remind us of His blessed Word when He knows it is necessary for the benefit of the Church. Favours of this kind, for a favour it is, illumine or make manifest a truth already known, giving a better understanding of it.

One could ask then, why did God call someone so limited and unworthy, totally disinterested and ignorant in church matters, who never aspired for God, to receive a "reminder of His Word"? Are not the priests and theologians called to do the same? Yes, I believe they are, and I, in no way ever intended to compete with the priests and theologians that God has called to do their duty; yet, I do believe that God has called me unexpectedly by a direct action from His part.

I have recently learnt that the second Vatican Council has underlined how important it is that the laity contributes to spreading the Good News through the various gifts God bestows upon His Church. In *Lumen Gentium*, the Council clearly states that the laity participates in the prophetic office of Christ and that Christ "fulfils this office, not only by the hierarchy but also by the laity. He accordingly both establishes them as witnesses and provides them with the sense of the faith (sensus fidei) and the grace of the word" (LG 35). Every lay-person, therefore, has a part to play in this service of the

---

[1] I heard at the same time the word "understanding".
[2] The Holy Bible.

Gospel according to the charism God has given him or her and through those gifts he or she is at once the witness and the living instrument of the mission of the church itself, "according to the measure of Christ's bestowal."

In most Classic works of Catholic Fundamental Theology there is a distinction between Revelation as a concept of reflection (Revelation with capital R) and revelation as a concept of experience (revelation with minor r, often revelations in plural). When I speak of my humble experience as "revelation", I speak of revelation with a minor "r" from the experiential point of view.

I do not speak of my experience as revelation from a doctrinal point of view in any way wanting to compete with Revelation. Just as with other "private revelations" or "prophetic revelations" my work adds nothing to the Deposit of Faith. On the contrary, God's calling to me aims at pointing to the fullness of the truth of the Deposit of Faith, to enter more fully into and live by this truth.

The constitution Dei Verbum of the Second Vatican Council has made it clear that the Public Revelation is complete and perfect and that "no new public revelation is to be expected before the glorious manifestation of our Lord, Jesus Christ" (Dei Verbum 4). On the other hand, Dei Verbum also makes it clear that the people of God constantly needs to deepen the appreciation of this truth:

> The Tradition that comes from the apostles makes progress in the Church with the help of the Holy Spirit. There is a growth in insight into the realities and words that are being passed on. This comes about in various ways. It comes through contemplation and study of believers who ponder these things in their hearts (cf. Lk. 2:19 and 51). It comes from the intimate sense of spiritual realities which they experience. And it comes from the preaching of those who have received, along with their right of succession in the episcopate, the sure charism of truth. Thus, as the centuries go by, the Church is always advancing towards the plenitude of divine truth, until eventually the words of God are fulfilled in her (Dei Verbum 8).

His Eminence, Cardinal Joseph Ratzinger has said very explicitly on the relationship between Christian prophecy and Revelation that the thesis that prophecy should end with the completion of Revelation in Christ harbours misunderstandings. His position was phrased in an interview on Christian prophecy and again in a commentary to the disclosure of the Third Secret of Fatima. I allow myself to quote him directly from the interview:

> The Revelation is essentially God who gives himself to us, who constructs history with us and who reunites us gathering us all together. It is the unfolding of an encounter that has also an inherent communicative dimension and a cognitive structure. This also carries implications for knowledge of the truth of Revelation. Understood in the proper way, the Revelation has attained its goal with Christ because – in those beautiful words of Saint John of the Cross – when God has spoken personally there is nothing more to add. Nothing more about the Logos can be said. He is among us in a complete way and God has nothing greater to give us, to say to us than Himself. But this very wholeness of God's giving of himself – that is, that He, the Logos, is present in the flesh – also means that we must continue to penetrate this Mystery. This brings us back to the structure of hope. The coming of Christ is the beginning of an ever-deepening knowledge and of a gradual discovery of what, in the Logos, is being given. Thus, a new way is inaugurated of leading man into the whole truth, as Jesus puts it in the Gospel of John when he says that the Holy Spirit will come down. I believe that the pneumatological Christology of Jesus' leave-taking discourse is very important to our theme given that Christ explains that his coming in the flesh was just a first step. The real coming will happen when Christ is no longer bound to a place or to a body locally limited but when he comes to all of us in the Spirit as the Risen One, so that entering into the truth may also acquire more and more profundity. It seems clear to me that – considering that the time of the church, that is, the time when Christ comes to us in Spirit is determined by this very pneumatological Christology – the prophetic element, as

element of hope and appeal, cannot naturally be lacking or allowed to fade away (30 Giorni, January 1999).

In the same manner, I do not claim in any way, a status or an authority of my writings coming close to Holy Scripture. The Holy Bible is inspired in an infallible way. I humbly believe that the Lord touched me to journey with Him through a direct action in my soul assisting me when called to write, but it is not inspiration in the same sense as Scripture is and the result is not infallibility, but this does not mean either that there should be doctrinal errors in my writings, which I am assured there are not.

In Fr. Marie-Eugène's book *I am a Daughter of the Church*, he reminds us how God can adapt Himself to the soul:

> God's direct action, being thus grounded in the human of which it makes use, is marvellously adapted to the psychological life of the soul. This adaptation of God should be underlined as an important characteristic of His interventions. God, who consents to speak the language of human signs to give us His light, pushes condescendence to the point of adapting Himself to our temperaments and our particular needs in the choice of these signs, so as to reach us more surely. For a faith that has kept its purity and its simplicity, He will speak in a language of external brilliant signs that will make faith vibrate. For a faith that rationalism has rendered prudent and critical, He will have a more intellectual language.[1]

Cardinal Ratzinger has said, "that being able to set oneself up as the word and image of interior contact with God, even in the case of authentic mysticism, always depends on the possibilities of the human soul and its limitations". I thus experience the Word of God without effort, in other words, without me forcing anything, it just comes. I receive these communications (interior words) namely in two forms. Please note here that in no way I intend to say I know perfectly well how to express this phenomenon and how God can do such things, but this explanation below is the best I can do:

> 1. Through the intervention of interior words, namely locutions. The words I perceive are substantial ones, much clearer than were I to hear them through my ears. One single word alone may contain a world of meaning such as the understanding on its own could never put rapidly into human language. Any divine word or instruction given to teach me, will not be in the manner of school teaching, that perhaps due to limited time cannot be wholly explained all at once, or because of human frailty may be forgotten, or even not quite understood. But the divine instruction or the word given, will be given in such lapse of time and engraved in the mind in such a way that it will be difficult to forget. The light it spreads is so vast, just like a bright light that sheds far and wide, giving you a wealth of knowledge instantly more than just the word itself. The word given is like a wide river that breaks into other rivulets leading you everywhere and in different places but always coming from the one river. Any normal teaching in a school would have taken me months to learn. While I experience the words so strongly, I am equally aware that the written form and the way I should express the words still depends on my limited capacities of language and expression.

> 2. The second way I receive the words of God is through a light of understanding in my intellect without any utterance of speech. It is like God transmits His thought into mine. I would immediately know what God wants, or wishes to say. Then I have to write down this "non-expressed message" as well as I could by selecting my own words.

I have been told later here in Rome, that St. Bridget of Sweden had similar ways of writing down her messages.

---

[1] Fr. Marie-Eugène, O.C.D., *I am a daughter of the Church*, Vol. II, Chicago, 1955. p. 283.

Why the Lord chose this special form of writing down the messages to which He even seizes my hand? I really do not know. The Lord just told me when I asked him why: "Because I like it in this way". So I do not know how this happens. I would like to point out though that theologians who are also expert graphologists and who have investigated the writings called them "hieratic", describing many groundbreaking differences between the way I write and the so-called automatic writing. I have later come to know that known mystics such as Theresa of Avila experienced raptures of her body or sometimes part of her body. I believe this to be a mitigated form of rapture of my hand and trust that the Lord has his own purposes in this.

Question 2. My relationship as Orthodox Christian to the Roman Catholic Church.

> You belong to the Orthodox Church and often exhort priests and bishops of that faith to acknowledge the Pope and to make peace with the Roman Church. For this, unfortunately, you are not welcome in some countries of your own persuasion. Why do you take up this mission? What is your idea of the Bishop of Rome and how do you foresee the future of Christian unity? One sometimes gets the impression in reading your works, however, that you stand above both churches without being committed to either. For example, it seems that you receive communion in both catholic and orthodox churches, but in your marital status you follow the custom of oikonomia. As I have said already, these observations are not meant as a personal censure as we have absolutely no right to adjudicate your conscience, but you understand our concern about the Catholic followers who may interpret these attitudes in a relativistic manner and are tempted to disregard the disciplines of their own church.

Motivations for taking up this work of unity

I do not believe I would have ever had the courage or the zeal to face the Orthodoxy to bring them to understand the reconciliation our Lord desires from them if I had not experienced our Lord's presence, neither would I have endured the oppositions, the criticisms and the persecutions being done on me by them. In the very beginning of God's intervention I was totally confused and feared I was being deluded; this uncertainty was truly the biggest cross, since I never heard in my life before that God can indeed express Himself to people in our own times and had no one to ask about it. Because of this, I tried to fight it away, but the experience would not leave and later on, slowly, with time, I became reassured and confident that all of this was only God's work, because I started to see God's hand in it.

This is why I stopped fearing to face opposition and criticism and have total confidence in our Lord, knowing that where I lack He will always fill, in spite of my insufficiency, and His works will end up always glorious.

Approaching the Orthodox priests, monks and bishops to acknowledge the Pope and to reconcile with sincerity with the Roman Church is not an easy task as our Lord says in one of the messages; it is like trying to swim in the opposite direction of a strong current, but after having seen how our Lord suffers in our division I could not refuse our Lord's request when asked to carry this cross; therefore, I have accepted this mission, yet not without having gone through (and still going through) many fires.

You have asked: "Why do you take up this mission?" My answer is, because I was called by God, I believed and I answered Him; therefore, I want to do God's will. One of Christ's first words were: *"Which house is more important, your house or My House?"* I answered, "Your House, Lord." He said: *"Revive My House, embellish My House and unite it."*

Some of the Greek Orthodox hierarchy totally reject me, first because they do not believe me,[1] secondly because I am a woman and thirdly because a woman should not speak. Some of the monks are suspicious of me saying that I am probably a Trojan horse sent and paid by the Pope, or that I am even a Uniate. Many do not want to hear of reconciliation or ecumenism. They consider it heresy if I pray with the Roman Catholics. That is where they see it as standing above both Churches without being committed to either. I am full and wholly committed to my Church but it is not heresy nor a sin if I live ecumenically and pray with other Christians to promote unity. The key to unity though, according to our Lord in the writings, is humility and love. Many of the people of the Churches do not have this key yet. Many of the Greek Orthodox lay people but as well as the simple priest around the corner, up to the monk in a remote monastery would call the Roman Catholic Church to this day heretic and dangerous; they are taught to believe this since their birth and it is wrong. Yet, I believe that in their rigidity they can change through a metanoia and the power of the Holy Spirit who will make them bend and through the prayers of the faithful. In our gatherings we pray to God for this change of heart.

Nevertheless, it is not a question of them alone bending. Everyone must bend in humility and love. The people of each Church should be willing to die to their ego and to their rigidity and then through this act of humility and obedience to the truth, Christ's presence will be shining in them. I believe that through this act of humility, the Churches' past and present failures will be washed away and unity will be accomplished. I never lose hope to approach the Orthodox and this is why I always keep returning to them to give them my testimony. My testimony is given reminding them of our Lord's words: "may they be one in us, as you are in me and I am in you, so that the world may believe it was you who sent me," (Jn 17:21). In this manner, despite the obstacles, a few ecumenical prayer groups were formed in Athens and in Rhodes with Orthodox priests included in them. All these prayer groups start by praying the Rosary, then other prayers. Nevertheless, it is not only rejection I get from the Orthodox hierarchy because of the reasons I mentioned above, but our Lord has provided me with a good number of Greek Orthodox clergy friends as well.

The Bishop of Rome

Our Lord gave me an interior vision of three iron bars symbolizing the three major Christian bodies, Catholics, Orthodox and Protestant Christians, calling their heads to meet by bending, so that they meet, but to meet they have to bend. This passage speaks of the attitude that is needed to arrive at the unity the Lord has been longing for since his prayer to his Father – "that all may be one". This passage of the TLIG messages does not pretend to speak of unity on an ontological level, indicating that there should be no differences in which extent the various Christian groups have retained the truth Christ conferred to his church. And it is not true I claim that this calling to humility amongst Christian brothers should imply a pan-Christian approach to unity and that unity should be advanced through a bargain of truth, (like a trader, selling and buying) leading to a levelling and a relativism of truth. On the contrary, I have often spoken on the importance of remaining faithful to the truth, and even more than my speaking, the message is nothing but a calling to live by the truth of the Gospel in the One Revelation of Christ, as expressed above. The writings contain many warnings against the contrary attitude, to the point of portraying a "false ecumenism" as a Trojan horse of introducing a lifeless image of Christ:

> *The figure daubed with assorted colours, this figure these traders are trying to make you revere to and follow is not me – it is an invention of perverted human skill to degrade the concept of*

---

[1] Although in our book of the doctrine of the Orthodox Church, Book I, published in 1997 by Mr. Trembelas, on p. 79 it reads: "Revelations are defined as an act taken by God by which He notifies His reasonable creatures about the mysteries of His existence, nature and will, according to their limited intellectual capacity..."

> My Holiness and My Divinity; it is a false ecumenism; it is a defiance of all that is holy. I suffer because of the sins of these traders. (22.10.1990)

Many messages on unity keep together these two vital aspects of ecumenism: The spiritual attitude implying humility and love towards other Christians together with the un-compromised quest for the truth of Christ. One example is a passage where the Virgin Mary speaks of the fabrics of unity:

> The Kingdom of God is not just words on the lips, the Kingdom of God is love, peace, unity and faith in the heart. It is the Lord's Church united in One inside your heart. The Keys to Unity are: Love and Humility. Jesus never urged you to divide yourselves – this division in His Church was no desire of His. (23.09.1991)

Further down in the same passage, Jesus speaks of the truth: "Always defend to death the truth. Scathed you shall be from time to time, but I shall allow it just enough to keep your soul pure and docile" (reiterated on 05.06.1992, 25.09.1997, 22.06.1998, etc.)

I have had a few meetings with Catholic clergy in the United States, Holland and Switzerland in particular who are very liberal and very much against the Pope. I had to defend the Chair of Peter and explain it to them as well as I could through powerful messages that came from Christ, showing them how confused their minds were. In the end many of these priests came to tell me how they appreciated these clarifications. I had one or two though who did not agree telling me that I am more Catholic than the Catholics… Although there are many unity passages that regard the unity between the Churches, there are also quite a number that especially are written for a lot of Catholic clergy who are rebelling against the Pope to bring them back to faithfulness to him. Here is one early example:

> I the Lord do not want any divisions in My Church. You will, for My sake, unite and under My Name love Me, follow Me and bear witness for Me. You will love one another as I love you; you will unite and become one flock under one Shepherd.[1] I have, as you all know, selected Peter – giving him the authority. I have, as you all know, given him the keys of the kingdom of heaven. I have asked Peter to feed My lambs and sheep – looking after them.[2] This authority was given by Me. I have not desired you to alter My wish. (19.03.1988)

Another message speaking of the future of unity puts it even clearer:

> I will then place into Peter's hand an iron sceptre with which he will guard My sheep, and for those who do not know and still ask themselves "why is it that we have to have a guide?" I tell you this – "have you ever seen or known of any flock of sheep without a shepherd? I am your Heavenly Shepherd and I have chosen Peter to keep My lambs until My return. I have given him the responsibility, so why all these disputes, why all these futile arguments?" And for all those who still do not know My words, I tell you to read them in the Scriptures – they are to be found in the testimony of John, My disciple.[3] I will then unite My Church and encircle you with My arms into one fold for today; as it is you are all scattered, developing too many communities, split sections. My Body you have torn apart and this CANNOT BE. I will unite you all. (16.05.1988)

Other messages speak of the Pope as the Vicar of Christ or the Vicar of the Church. Here is one example:

---

[1] The Pope.
[2] John 21:15-17.
[3] John 21:15-17.

> *Pray for the whole Church. Be the incense of My Church and by this I mean that you pray for all those who are proclaiming My Word, from the Vicar who is representing Me to the apostles and prophets of your days, from the sacerdotal souls and religious souls to the laymen, so that they may be ready to understand that all of you whom I mentioned are part of One Body, My Body. (10.01.1990)* (More references in 01.06.1989, 02.03.1990, 10.10.1990, 18.03.1991, 20.04.1993, 20.12.1993, 15.04.1996, 22.10.1996, 20.12.1996.)

The writings contain no references to how the role of Peter will relate to the roles of the various patriarchal sees, and so I cannot speak about this. But I am aware that the Pope himself in the Encyclical "Ut unum sint" does open up for a discussion of this sort:

> It is nonetheless significant and encouraging that the question of the primacy of the Bishop of Rome has now become a subject of study that is already under way or will be in the near future. It is likewise significant and encouraging that this question appears as an essential theme not only in the theological dialogues in which the Catholic Church is engaging with other Churches and Ecclesial Communities, but also more generally in the ecumenical movement as a whole. Recently the delegates to the Fifth World Assembly of the Commission on Faith and Order of the World Council of Churches, held in Santiago de Compostela, recommended that the Commission "begin a new study of the question of a universal ministry of Christian unity". After centuries of bitter controversies, the other Churches and Ecclesial Communities are more and more taking a fresh look at this ministry of unity.[1]

The same encyclical confirms the necessity of East and West reuniting, allowing differences between the two communions while being in full communion:

> In view of all this, the Catholic Church desires nothing less than full communion between East and West. She finds inspiration for this in the experience of the first millennium. In that period, indeed, "the development of different experiences of ecclesial life did not prevent Christians, through mutual relations, from continuing to feel certain that they were at home in any Church, because praise of the one Father, through Christ in the Holy Spirit, rose from them all, in a marvellous variety of languages and melodies; all were gathered together to celebrate the Eucharist, the heart and model for the community regarding not only spirituality and the moral life, but also the Church's very structure, in the variety of ministries and services under the leadership of the Bishop, successor of the Apostles. The first Councils are an eloquent witness to this enduring unity in diversity."[2]

Although the writings do not speak of structural issues regarding East and West, there are many references to the importance of the Eastern Church. Thereby, the un-compromised underlining of the importance of the role of Peter is paired in later messages by an insight that spiritual renewal very well could be inspired by the Eastern Church. Thereby it becomes even more evident why the Body of Christ needs to breathe with both its lungs - that of the western and eastern presence of the Church:

> *House of the West, you have realized, through the Light of My Spirit, that a body needs its two lungs to breath freely, and that My Body is imperfect with one lung; pray that My vivifying Spirit will join you together, but what have I to suffer before!*[3] *(27.11.1996)*

---

[1] Encyclical Letter Ut Unum Sint of the Holy Father John Paul II on Commitment to Ecumenism, 89.
[2] Encyclical Letter Ut Unum Sint of the Holy Father John Paul II on Commitment to Ecumenism 61, ref. to Apostolic Letter *Orientale Lumen* (2 May 1995), 24: *L'Osservatore Romano*, 2-3 May 1995, 18: *loc. Cit.*, 4.
[3] I understood at the same time "what have we to suffer before!" The "we" was meant for Pope John Paul II together with Jesus.

And another similar message:

> *pray for the house of the east and the west to join together, like two hands when joined in prayer; a pair of hands, similar, and in beauty when joined together, pointing towards heaven, when in prayer. Let those two hands, belonging to the same body, work together and share their capacity and resources with each other... let those two hands lift Me together... (15.06.1995).*

Another message speaks of the role of the East in bringing the two houses together again, unifying the Body of Christ:

> *Listen and write: glory will shine from the Eastern bank - that is why I say to the House of the West: turn your eyes towards the East. Do not weep bitterly over the Apostasy and the destruction of your House; do not panic, for tomorrow you will eat and drink together with My shoot from the Eastern bank - My Spirit will bring you together. Have you not heard that the East and West will be one kingdom? Have you not heard that I shall settle for one date?[1]*

> *I am going to reach out My Hand and carve on a stick the words: West bank, House of Peter and all those who are loyal to him; then, on another stick I will carve: East bank, House of Paul, together with all those who are loyal to him. And when the members of the two Houses will say: "Lord, tell us what you mean now", I will say to them: "I will take the stick on which I carved Paul's name together with all those who are loyal to him and put the stick of Peter and his loyal ones, as one. I shall make one stick out of the two and I shall hold them as one; I shall bind them together with My New Name; this will be the bridge between the West and the East. My Holy Name will bind the bridge, so that you will exchange your possessions across this bridge – they will no longer practise alone, but together, and I shall reign over them all.*

> *What I have planned shall happen, and should men say to you, daughter, that these signs are not from Me, tell them: "do not fear - have you not heard that He is the Sanctuary and the stumbling stone as well? The Rock that can bring down the two Houses but raise them up again as one single House?" (24.10.1994)*

Again, this message takes nothing away from the role and authority of Peter, but it highlights the importance of having the eastern and western parts of the Body of Christ united so that the World may believe.

The Future of Christian Unity

Although the message confirms the primacy of Peter, the Bishop of Rome, known in both Orthodox and Catholic tradition, it does not speak of questions of jurisdiction. I believe I have not been called to speak on this issue and so I refrain from doing so in any way.

My calling is to confirm the Pope's importance and defend his Chair against all those who tend to disobey him and rebel against him, while inspiring the construction and strengthening of the interior fabrics of unity. My primary approach to unity is that of unity through spirituality. The message is a calling for unity both intra nos and extra nos - a calling to strengthen the spiritual dynamics of unity both within the particular churches and between them.

---

[1] I understood that Christ was referring to all of His messages of unity, calling us all to unify the dates of Easter. This alone seems to "settle" Him and satisfy His thirst for unity. Christ promised us that if we unify the dates of Easter, He will do the rest.

I do not know what the future structures of the unified church will look like, as the Lord has chosen not to speak on this nor did He favour me to give me any light on this, but I believe it will come through spirituality; and I believe I have been granted a foretaste of the grace of that future unity in various ecumenical gatherings.

In March 2000, for instance, the Lord permitted our prayer groups to gather in his birthplace, Bethlehem. 450 people came from far and wide; yes, from more than 55 countries and from 12 different churches to an international meeting of prayer for peace and unity. We gathered as one single family. With us we had 75 clergy also from 12 different churches that came, but also other clergy from the Holy Land, who, hearing of this prayer meeting joined us as well. This ecumenical event was co-ordinated by some Jews and Palestinians who were touched by the writings of "True Life in God". They believed in the redemption of Christ and of his saving plan in our days and volunteered to organize this meeting. When one knows how in our days, Palestinians and Jews are fighting against each other, their reconciliation is a sign of the power of the Holy Spirit who joined those two nations to work for a meeting for peace between the divided Christians. As Scriptures say: "Peacemakers, when they work for peace, sow the seeds which will bear fruit in holiness" (Jm 3:18). This is a lesson for all of us.

We lived and had a foretaste of what unity will be like one day between Christians. We had speeches given to us from clergy of different churches on unity. Their speech resounded like they came from one voice and one mind. We sensed the great desire of all of us being one, during their talks. We saw and we watched the thirst of the laity and the clergy, they have for unity. But we sensed at the same time the great external wounds our division has produced on the Mystical Body of Christ.

The majority of us are tired of this division, because it is not according to our Lord's law of love. Christ is even more tired of seeing us divided. The cheers and acclamations of joy of all these nations who were bonded together, appealing for a complete unity among Christians exposed that this division is not only a sin but an anti-testimony as well. Yet, the biggest sin against unity is to have the dates of Easter separated. How good it will be when we all cry out together: "Christos Anesti" in one voice all in one day. We all say, "Thy Will be done on earth as it is in heaven…" Jesus Christ united us together by his Blood, so how can one deny this unity? "He is the peace between us, and has made the Gentile and the Jew into one and broken down the barrier which used to keep them apart, actual destroying in his own person the hostility caused by the rules and decrees of the Law." (Ep 2:14-15). How can we say "no" to God, if He wants us to unite? Could it be because our hearts have hardened? Have we forgotten the Holy Father's words when he said: "The elements that unite us are far greater than those that divide us"? So we should take up those elements and use them to smoothen up the way to a complete unity.

The Holy Eucharist and eucharistic sharing

In the Catechism of the Catholic Church it is said with reference to St. Augustine regarding the Eucharist:

> Before the greatness of this mystery [the Holy Eucharist] St Augustine exclaims: *"O sacrament of devotion! O sign of unity! O bond of charity!"* The more painful the experience of the divisions in the church which break the common participation in the table of the Lord, the more urgent are our prayers to the Lord that the time of complete unity among all who believe in him may return (CCC 1398).

The Lord urges us to reconcile and reunite. As a well-known Catholic cardinal said recently to an Orthodox priest friend of mine from New York who attended the cardinal's mass in Rome, so it is my conviction that it *must* be possible to obtain again that union around the Lord's table between

Catholics and Orthodox, as we share the same sacraments and have virtually the same faith, albeit clothed in different expressions of faith and worship. I have come to experience from the flaming love of Our Lord the depths of his desire for the perfect union of his Body and believe He is in pain over our lack of love and communion. Therefore, I have no bigger desire than to see his Body reunited and I am convinced that we, Christians, if we really love Jesus Christ, must do all that is in our power to work for the reconciliation of the separated members of Christ's body.

Meanwhile, I know this union will not come easy but only through a miracle of Our Lord. Although we must do all we can to advance unity, He has promised to give us that union that will be the Holy Spirit's work for, as I once said back in 1992, it will come as sudden as the fall of the Berlin wall: *"Mercy and Justice is working with such wonders as has never happened among many generations, and Unity shall come upon you like Dawn and as sudden as the fall of communism - it shall come from God and your nations shall name it the Great Miracle, the Blessed Day in your history."* (10.01.1990)

The Church of Christ is one in the sense that Christ is one and only has one Holy Body. It is the people of the church who are divided. If Christians are able to go beyond the negative obstacles that separate them, obstacles that according to Scriptures are against the fulfilment of the unity of faith, love and worship among us, the Father will hear the prayer expressed already of his Divine Son, when he said: *"may they be one in us, as you are in me and I am in you, so that the world may believe it was you who sent me"* (Jn 17: 27).

While waiting for this grace I follow as good I can the principles in the present state of affairs and am convinced not to infringe on the conscience of the members of any church. In the question, it says the following, "one sometimes gets the impression in reading your works, however, that you stand above both churches without being committed to either…" There is no ground in the written work to get the impression that I stand above both churches. As you write it, it seems that it is more on the practical level.

As to the way I practise my faith, I am an Orthodox and am committed fully to my Church. Whenever there is an Orthodox church nearby I never fail to follow its Sunday Mass, unless of course there is none, like in Dhaka, Bangladesh where I lived. Just before coming to Rome, where I live now, I lived 11 years in Switzerland. Every Sunday I went to our Orthodox Church and the Greek priest of Lausanne, Fr. Alexander Iossifides is my witness as well as the faithful who were in the church and saw me regularly, unless of course I travelled. Abroad, during my travels when a program has been set-up for me to follow and give my witness, sometimes, and I would add, rather rarely, it could happen that the Catholic priests or Bishops of the place who invited me to speak, have programmed a public Holy Mass to follow in the same place where I spoke; I then remain with the people for the Mass as it is in the program and receive Holy Communion there.

Here in Rome I live out from the centre and quite far from my Greek Orthodox Church which is in the centre of Rome. There is a Slavic Orthodox church at the Tre Fontane, which I attended but I do not understand the language. And so I allow myself once in a while, since half of the time I am away, to receive Holy Communion in the Sanctuary of the Madonna del Divino Amore which is 3 km from my place.

I believe the Second Vatican Council allows me to do this when, as reiterated in the Catechism of the Catholic church says: "a certain communion *in sacris*, and so in the Eucharist, given suitable circumstances and the approval of church authority, is not merely possible but is encouraged" (CCC 1399).

In the Decree *Orientarium Ecclesiarum* of Vatican II it states: "When Eastern Christians separated in good faith from the Catholic church, request of their own accord and are rightly disposed, they may be admitted to the Sacraments of Penance, Eucharist and Anointing…"

The Catholic Code of Canon Law states:

> Catholic Ministers may lawfully administer the Sacraments of Penance, Eucharist, and Anointing of the Sick to members of the Eastern (Oriental) churches which do not have full Communion with the Catholic church, if they ask on their own for the Sacraments and are properly disposed. This holds also for members of other churches, which in the judgement of the Apostolic See are in the same condition as the Oriental churches as far as the Sacraments are concerned. (Canon 844.3)

Pope John Paul II's encyclical letter "Ut unum sint" continues these assertions with reference to *Orientalium Ecclesiarum*:

> By reason of the very close sacramental bonds between the Catholic church and the Orthodox churches, the Decree on Eastern Catholic churches *Orientalium Ecclesiarum* has stated: "Pastoral experience clearly shows that with respect to our Eastern brethren there should and can be taken into consideration various circumstances affecting individuals, wherein the unity of the church is not jeopardized nor are intolerable risks involved, but in which salvation itself and the spiritual profit of souls are urgently at issue. Hence, in view of special circumstances of time, place and personage, the Catholic church has often adopted and now adopts a milder policy, offering to all the means of salvation and an example of charity among Christians through participation in the Sacraments and in other sacred functions and objects."[1]

As to the relationship to the churches of the Reformation things are a bit more complex. Many people of Protestant upbringing who read TLIG became Catholics due to their free choice, mainly due to the issues around the Eucharist. Jesus does not speak in the messages of the validity of their sacraments, but he urges Protestants once again to love the Mother of Jesus and to recognize the role of Peter:

> *Vassula, the time has come to unite My Church. Come together again beloved, come and rebuild these ancient ruins; rebuild My old foundation, a foundation established by My own Hand. Honour My Mother as I, who am The Word, and above all honour her. Would I then not desire you, who are dust and ashes, recognize Her as Queen of Heaven - honouring Her? My grief of today is to see how little My creation know of Her importance. Most of My devoted ones who are under the name of Luther and who have isolated themselves entirely, must return to Peter. (22.12.1987)*

In another message, Christ reprimands those Christians who fail to see the greatness of the mystery of the Eucharist and Christ's Divine Presence therein:

> *…so I tell those churches whose clergy have not accepted My Mystery: "come to your senses and seek Me earnestly. Master you resentment, as well, against My Mother. May every race know that My flesh and My blood come from My Mother. Yes, My Body comes from the most Holy Virgin, from pure blood; blessed be Her Name! To save all the humble of the earth who receive Me and to give them imperishable life I became Bread to give Myself to you; and through this Communion I sanctify all who receive Me, deifying them to become the flesh of My Flesh, the bones of My Bones (...) through My Divinity I deify men (...) now I am judged by men; the Garment[2] that can cover you, adorning you majestically, giving you a metamorphosis,*

---

[1] Encyclical Letter Ut Unum Sint of the Holy Father John Paul II on Commitment to Ecumenism, 58.
[2] A symbolic name for Christ.

divinizing you, is rejected by those churches who cannot comprehend My Mystery...today again I cry out from heaven: "Brothers, why are you undermining My Divinity? If you claim that you are the ones who know what is right, then why is your spirit plundering My Church? (...) I am inviting you to celebrate Mass and partake of the Divine Mystery in the manner I truly instituted (...) They affirm My might, proclaiming My fearful power, singing their praises to Me, acknowledging My Omnipotence and My mighty wonders, but I become a stumbling stone when it comes to measure the magnificence of My Divinity and of My Presence in the Eucharist. (16.10.2000)

Marital Status

Further down in your question, you say about me receiving Holy Communion sometimes in the Roman Catholic church: "our concern about the Catholic followers who may interpret these attitudes in a relativistic manner and are tempted to disregard the disciplines of their own church." If according to the Canon Law which I have quoted above proves that I am in total concordance with the Catholic Church's canon Law, I see no reason for the Catholic people to react relativistically.

I am not in favour of divorce and am not seeking to promote the doctrine among Catholic Christians that remarriage of divorced people should be permitted. My divorce and civil remarriage was prior to my conversion. After my conversion under the light of the TLIG messages I discovered that my marital situation was not regular. However, nobody knew about this situation except myself and it was again by myself that I deplored it publicly. I have denounced my own situation when in fact nobody knew anything about it. Having realised my mistake, I approached my church authorities in Lausanne and went through a process of having everything cleared according to Orthodox marital regulations. I am thus an Orthodox Christian at peace with my Church and its regulations as any other Orthodox Christian and as such am allowed to receive the Eucharist in my own Church and in the Catholic Church according to the principles mentioned above. I in no way disregard the marriage regulations of the Catholic Church. For your information, I attach my Marriage Certificate with this document (Attachment 1).

Question 3. Confusion of terminology in regards to the persons in the Holy Trinity.

In your earlier writings, as observed in the Notification there was some confusion of terminology regarding the persons of the Holy Trinity. We are sure that you subscribe to the teaching of your church. Do you think you could help us clarify these expressions? When dealing with matters of faith would it not be useful to follow the official terminology of standard catechisms to avoid confusion in the mind of the readers of TLIG?

In view of this I would try my best to explain the dilemma of language, reminding you that I am not a theologian who could express herself in a technical manner or receive words from above in an official terminology. It is clear that our Lord has expressed Himself in the manner that I would understand by adapting Himself to reach me. He does not speak to me either in a scholastic theology, but then neither did He when on earth, when He said: "The Father and I are One," (Jn 10:30) nor that of St. Paul when he wrote: "the Lord is the Spirit" (II Co 3:17). To Bernadette of Lourdes, Mary spoke in the local dialect, which was not good French. Even in the inspired books of Scripture, I have learnt that there is a noticeable difference between the refined Greek of St. Luke, and the simple language of St. Mark. St. Catherine of Siena, in her Dialogue, once explained: "You are my Creator, Eternal Trinity, and I am your creature. You have made of me a new creation in the blood of Your Son."[1] To

---

[1] St. Catherine of Siena's Dialogo della Divina Providenza, no. 167. This passage is cited by the Roman Breviary in the second reading for April 29th.

call Christ the Son of the Trinity sounds heterodox but we take this part as far as possible in a good sense...

So it is perfectly normal if Christ uses my level of vocabulary in the beginning rather than the language of a theologian. I sometimes expressed words out of my personal experience of God, and uttered what I had felt in the terms that come to me spontaneously without much critical reflection on how this will sound to others, or whether it might be misunderstood. To articulate divine mysteries was hard enough for me, even more of how one should express these divine mysteries that would be fitting with the traditional language. Theologians, on the contrary, use a vocabulary that has been carefully refined by many centuries of discussion.

I do not know exactly which parts of the earlier writings the question is referring to, but I could imagine it deals with Christ being called "Father". Christ is the Son of the Father. In these parts of the revelation the writings do not refer in an ontological or doctrinal way to the person of Christ. Rather, it is affectionate and paternal language, the same language, Jesus used to his disciples: "My children..." (Jn 13:33). Already Isaiah described the Messiah as the "Wonderful Counselor, the Mighty God, the Eternal Father" (Is 9:5).

From the very beginning I never mixed up the Father, the Son and the Holy Spirit. Christ's presence (attitude) with me was with fatherly affection. When in a passage I called Jesus "Father" it was because of the fatherly way He spoke to me. It was like those instances when fathers are explaining and teaching certain things to their children with patience and love for their growth and development. Here is one example of Christ's words: *"Grow in spirit Vassula, grow, for your task is to deliver all the messages given by Me and My Father. Wisdom will instruct you."* I then answer: "Yes Father!" Jesus replies: *"How beautiful to hear you call Me 'Father'*! I longed to hear from your lips this word: 'Father'" (16.02.1987). In the Litany of the Most Holy Name of Jesus it calls Jesus: "Father of the world to come". The Sequence for the Mass of Pentecost names the Holy Spirit, "Father of the poor".

I chose St. Symeon, a theologian and saint very dear and important to my Orthodox tradition, in order to give you some more similarities. This is what he says: "For those who have been weaned, He (Christ) plays the role of a loving Father who watches over His children's growth and development" (Theological Ethical Orations 4. 269-270).

Also, the critique may refer to one particular message in the beginning when the Lord wanted to teach me of the unity of the Holy Trinity. The message that might be questioned was: *"I am the Father and the Son. Now do you understand? I am One, I am All in One" (02.03.1987)*. Here, our Lord wanted me to understand the perfect and ontological unity of the Most Holy Trinity; how the three divine Persons are undivided and so completely one in nature. Like St. Symeon said in his Hymn 45. 7-21: "Three in one and one in three... How could I have known, Lord, that I had such a God, Master and Protector, Father, Brother and King...?" Gradually any non-official terminology was being crystallized with time so if anyone might have had any confusion it became clearer later on.

Remember how pope Benedict XIV long ago took note of questionable passages in the writings of the Fathers of the church and the saints, and direct that:

> ...what these have said should be taken, as far as possible, in a good sense... obscure points in one text are to be explained otherwise by clearer texts... seek the mind of the writer, not from a particular phrase, but from the whole context of the work; benevolence should be joined to severity; judgment about views one does not agree with should be made, not on the basis of one's views but according to the probability of the doctrine (Constitution of introduction of the Index).

In one of the earliest messages, I tell how Jesus asked me to "design how the Holy Trinity is". I describe having a vision of light. Then one light coming out, then another one, making three. Then I commented: "When the Son is in the Father, then they are one. The Holy Trinity is ONE and the same. They can be 3, but all 3 can be one. Result, One God." This statement employs, I learnt, a metaphor that goes back to the Nicene Creed which declares that the Son came forth from the Father as "light from light". This image has since become classic in Christian thought. For example Symeon the Theologian, writes of "the One who was in the beginning, before all ages, begotten of the Father, and with the Spirit, God and Word, triple in unity, but one light in the Three" (Hymn 12, 14-18).

Sometimes God the Father speaks and it is obvious to any reader who knows the Scriptures that it is indeed the Father who speaks since He would mention words like, "My Son Jesus" etc. Then, it could happen later in the same day that Christ calls me to continue the message and speaks. Again, the reader who knows Scriptures would understand that it is Christ speaking because He would speak of His Wounds or Cross. As for the messages that would start e.g. with the Father, then later on continue with the Son, it would usually contain a reference saying, "later on". If I did not put any reference to help the one who reads it was because it appeared to me so obvious from the words uttered who was actually speaking that I left them as they were. From the thousands of readers I never received a letter from anyone who asked for clarification on the subject and no-one came to tell me they were confused. Only two clergy in the United States read the message in the wrong way, publishing their views in newsletters over and over again, without ever meeting me.

In one passage in the True Life in God writings, Christ says: "I am the Trinity". Here Christ identifies Himself with the divine nature of the Trinity that is One. Christ is one of the Trinity. Christ speaks as the <u>divinity</u>, since it is one in nature, communicated by each of the three persons.

In one of the passages of True Life in God it was Christ speaking: *Be blessed My child, I, Your Holy Father love you. I am the Holy Trinity*, then He added, You have discerned well. I discerned while Jesus was saying *I am your Holy Father*, a "triple" Jesus, like those fancy pictures of one person but made as though they are three, one coming out of the other, all similar and all three the same. *"I am the Holy Trinity all in one" (11.04.1988)* (Unique, undivided, one essence, one substance.) If one looks just at the initial statement attributed to Jesus, one might wonder if He is not identifying Himself with the Father and then with the entire Trinity. But when one reads on, it is clear He is not.

Christ was trying to teach me the oneness of the Holy Trinity, how the Three Persons are undivided and so completely one. The oneness of the Trinity comes out not primarily from the fact that the three persons are undivided (like inseparable friends!) but from the fact that each one of them possesses the same unique divine nature and are distinguished only by their mutual relations.

In another passage of the True Life in God, Christ teaches me how the Trinity is recognized in each of them as One and the same substance: *"...am I not Bountiful? Am I not the highest? So have confidence for you are in your Father's Arms. I, the Holy Trinity am One and the Same (substance)..." (25.07.1989)*.

In order to express this in the way of thinking of the tradition of the Orthodox Church, it may be useful again to turn to Basil Krivoscheine's book on St Symeon. Here, the words are expressed in a better way than were I to express them. "God is beyond names. He is Trinity, yet the One and its Unity cannot be expressed" (p. 284). And from St. Symeon himself:

> Whatever multifarious names we call You, You are one being... This one being is a nature in three hypostases, one Godhead, one God is a single Trinity, not three beings. And yet the One is three according to hypostases. They are connatural, the one to the other according to nature, entirely of the same power, the same essence, united without confusion in a manner that

surpasses our understanding. In turn, they are distinct, separated without separation, three in one and one in three. (Hymn 45. 7-21)

And in another passage of TLIG, Christ insists on Their Divine Oneness: *"I-Am-He-Who-Saves, I am your Redeemer, I Am the Holy Trinity all in One, I Am the Spirit of Grace..." (28.07.1989)*

Here Jesus was telling me that He is in the Father with the Spirit, likewise the Father and He are in the Spirit. He, the Son, is and remains co-eternal in the Father, with the Holy Spirit. We may remember Christ's words: God is a Spirit: and they that worship him must worship him in spirit and in truth (John 4, 24). Of vital importance are also St. Paul's words: "...Now the Lord is that Spirit: and where the Spirit of the Lord is, there is liberty" (2. Cor. 3:17).

One will never find the Father separated from the Son or the Spirit, nor the Son separated from the Father and the Spirit, nor the Spirit excluded from the union with the one from whom He proceeds. Thus, the expression of: *"I Am the Holy Trinity all in One,"* and other expressions in the writing that are similar to this one. Likewise in another passage of TLIG, I specify: *"The Son is in the Father. They are only one. The Holy Trinity is one and the same: three Person but a single God: one and three"* (23.11.1987).

I would like to explain especially these two expressions that came often in the writings of True Life in God. Christ speaks: *"...be one as the Holy Trinity is One and the same" (10.10.1989)*. Or the other expression: *"Pray that My Fold be one, as I and the Father are One and the same" (29.03.1989)*.

There is a very important factor here. When Christ uses the word "the same" it is different if one translates this word in Italian or French because the meaning changes, and I would like to point out that there have been weaknesses in translation, but I cannot be held responsible for this. In English (which is the original language of the writings) it does not mean "the same person" but it means "equal" in the sense of "the unity of essence," "substance".

Then there are passages when in turn the Holy Trinity speaks in one voice. But even so it is very clear. For example here is one passage: *"Your terrified cries pierced through the heavens, reaching the Holy Trinity's ears... My child!"* The Father's Voice, full of joy resounded through all Heaven. Then the Son said: *"Ah... I shall now make her penetrate My Wounds and let her eat My Body and drink My Blood. I shall espouse her to Me and she will be Mine for eternity. I shall show her the Love I have for her and her lips from thereon shall thirst for Me and her heart shall be My Headrest."* The Holy Spirit said immediately after: *"And I, the Holy Spirit, shall descend upon her to reveal to her the truth and the depths of Us. I shall remind the world through her, that the greatest of all the gifts is love."* And then the Holy Trinity spoke in one voice: *"Let Us then celebrate! Let all Heaven celebrate!" (22.12.1990)*

The mystery of the Most Holy Trinity, its oneness combined with the distinct traits of each of the three persons and the relationship between them, is one of the greatest mysteries of the Christian Faith. However, the fact that the Trinity is such an infinite mystery should not make us shrink back from praising its marvels and avoid talking of it, although human language never will be able to express the beauty and immensity of the One but Triune. For the mystery of the Most Holy Trinity is so central to our faith that it stands above and sheds light upon all the other mysteries of faith. This has been pointed out again most clearly in The Cathechism of the Catholic Church:

> The mystery of the Most Holy Trinity is the central mystery of the Christian faith and life. It is the mystery of God in himself. It is therefore the source of all the other mysteries of faith, the light that enlightens them. It is the most fundamental and essential teaching in the "hierarchy of

the truths of faith."[1] The whole history of salvation is identical with the history of the way and the means by which the one true God, Father, Son, and Holy Spirit, reveals himself to men "and reconciles and unites with himself those who turn away from sin".[2] (CCC 234)

Question 4. Protology and Eschatology.

There are also some difficulties regarding protology and eschatology. In what sense does the soul have a "vision of God" before being infused into the body and how do you envision of the new Pentecost within the history of salvation in relation to the parousia and the resurrection of the dead?

Protology: I do not believe in any form of reincarnation. On the contrary, my writings speak against reincarnation and New Age: *"These doctrines of Satan teach you to believe in reincarnation, whereas there is no reincarnation; they keep up the outward appearance of religion but have rejected the inner power of it - the Holy Spirit and the Holy Communion" (19.04.1992)*. The passage that you are referring to might be the following:

> ...then, in the midst of this dazzling Light, your soul will see what they had once seen in that fraction of a second, that very moment of your creation... They will see He who held you first in His Hands, the Eyes that saw you first, they will see the Hands of He who shaped you and blessed you... they will see the Most Tender Father, your Creator... (15.9.1991)

The passage is one of poetic and mystical language. What is being said here is in no way the pre-existence of the soul. Rather it speaks of how God blesses and loves any soul from the very instant of its creation. I believe we are created in the image of God and have His imprint in the depth of our souls wherefore humans have a natural longing for their Creator, which only He can satisfy, as Saint Augustine says: "The heart was made for God; neither can it rest until it rests in God." The important thing I intended to communicate through that sentence is: We carry the image of God in the depth of our being from the moment of our conception.

Eschatology: It has been said that I advocate a wrong kind of millenarianism, wanting to establish a new order, a material "New Heavens and New Earth" *before* the Second Coming of Christ. This is wrong and can be nowhere found in the messages. I am well aware that the Catholic Church has condemned such kind of millenarianism as written in the Catechism of the Catholic Church:

> The Antichrist's deception already begins to take shape in the world every time the claim is made to realize within history that messianic hope which can only be realized beyond history through the eschatological judgment. The Church has rejected even modified forms of this falsification of the kingdom to come under the name of millenarianism, especially the 'intrinsically perverse' political form of secular messianism. (CCC 676)

There are many passages with terms such as: New Heavens and a New Earth as well as a Second Pentecost, or sometimes with the term of New Pentecost, in the True Life in God writings, but they are to be understood metaphorically. The realization of these words is not to be found in a break with this regular history of ours before the Second Coming establishing a second economy of history. The words express the supreme hope that Christ will renew us from within in the power of the Holy Spirit. It is a revival of faith and a renewal of the church that we so much yearn for. And the fruit we hope from this renewal is the healing of the schism in the Body of Christ. Already Pope John XXIII envisioned such a renewal when he prayed for a Second Pentecost: "O divine Spirit...renew in our

---

[1] *General Catechetical Directory* 43.
[2] *General Catechetical Directory* 47.

own days your miracles as of a second Pentecost." And also our present Pope John Paul II has used the term on several occasions, as in a letter to the Most Reverend Father Joseph Chalmers, Prior General of the Brothers of the Blessed Virgin Mary of Mount Carmel, 08.09.2001: "…I invoke an abundance of divine grace on you. Just like a second Pentecost, may the Holy Spirit descend on you and illuminate you so that you may discover the will of your heavenly and merciful father. In this way you will be able to speak to men and women in forms which are familiar to them and efficient" (cf Acts 2:1-13).

Likewise, my writings speak in metaphorical language of a revival of faith, so that the Lord is able to erect his Throne and build his kingdom in our souls: *"Come and learn: the New Heavens and the New Earth will be when I will set My Throne in you, for I will give water from the well of Life free to anybody who is thirsty"* (03.04.1995, ref. to Apoc. 21:6).

I believe the renewal promised to us has already started and it is through grace only that the Mercy of God is upon us to pour out His Spirit on all mankind like never before in history and its growth will continue as grace in our days shines on us like the rays of the sun to heal us.

The Lord favoured me to show me the state of the faith of the Christians in our times. It was deplorable and that is the least one could say. Many of the messages are filled with grief describing the apostasy that has fallen on the Christian world. But the Lord gives us hope, by sharing with us that there will be (there is) a renewal, a transfiguration and a revival by the action of the Holy Spirit. A thirst of God will be given by grace through the Holy Spirit. Here are some extracts: *"My Holy Spirit shall lift you out of your great apostasy, to wed you; your era's wretchedness shall peel off you because with My Own Hand I shall unwrap your death shroud to clothe you in the garments of your wedding…"* (20.10.1990). *"I shall make the whole creation new, I shall renew you all with my Holy Spirit"* (27.6.1991).

My writings do not speak about when this will happen or to what an extent the Lord will be able to build his kingdom as we all hope and pray for when we pray the Lord's prayer: "Thy Kingdom come". I believe it has already begun inside us, and its growth will always include our collaboration and good will. I believe that a renewal has already started but it comes slowly like the tide in the sea, that no one can stop.

The New Pentecost or Second Pentecost is the hope of our renewal. It is an outpouring of the Holy Spirit that will renew the creation. In the True Life in God it is compared to Apoc. 21. Here is a passage:

> *Come and learn: the new heavens and the new earth will be when I will set my throne in you for I will give water from the well of life free to anybody who is thirsty. Allow my Holy Spirit then to draw you into my kingdom and into eternal life. Let evil win no more power over you to die… Allow my Holy Spirit to cultivate your soil and make a terrestrial Eden in you. Let My Holy Spirit make a new earth to prosper in your soil so that your first earth, that was the devil's property, wears away. Then once again My glory will shine in you and all the divine seeds sown in you by My Holy Spirit will sprout and grow in my divine light (…) so allow My Holy Spirit to turn your soul into another paradise, a new earth where We (the Trinity) will make our home in you…*

(My question) What about the new heavens?

> *The new heavens? They too will be inside you when my Holy Spirit will govern you in holiness. My Holy Spirit will shine in your darkness like a splendid sun in the sky, because the Word will be given to you to express thoughts and speech as I would wish you to think and speak. Everything expressed will be in accordance to My Image and thought, everything you will do*

will be to our likeness because the Spirit of your Father will be speaking in you. And your new universe will march with my Holy Spirit to conquer the rest of the stars (Symbolic for people) for My Glory and those who had not observed My Law and were fully drawn away like a passing shadow into darkness, never knowing the hope and holiness I was reserving for your times.

The new heavens will be when my Holy Spirit will be poured out to you all from above from the highest heaven. Yes, I will send My Spirit in you to make a heaven out of your soul, so that in this new heaven I may be glorified thrice... and as the paths of those who received My Holy Spirit will be straightened so will their darkness and gloom too be enlightened and restored into blazing stars illuminating their darkness for ever and ever. Soon, this earth and heaven will disappear because the radiant glory of My Throne will shine in you all. (03.04.1995)

As you may see, this is all symbolic imagery language as well as poetic to describe a renewal, or a new Pentecost. I had been explaining to the people that they should never wait from God sensational events because God rather works in a discreet way, although His language can be expressive and powerful. Many events, like a new Pentecost, should not be expected as visible flames above our heads or the like. When God is in action He does it in such a smooth and discreet way that many who expected sensational events would not even notice them immediately.

Question 5. TLIG as movement?

What is the real identity of the TLIG movement and what does it require of its followers? How is it structured?

<u>True Life in God is not a movement but an apostolic call</u>

True Life in God is not a movement, nor has it got an office. It is simply a calling for reconciliation and unity for everybody, no matter who they are. The calling does not apply only to Christians, but it has drawn inside it non-Christians as well to become Christians. After reading the inspired writings of True Life in God, several Jews, Moslems, Buddhists and Hindus have been baptized, although its spirituality is a Trinitarian contemplative spirituality and totally imbued in Christianity. Christ had prayed to the Father for this and said: *"I pray not only for these but also for those who through their teaching will come to believe in me." (Jn 17:20)* So through grace, God is opening many doors. For instance, from the very beginning I was told that this apostolic work would happen.

God will give you his peace and His strength when the time comes to show the messages. God will want you to give the messages to everyone... (My angel speaking 06.08.1986). *You need not fear. You will be working for Jesus Christ. You will be helping others to grow spiritually...*(My angel 07.08.1986). *When you will be filled with My Holy Spirit you will be able to guide others to Me and you shall multiply...* (Jesus speaking 05.09.1986) *By calling you in this way I mean to conduct others too, for all those who abandoned Me and do not hear Me, because of these reasons this call is in written form...* (The Father 18.11.1986).

The Hiroshima Buddhist monks too got to know of the messages and invited me to speak in their temple. The Catholic Bishop was there as well. It was the memorial day of the atomic bomb. They were presented with a totally Christian message; then I offered them, an enormous Rosary to hang on the wall for their meditation and a statue of our Lady of Fatima which they placed in their yard.

Jews who read the True Life in God messages, asked for baptism and one of them translated the first volume of True Life in God in Hebrew. It is now at the publishers to be published. They all live in Israel.

Recently, Bangladesh wanted me to address the people in Dhaka in an open field. They invited an Imam from the mosque who accepted their invitation to open the meeting with a prayer and many Moslems were there. There were Hindus and Buddhist representatives and Catholic priests as well. The message again was totally Christian (taken from the inspired writings of True Life in God). The central and essential message that I gave was to reveal God as Love, to make peace with God and neighbour, to reconcile and to learn to respect one another. After the meeting was over though, two Moslem men wanted to become Christians and get baptized. *"I want all the nations to hear My Words. I will instruct you and tell you the way to go..." (10.01.1987)*

Contemplative teachings

The inspired writings teach the readers to know God and understand Him. Many people believe in God but do not know God, so it encourages us to have an intimate relationship with God, which leads us to unitive life with Him. United thus through the Holy Spirit, in Christ, the faithful are bidden to live one and the same life, the Christ-life.

Scriptures say: *Let the sage boast no more of his wisdom, nor the valiant of his valour, nor the rich man of his riches! But if anyone wants to boast, let him boast of this: of understanding and knowing me. (Jr 9:22-23)*

Formation of prayer groups

The writings of "True Life in God" teach us to practice the simple prayer of the heart and to turn our lives into an unceasing prayer, which is to live perpetually in God and God in us. But it has a strong call to forming prayer groups as well, all around the world. Since people in over 60 countries arranged meetings that I testify, in all these countries now prayer groups have been formed. There are several in each country. For instance, in France, there are 48 ecumenical prayer groups inspired by the spirituality of True Life in God. In Brazil which is a bigger country, there are more than 300 ecumenical prayer groups. Every prayer group, whether the Christians are Orthodox or Lutherans or Anglicans or Baptists, they all start with the Rosary together.

"How I long for this day! The day when I will send you to all mankind, they will learn to love Me and understand me more; Wisdom will share her resources with all mankind..." (Jesus speaking 25.01.1987).

Faithfulness to the teachings of the church stimulated

In reading the writings one learns how to remain faithful to the church. I tell people, "even if they throw you out of the church, climb from the window but never leave the church." They teach us to visit the Blessed Sacrament and be with Jesus in adoration. They teach us to follow the Sacraments of the church and to keep the Tradition, to learn self-denial, penance, fasting and practice especially the Sacrament of confession. They draw us to be eager to attend Holy Mass if possible daily. They explain to us the importance of the Eucharist.

"Through this Communion I sanctify all who receive Me, deifying them to become the flesh of My flesh, the bone of My bone. By partaking Me, I who am divine, you and I become one single body, spiritually united; we become kin, for I can turn you into gods by participation. Through My divinity I deify men..." (Jesus speaking 16.10.2000.)

Activities : Charity houses run by the readers

Back in 1997, after I had been given by grace a vision of our Blessed Mother, while standing outside the Nativity Place in Bethlehem, I heard her say that spiritual food does not suffice, but that one has to think of the poor and nourish them as well. So immediately when I announced this to our prayer groups, many volunteered to assist me in opening charity houses to feed the poor. They are called "Beth Myriams". There is one in Bangladesh, four in Venezuela, three in Brazil, two in the Philippines, one orphanage in Kenya and soon one will open in Puerto Rico, one in India, one in Romania and one orphanage in Ukraine. I am enclosing some information on this (Attachment 2). All the work done is on volunteer basis. The Beth Myriam's are functioning only by donations. They are all local initiatives, local houses without any structure linking them. They are self-supported and the same people (the prayer groups) are the ones who run them and take the task to serve the poor themselves. They are progressing not only to feed the poor, but to give them as well medical services, clothes and education for the children. Lastly, they are run in a constant spirit of prayer, and they are always ecumenical in nature.

Establish our Beth Myriams everywhere you can. Lift the oppressed and help the orphan, protect Me, rescue Me from the gutter, shelter Me and feed Me, unload my burden and fatigue, support me and encourage me; all that you do to the least of my brethren, you do it to me... I bless the supporters of My life, may they remain virtuous and all-loving, I am with you... (Jesus speaking 27.03.2002.)

Calling to evangelisation

Some of the readers of True Life in God who were touched feel that they can become witnesses across the world to contribute to spread the Good News. Having become the docile instruments of the Holy Spirit who provides them with the grace of the word and the sense of the faith, they are capable now to go and witness around the world inviting people to a life of prayer and teaching them to form prayer groups. The aim is to bring them to change their lives and live their life as an unceasing prayer. A few from the prayer group in Dhaka go out in the villages (to Moslems) and read out to them the messages. Many believe and want to become Christians.

"I want to make out of each one a Living Torch of Love's Furnace. Honour Me now and evangelize with love, for love." (Jesus speaking 27.01.1989.)

Devotion to the Virgin Mary

True Life in God brings us to become the child of the Mother of God since Her Immaculate Heart is never separated from the Sacred Heart of Jesus but is in perfect union with His. Our Mother is our support and we know it. Any one who joins the prayer groups, may they be Protestants, Calvinists or others, all are taught to honour our Lady, our saints, and pray to them.

"Have you not noticed how My Heart melts and favours always Her Heart? How can this Heart who bore your King be denied anything She asks from Me? All the faithful bless Her Heart for in blessing Her Heart you will be blessing Me" (Jesus speaking 25.03.1996.)

True Life in God Associations

If in some countries there are Associations of TLIG it is for legal purposes only, in connection with supporting this work of evangelisation and publishing the books. If we have founded associations in certain countries it was just to obey to local laws. Just to mention one example: opening a post office box in connection with the name of TLIG. But I have never thought of forming a movement. The books are translated in 38 languages and I have received no royalties from any except from PARVIS publication as the editor said it is in his rules. This money goes for the charity works, for covering costs for books and for travel expenses to witness in third world countries that do not have the means.

Other activities

Every two years, volunteers of the prayer groups volunteer to help me put up an international symposium on ecumenism. At the same time we have it as a pilgrimage. Till now four of these have been done. The largest we had was in the year 2000 in the Holy Land (while the Holy Father was there), where 450 people came from 58 countries. There were with us 75 clergy from 12 different churches. This year we are trying to do it in Egypt.

All in all, I love the House of the Lord and above all I love God. I am in debt to Him for the graces that He has given me. He once told me: "I have given you freely, so freely give." So this is what I am trying to do; I transmit His Words freely to whosoever wants to listen.

I thank you again for allowing me to shed light on the questions with regard to my writings and my activities. On the web-site www.tlig.org you will find more information. I kindly ask you to greet from my part H.E. Cardinal Joseph Ratzinger, H.E. Mons. Tarcisio Bertone and Mons. Gianfranco Girotti, as well as Their Excellencies from the Consulta of the Congregation for the Doctrine for the Faith, thanking them again for granting me this occasion of explaining my work. I hope I have done this in the expected way. I am but willing to answer orally or in written form to any more questions you may have. And I am ready to accept any suggestions you might make to clarify certain expression contained in the TLIG books. If necessary I can add such clarifications in the new editions of my books. With this, I send my heartfelt compliments and most cordial wishes and greetings.

Yours sincerely in Christ,

Vassula Rydén

Messages of TRUE LIFE IN GOD

Discover more resources at our website or take the next step and continue reading

tlig.org/next

For a complete set of The True Life in God Books

The complete True Life in God Messages, received by Vassula Rydén between 1986 and 2021 are available in two volumes. They are published in the original English and various other languages.

1986 - 2003

2003 - 2021

www.tlig.org